(67-22473)6-30-65

The
New
Liberia

A Historical and Political Survey

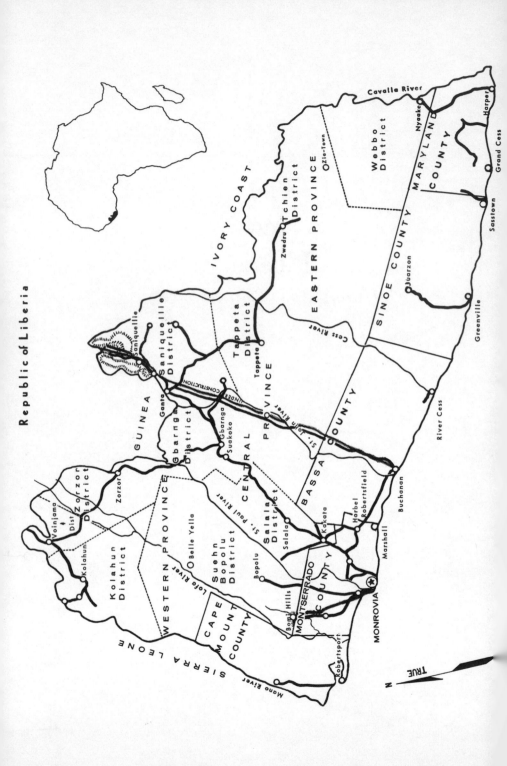

Republic of Liberia

The New Liberia
A Historical and Political Survey

LAWRENCE A. MARINELLI

With an Introduction by
Léopold Sédar Senghor

Published for the Africa Service Institute of New York

by

FREDERICK A. PRAEGER, *Publishers*

New York • London

FREDERICK A. PRAEGER, *Publishers*
111 Fourth Avenue, New York 3, N.Y., U.S.A.
77–79 Charlotte Street, London W.1, England

Published in the United States of America in 1964
by Frederick A. Praeger, Inc., Publishers

© 1964 by the Africa Service Institute of New York, Inc.

Library of Congress Catalog Card Number: 64–22493

Printed in the United States of America

To
My Family
and
T. P. M.

ACKNOWLEDGMENTS

I wish to express my deep appreciation and indebtedness to Dr. Thomas P. Melady, who, by his interest and inspiration, has made this book possible. I should also like to thank the Africa Service Institute of New York, Inc., whose grant financed my travel to, and stay in, Liberia; St. John's University for permitting me a one-year leave from my graduate studies; Dr. Hugh C. Brooks, Director of the African Institute at St. John's, for his much appreciated cooperation; Mr. Edward Wakin for his helpful editorial criticisms; Mr. E. Reginald Townsend, Director-General of the Liberian Information Service, for his gracious assistance in locating and making available research materials in Liberia; and President William V. S. Tubman of Liberia for granting me several lengthy interviews.

To my many friends in Liberia, whose kindnesses and warm understanding immeasurably eased the work involved in preparing the manuscript and made my first visit to the African continent a memorable one, I extend my heartfelt gratitude.

The author accepts full responsibility for the opinions expressed and conclusions drawn, which, of course, are not necessarily in agreement with those of the persons and institutions named above.

LAWRENCE A. MARINELLI

CONTENTS

The
New
Liberia

A Historical and Political Survey

William Tubman:
The Building of a Nation

by Léopold Sédar Senghor

I have no intention here of recounting the life of President Tubman. That task is fulfilled in the book that follows. It is not even a question of analyzing his work as a statesman. It is a question of explaining the meaning of this work.

Beneath the smiling visage of the President of the Republic of Liberia, behind the ever-present cigar, behind the gentleman's airs, it is difficult at first to see a revolutionary. But what is revolution, if not the radical transformation of mentalities and, therefore, of the social structures of a people? Here, ideology matters less than deeds, yet President Tubman has also proposed a new ideology to his people, a "New Frontier."

To appraise President Tubman's grand design, we must recall what Liberia was when he was first inaugurated in January, 1944. At that time, the situation of Liberia was that of a particularly underdeveloped African country. It had not been colonized by a Great Power, but by philanthropic endeavors with more good will than technical or financial means. For—and we cannot recall it too often—the misfortune of Africa lay less in European colonization than in the slave trade. The

3

European conquest, bloody as it sometimes was, caused, after all, the loss of few human lives. The moral devastations that came with the break-up of traditional societies were the most terrible—draining Africa's spiritual sources: her religion, her art—because of the communal values of civilization. That is the negative aspect of colonization, but there is, happily, a positive aspect: the economic infrastructure, industrial cultures, schools, hospitals, and, above all, the *modern spirit*— the spirit, both analytic and synthetic, of method and organization.

From these positive assets, Liberia had scarcely benefited before 1944. After all, what could several thousand impoverished Americano-Liberians do, quartered as they were in a few towns along the Atlantic coast and faced with almost two million natives who were still living in the Middle Ages? Very little—unless there appeared among them a great politician with a grand design offering them reasons for living, and, above all, for action. Such a man, in 1943, was William Tubman, who was going to revolutionize Liberia, and give it not only a modern *ideal* but modern means to achieve it.

But first, a modern ideal: the one ideology that can rouse, that *does* rouse the people beyond—or, I should say, this side of—the capitalist and Communist catechisms. The ideology is that of the *Nation,* more precisely, of *national construction.* For we are speaking here of an underdeveloped country.

In 1943, during his first electoral campaign, William Tubman began to define this new ideology, never hesitating to upset the century-old fetishes, the "creole" prejudices, and the segregation that had resulted from them. "Our efforts," he announced, "will be directed toward educating the population in these regions [the tribal peoples in the hinterland] into citizens, who are one people with us all, having equality of rights and privileges, and deriving identical responsibilities, benefits, and protection; hence, I believe it to be of the greatest importance that they receive the training that will inspire in them the *principles of devotion to one authority, to their only native land, Liberia."* I have emphasized the last words, since they define both the Liberian Revolution and the modern concept of Nation. Without demagoguery.

The *Nation,* then, is the totality of persons who, despite a diversity of races, classes, castes, languages, or religions, form "one people" subject to "one authority, one native land." But for the various tribes to become "one people"—I mean, to aspire and conspire in a "common will of communal life"— they must share a common *soul,* which they can only create through education. William Tubman saw clearly, and this is what distinguished him from a demagogue, that theoretical equality would not become real, and political, economic, and social rights would not be effectively practiced, without education.

As a true revolutionary, Tubman, once elected, tried to fulfill his electoral promises. In 1944, he launched the National Unification Program, which aimed to make firm that cornerstone of the national edifice: *national sentiment.* Conforming his acts with his words, he had the Constitution revised the following year so as to give representation in the Legislature to the tribal population and the vote to women. Even more important, in that same year he created National Unification Councils in each district of the country, councils that inaugurated his policy of decentralization—a necessary adjunct to his policy of giving citizen rights to the native population.

The first of these reforms gave Tubman the opportunity, as a *reformer,* to visit the provinces of Liberia as no President had done before him, an opportunity he used to advantage in controlling and overseeing the actual application of those reforms. In numberless and lengthy conversations, he listened to his people pour out their grievances, he arbitrated disputes, he redressed administrative wrongs, and he penalized the wrongdoers. The most positive result of these activities is—I have witnessed it myself—that there are no longer "Americo-Liberians" or "natives." There is a Liberian nation to which all its citizens are proud to belong. National sentiment, born in Africa of anticolonialist resentments, is unquestionably here the result of the historical phenomenon of decolonization, but above all, it is the work of William Tubman, the achievement of his life and his political activity.

That is surely enough glory for one man—to have created a nation. But the accomplishment would have been a fragile one if it had depended only on political reforms. For how can a country be educated without schools? How can one forge a "common will of communal life" if it leads to nothing but a life of poverty? How, in short, is one to vanquish the three-headed hydra of ignorance, sickness, and misery, if one does not begin by bringing the economy to the point of takeoff?

Here, as elsewhere, William Tubman disdains outworn dogmas. Relying on solid, Negro-African good sense, he rejects ready-made formulas. An American education marks him, of course, as we French-speaking peoples are marked by a French education. Naturally, too, his financial and economic policy of the Open Door is inspired by the United States, but less than one would think at first.

In a message to the Legislature in 1944, William Tubman defined his Open-Door policy in these terms: "We shall encourage foreign capital investments for the *development of our country's resources on a co-operative basis* according to priorities, and we shall assure the foreign companies who bring their capital here of the protection and treatment they desire." (My italics again.)

Thus it is clear that the Open Door is not the transposition, pure and simple, of liberal capitalism's laisser-faire and laisser-aller. The development of resources on a cooperative basis presupposes concerted and flexible planning. Indeed, a nine-year plan for economic development was drawn up with the aid of the National Production Council, created in 1956. To draw up a plan, of course, is not difficult: To realize it, though, one needs investment credits and cadres, a need to which the Open-Door policy and its corollaries responded with the Investment Code and the Industrial and Agricultural Credit Corporation—with the development, in other words, of technical assistance as well as national education.

Today, one can measure the positive results of this policy of economic expansion. The national budget, which in 1944 amounted to about $1 million, came to $50 million in 1963, with a gross national product of about $200 million.

Nevertheless, national unity and economic growth are not ends in themselves, but only means. The end that President Tubman continues to advocate is *development*—but of integral man, body and soul. If part of the national budget was devoted to productive investments, another not inconsiderable part was devoted to public health and national education.

The figures are there, elegant in their simplicity. In 1944, Liberia had a total of 240 schools for 10,200 students; 18 years later, in 1962, there were 841 schools for 80,321 students. Since that time, the pace of construction and academic achievement has rapidly accelerated. As for Liberia's public-health system, there were throughout the country 23 hospitals with 1,200 beds in 1957, without counting 8 leprosariums and 106 clinics. Here too, in the past six years, Liberia has moved forward strongly.

Before ending, I should like to emphasize the humanism of that great democrat, William Tubman. *To nurture the body in order to shape the soul*—heart and spirit—would hardly be a worthwhile aim if done according to the European white example, or rather, the American white example. Hence the emphasis on African civilization, or, better, on Negro-African civilization; hence the emphasis on the history and geography of sub-Saharan Africa, especially on art and the artisan. Education can be humanism only when it takes root in the man of flesh and blood—the fruit of spatio-temporal determinations, ripe and succulent only when there are deep roots to sustain him and a reaching forth into new life.

Thus do we view William Tubman. Leader of his people,

founder of the Liberian nation, and creator of its modern economy, he has done more alone than all his predecessors did together. We do not smile at Liberia the way we did before 1944. Today, Tubman is among the African heads of state who are most listened to, most respected. In his lifetime, he has entered into the history of the continent; never will he leave it.

Dakar, Senegal
May 16, 1964

1

The People and Their Past

Liberia has been an object of curiosity and bitter debate for nearly a century and a half. For the early part of its history, the colony was watched closely as a possible answer to the problems arising out of the existence of free people of color in the United States. Later, as an independent republic, it was assigned the task in the minds of many of proving that a black government could function as well and as successfully as the white governments to the north. Vast differences in size and economic potential between Liberia and the white world powers were conveniently ignored by those convinced of the Negro's inability to govern himself. In the 1930's, when the Liberian Government was on the verge of financial bankruptcy and faced world moral indignation for having participated in remnants of the slave trade, most whites and Negroes, though perhaps for different reasons, wrote off the "Land of the Free" as a failure. Throughout Liberia's uncertain history, it was the complex, almost mystical, national determination of the Liberians themselves that prevented their country from meeting the ignominious fate predicted for it by the outside world. Who are the Liberians and what is their past?

THE COUNTRY AND ITS PEOPLE

Liberia today remains a country of great ethnological and linguistic complexity, of highly diverse tribal structure with a proliferation of secret societies, of traditional village life existing side by side with modern urban life. Its topography, too, is unusually complex. For all this, Liberia is a small country, the fifth smallest state of independent Africa. (Only Sierra Leone, Togo, Rwanda, and Burundi have less area.) The country's area of 43,000 square miles is roughly equivalent to the states of Ohio or Pennsylvania. Bordered by Sierra Leone, Guinea, and the Ivory Coast on the west, north, and east respectively, Liberia has a coastline of 350 miles along the Atlantic Ocean between the Mano and Cavalla rivers.

Lying between 4°30′ and 8°30′ north of the Equator, Liberia has a tropical and humid climate, with a fairly constant mean temperature of 82° F. It has never known earthquakes, droughts, hurricanes, or other natural disasters. Its seasons are given the traditional classification of rainy and dry, the latter running from November to April. Rainfall is heaviest along the coastal belt, where it reaches 200 inches annually, and gradually decreases to about a third of that amount in the interior. The relative humidity is lowest (30 per cent) between the months of December and March when the Harmattan wind blows from the Sahara.

Topographically, there are three main zones stretching in an east-west direction parallel to the shoreline. The first is a coastal, or littoral, belt between forty and fifty miles in width, which is generally low and marked by shallow lagoons, white sand beaches, and mangrove marshland. Next is a very dense rainforest belt rising gently to an elevation of 1,000 feet above sea level. The last zone is a vast undulating plateau at an elevation of about 2,000 feet. The highest points of the country, the Nimba and Walo mountains, are located in the north near the Guinea border. The bedrock is Pre-Cambrian and generally consists of gneisses, granitic gneisses, sand, and schists. The younger rock formations are granitic, pegmatitic, and dioritic, the last mainly in the littoral zone.

The country drains into the Atlantic by way of six principal rivers: the Mano, Lofa, St. John, St. Paul, Cavalla, and Cestos. Smaller rivers include the Sinoe, Junk, Sanquin, Farmington, and Dukwia. None of Liberia's rivers are navigable for more than a few miles; nor can they be entered from the sea because of sand bars and perilous rock formations.

The soil is generally very fertile but subject to leaching; the flora is typical of tropical Africa. The evergreen forests, among the greatest on the continent, contain 235 different species. So far, only twenty-six of these are being used commercially, including the most valuable income producer, the rubber tree. The long list of natural or wild food crops includes coffee, citrus fruits, cacao, pineapple, avocado, cassava, and rice.

The fauna sustained by the land is varied. More than 200 species of birds make Liberia an ornithologist's paradise. The pigmy hippopotamus, found only in Liberia, is sought after by zoos the world over. Elephants and water buffaloes have all but disappeared, but leopards and several species of antelope are still found in large numbers.

Administratively, the country is divided into the coastal and interior regions. The former is further broken down into five counties and four territories. The five counties are: Maryland, Montserrado, Cape Mount, Bassa, and Sinoe. The four territories are: Marshall, River Cess, Sasstown, and Kru Coast. The interior region has three provinces, the Western, Central, and Eastern, each containing a number of districts.[1] Each district is made up of several chiefdoms headed by a Paramount Chief who is elected by the tribal elders and approved by the President. These divisions differ mainly in legislative representation. The territories and provinces are represented only in the House; counties are represented in both the House and the Senate.

In addition to the settler-descendant elite whose history will be discussed, there are at least twenty distinct tribes in Liberia. Ethnologists use linguistic similarities to divide them into four main groups: Mande-tan, West Atlantic, Mande-fu, and Kru.[2] The country's population has been estimated at anywhere between 1 and 2.5 million; the *Population and Vital Statistics Report* published by the United Nations (April, 1962) places it at 1.29 million. In 1962, the Bureau of Economic Research and Statistics,[3] with the assistance of various U.S. and U.N. demographic experts, conducted a census. At the time of this writing, this is in the postenumeration survey stage and figures are expected to be released in mid-1964. The results of a pretest census made by the Bureau in October, 1961, though not made public, are said to have reached a figure substantially less than 2.5 million. One official unofficially placed the total at about 900,000. But President Tubman told a press conference in November, 1963, that preliminary survey estimates place the population total at no less than 1.5 million.

The Mande-Tan Group

The Vai tribe, situated in the Western Province, is the only Liberian tribe classified in this group. The Vais are descended from the Mandingo people who left what is now the Sudan in the Middle Ages to settle in Timbuctu, then the center of Islamic learning and influence. According to their legends, when they found they could not live in peace with the Arabs, their great Prince Duamani Kamara led his people from Timbuctu to settle the sparsely populated and fertile land along the "Great Sea." The journey took many years, and a group who despaired of reaching the goal was permitted to drop out along the way, while the Prince and the others followed the route to the sea. When the Prince sent for these people to help settle the new land, they chose to remain where they were. Today the two groups are known as the Kono and the Vai tribes. Translated from their respective dialects, these words mean "to wait" and "forward." Descendants of the Kono are believed to be living near the Guinea-Mali border to the north of Liberia.

The Vais are believed to number about 100,000. They are

generally tall, sturdy, and fair to dark brown in color. They are intelligent, proud, and honest; and the fact that they evolved a script makes them one of the more progressive tribes on the continent. The script is said to have been devised by a remarkable individual named Momolu Dualu Bukele in the year 1814. Born toward the close of the eighteenth century in Bandakolo, a village of the Gawula Chiefdom, in present-day Cape Mount County, he worked as a boy on European merchant vessels (perhaps Portuguese), and was impressed with their system of written communication. As the story goes, he became a mystic recluse upon his return home, and devoted his life for the next few years to fasting and prayer for knowledge. Finally he saw the script in a dream. When he awoke he immediately began writing down as much as he could remember. Using this as a basis, he recruited the assistance of several friends to fill in the gaps.[4] After a number of weeks, they produced a chart with over 200 characters.[5]

In 1849, Lieutenant F. E. Forbes of the British Navy stopped at Cape Mount and saw the strange writing on the walls of huts and chiseled in rocks. He reported his find to Dr. S. W. Koelle, a German linguist at Fourah Bay College at Freetown. Koelle subsequently made several trips to learn the script, and a few years before his death he wrote a Vai grammar. In 1924, Momolu Massaquoi, then Liberian Consul General in Hamburg, interested Dr. August Klingenheben of Hamburg University in the script. Soon it was included in the curriculm of the university's African Language Studies program. With the outbreak of World War II, it was quickly removed from the curriculum and used as a secret code. It is said that the Allies were not successful in cracking it.

Though their forefathers lived in and around the Moslem center of Timbuctu, the Vais did not take to the teachings of Mohammed in great numbers until recent years. Probably as many as 90 per cent of the Vais have now adopted the Moslem faith. However, they have not completely rejected the ani-

mism of the past generation; their religion today is an amal-
gam of the two. For example, although the Sambolaa clan in
Tewo are Moslem, they refuse to kill or eat alligators because
they believe they contain the spirits of their departed fathers.

Life in a Vai village, except for a few transistor radios, is
still primitive and severe in its simplicity. One of the main
weekly events is the five-minute Vai-language news broadcast
on Tuesday afternoon, when as many as fifty villagers will
gather around a single radio. Their homes are thatch-roofed
huts, usually round, with front and back doors; they are still
built close together as in the days when the villagers had to be
constantly on guard against attack. A father has responsibility
for and control over all his children, whether single or married, and each is expected to make contributions to a common
treasury over which the father has custody. When the father
dies, the eldest male member of the family takes control, and
the treasury remains intact for succeeding generations. While
individual wealth is traditionally judged by the number of
wives and cattle, the dollar is rapidly becoming the sole
criterion. In earlier years, slaves were used as a medium of
exchange.

The main Vai occupation is subsistence-level agriculture
and livestock raising. Methods are crude and only three tools
are used—the bush knife, the hoe, and the axe. The farming
season begins around mid-January. The first three months are
used to clear the land and burn the bush. Rice is the staple
crop, traditionally planted by tribal specialists to the accom-
paniment of chanting and drum rhythms. Eggplant, cassava,
corn, pumpkin, cotton, sweet potatoes, and other crops are
sown without ritual. The women, who are responsible for
the weeding and over-all maintenance of the farm, also do the
planting and harvesting of all crops except rice. For this
reason, as the Vai man's farm grows in size, so does the number of his wives.

Like agriculture, livestock raising among the Vais is very
unscientific. The herdsman's main concern is breeding or

buying as many cattle, sheep, and goats as possible. Quality is ignored, for the number of livestock possessed is a status symbol. More often than not the animals take shelter in the family hut when it rains; otherwise they roam freely. Little care is given to the animals and the incidence of disease is quite high.

The women of the Vai tribe, as is the case in most of Africa, have an inferior position. They do most of the burdensome work of the village and the farm, in addition to the household tasks. In effect, the woman's role approaches that of a servant. According to tribal law, her only right is to an equal number of nights in her husband's bedroom if he has more than one wife. In case of divorce, the husband keeps all of the property or belongings that the woman brought into his home. In the event of the husband's death, the woman remains the property of his family and must marry one of his brothers.

The West Atlantic Group

Northwest of the Vai, but still within the Western Province, are the Gola and Kissi tribes, which comprise the West Atlantic group. These were perhaps the earliest tribes to settle in Liberia. Emotionally high-strung and ruthless fighters, early in their history they left the Upper Sudan in search of more fertile land. Their legends say that they always went through and never around tribes blocking their path. This martial pride is still with them; disappointment over defeat in combat often culminates in suicide.

Each tribe numbers about 50,000. Their dialects differ slightly; their traditional views about women and the family are the same. Whereas the Gola occupy an area ten times as great and have villages separated by three or four days' journey, the agricultural Kissi have villages relatively close to each other. Gola villages are notably well kept and neat; the opposite is true of the Kissi.

Rather than fearing death, these tribesmen look forward to it as a deliverance. They believe that the dead become part of an eternal communal soul and can communicate with the living by means of a "Piomdo," which can be anything from a rock to a rice paddy. According to this belief, the deceased appears to a friend in a dream and identifies the Piomdo; the friend then informs the village doctor, or medicine man, who helps find it. Once it is found, various sacrifices are made to the Piomdo, and if it is portable it is placed on a white tray and borne to the center of the village. The village doctor conducts a series of ceremonies to prepare the villagers for its sacred message. It is then placed on a man's head, usually the one to whom the dream appeared, and he conveys the message to the gathering or particular member of the tribe.

The Mande-fu Group

To the north and west of the Golas is the Mande-fu group of tribes.[6] Numbering about 400,000, they occupy the upper third of the Western Province and all of the Central Province.[7] Eight major tribes, differing widely in color, size, and facial features, make up this group: the Dey, Bandi, Belle, Loma, Mende, Kpelle, Mah, and Gio. They are grouped together because their dialects are basically similar; for example, all use either "fu" or "vu" for the word ten.

The Dey. Dey legend says that the tribe descends from water people. The first father, Zie, came from the water, and Dewulo, his wife, came from a cave in the mountains. Scientists interpret this as meaning that their ancestors came from the Sudan by a water route and intermarried with the local inhabitants, who probably were hill people.

The Deys have three types of settlements: the goonvo, the kosa, and the kpakai. These roughly correspond to our concept of city, suburb, and rural-farm village. The goonvo has a market place and is the center for recreation and tribal ceremonies. Before the construction of any village, the duluma (doctor) buries some "medicine" to protect it against evil spirits. The goonvo is then built around this spot. It is ruled by a "goon-kan," or town chief, with the advice of a council of elders. Communal cooperation is employed for major tasks like farming or building a new house, but the wives alone must keep the village and its surroundings clean.

The Deys do not believe that they can communicate with the spirits of the dead, but they do maintain that there is an after-life in which the good are rewarded and the evil punished. Each year the tribe has a feast to commemorate the death of important men.

The Bandi. Throughout most of their history, the Bandis were enslaved by the Kissi tribe of the West Atlantic group, and there is still much bitterness between the two. Though they are the most superstitious people of the Liberian hinter-land, the Bandis take readily to education. They are one of the few tribes on the continent where Christianity is outstrip-ping Islam in conversions.

Legend says that the first Bandi was Chief Yallawalla, who was created by Ngala, an omnipotent being. Yallawalla fathered Harlingi, who had many wives and many children. The children's children called themselves the Bandi. They believe that their ancestors are still with them and that death is not final. Food is periodically placed on graves so that the spirits may sustain themselves.

Bandi music and dance reflect the meek personality of the people. The drive and violent rhythm characteristic of most native music are absent and the style is almost oriental. Their dances are graceful and effeminate.

The Belle. The Belle tribe is located just south of the Bandi in the Western Province. Its other neighbors are the Loma, on the east, and the Gola, on the south and west. The Belle man is something of a linguist and can speak all of the dialects of his neighbors, plus Kpelle, Dey, and Kissi. The Belle women are famous for their beauty and take particular pride in their hair styles. While they are not as superstitious as the Bandis, the men are frequently organized in the middle of the night to hunt down an evil spirit that may have in-vaded the village.

The Loma (or Buzi). The Lomas, located at the northern extremity of the Western Province, are the most populous tribe in their province. They are bounded on the south by the Kpelle and the Gola; on the east by the Belle and Bandi; and on the north by the Republic of Guinea. They are divided almost equally into the Gbaleng-vala and the Gizima-ziama chiefdoms.

They are an industrious people and, like the Vais, have developed a script, though it is not as precise nor as standardized. The tribe is alternately known as the Buzi, after a trader who transported large groups of these people to the coast for cheap labor. They are conscientious and reliable, and theirs is one of the few tribes that did not at any time oppose the central government.

The Mende. The Mendes, a splinter group of the vast Mende tribe which settled in Sierra Leone, are situated in the northwest corner of the Western Province along the Sierra Leone border. Their traditions are among the richest of West Africa. They are the originators and have the highest order of the Poro Cult, which is discussed at the end of this section. Their highly emotional songs and dances have been adopted, at least in part, by most of the Liberian natives. Mende masked dancing devils can be seen performing in all of Liberia's major cities.

The Kpelle. The Kpelles are found mainly in the Central Province, although some spill over into the Western Province. They are considered to be indolent and irresponsible. Hut taxes and other debts frequently go unpaid. They produce a superabundance of rice, but the excess seldom reaches the market place. In line with their earthly view of life, they consider death to be a relief from the tensions of living and the beginning of a new life in a perfect state of inactivity.

The Mah (or Mano) and the Gio. The Mahs and Gios live side by side in the northernmost corner of the Central Province. The people are muscular and thickset, in color almost black, with pure Negroid features. Their lives and ways are still quite primitive, due mainly to their geographical location. They have not had as much contact with outsiders as the coastal Vais or the Bandis, whose territory is the crossroads for the tribes of the Western Province. Their farms produce at lower than subsistence level, and their protein-deficient diet is perhaps the poorest of any of Liberia's native population.

Kru Group

The largest of the four major groups, the Krus also inhabit the largest area, taking in the Eastern Province, part of the Central Province, and three-quarters of Liberia's coastal zone. They number roughly 650,000. The distribution is densest along the coast, where the Grebo, Bassa, and Kru tribes live. The important upland members of this group are the Sikon, Sapa, Tchien, and Putu.

The Grebo (or Glebo).[8] The Grebos inhabit the southwest corner of the Republic, known as Maryland County. They are descended from the Gbobos who, according to legend, came to West Africa from the Sudan in dugouts. The word Grebo is apparently a corruption of Glebo, which means "those who survived the waters." At one point during their journey from the Sudan a large number capsized in rough water and these became known as the Wlebo ("capsizers"). It is not clear from legend whether the latter survived.

Grebo villages are not organized in any noticeable fashion and their huts vary in size and design. Only the important men have beds and the people usually sleep on thin straw mats. The tribe's main source of income for the past quarter-century has been agriculture. Prior to that time, it was derived from fishing and salt-making. Their religion tends toward animism but there is an acceptance of the idea of a supreme being called Nyesoa. They worship spirits found in trees and rocks and believe Nyesoa created and placed them in these objects.

The Bassa and Kru. The Bassas and Krus are first cousins

by origin, language, and tribal structure. They live side by side in the coastal-belt counties of Bassa and Sinoe, respectively. It is possible that their ancestors lived near Timbuctu and traveled to West Africa via the Niger River, working their way westward along the coast until they settled in Liberia. However, this is only theorizing and their exact origin is uncertain.

The Krus are the more famous of the two because of their celebrated skill as freight-handlers. Before the construction of ports along the West African Coast, they did the loading and unloading of freight at all surf ports from Ghana to Guinea. They carried fantastic loads over the treacherous surf to and from merchant vessels anchored a good distance from shore. They are individualists, enterprising and proud. In the days of the slave trade, they were quick to sell their fellow black men, but they themselves were of little value as slaves because they did not hesitate to commit suicide when faced with bondage. They were the last of Liberia's tribes to accept the authority of the central government, and this only after several years of bitter fighting.

The Sikon, Sapa, Tchien, and Putu. The hinterland tribes of the Kru group make up probably less than a quarter of the group's total population. They occupy all of the Eastern Province and roughly a fifth of the Central Province, just north of the Bassa tribe. Scientists believe that they settled first in the Ivory Coast, but that wars with neighboring tribes forced them westward across the Cavalla River. Their main occupation is agriculture. They are jealously retaining their tribal traditions and insist on doing things the same way their ancestors did them. As a result, their agricultural methods are among the most primitive in the country and English is spoken only by those for whom it is a necessity.

The Poro and Sande Cults

One universal aspect of tribal life in Liberia is the highly secret cult society. The number of societies and degrees may vary from tribe to tribe but all have a Poro society for men and a Sande society for women.[9] Today they are essentially initiation schools to teach the pre-puberty youth practical aspects of life and the ancient traditions of their tribe. Classes are held at a secret area in the bush and may last anywhere from four to twenty-four months. Formerly these classes were begun with a human sacrifice (usually one of the initiates) to make medicine for the success of the gathering and to drive the evil spirits from their midst. Today the sacrifice is in the form of a chicken or goat.

Each important village has its Poro and Sande "bush" or meeting site, which is usually well marked with ferns or evergreens. It is strictly forbidden for a woman to enter the Poro area or for a man to enter the Sande area. In cases where this rule has been broken, a severe beating or death has been the penalty. The cults are controlled and instituted by a Zo, or priest, who inherits his position. The head of the Vai Poro is called Dazowo; the head of the Vai Sande, a woman, Mazowo. Very powerful figures in tribal and intertribal affairs, they have been known to send their members to war and at times have even overruled or deposed their chiefs. The Zo is usually assisted by a deputy called Dakpana (for the Poro) or Zowogbilia (for the Sande), who is messenger, secretary, adviser, and spokesman all in one.

When the bush school is ready to begin a new session, all of the uninitiated youth of the appropriate age are gathered, sometimes involuntarily, and escorted into the bush. Except in areas where the people are not animists, the first ceremony of the Poro is circumcision; for the Sande, excision of the clitoris. This is closely followed by cicatrization (scarification) of the skin.[10] If the child does not die from blood poisoning, he has earned the right to be an initiate. If death occurs, it is attributed to evil spirits and several parts of the body are cut off and burned. The ashes are then placed in a goat's horn and used as medicine to protect the others. The whole affair is very painful, but it must be accepted by the initiate while fully conscious. The penalty for running away is death.

After their wounds heal sufficiently, the initiates are given instructions on how to be a good spouse and an upstanding member of the tribe. They are told most of the secrets of the society and their obligations and rights as members. When the instructions are completed, there is an elaborate coming-out ceremony. The initiates, covered with white clay from head to foot, enter the village, led by the Zo, in a slow, solemn procession. Each is announced to the village under a new name, signifying a rebirth. Several days of festivities follow, after which they assume their new role as adults.

A NATION IS BORN

Europeans and the Grain Coast

To that part of the "Grain Coast" in West Africa now known as Liberia, the European has come variously as friend and foe, explorer and exploiter, since the arrival of a Carthaginian named Hanno sometime between 520 and 470 B.C.[11] Like those who followed him through the centuries, Hanno was sailing the seas in pursuit of trade. After completing an inspection tour of the already well-established trade settlements of North Africa, he set out with several ships manned by Phoenicians and Moors to explore and develop markets along the West African Coast. At or near Cape Mount, situated in northwestern Liberia and probably the southernmost point of the journey, he bartered with the aboriginal black inhabitants.

Because there is no historical evidence of further contacts, it is generally assumed that for all practical purposes no intercourse between Europe and West Africa took place from the second century A.D. until about the twelfth century.

With the decline of Frank strength and authority in the tenth century, Norman fleets gradually gained control of the Atlantic and Mediterranean coasts of Europe. After pillaging and temporarily disrupting Saracen strongholds along the Moroccan coast, several expeditions were commissioned to explore West Africa. These continued even after Normandy rejoined the French Empire and, in 1365, a quarter-century after the English had captured the key port of Dieppe, two Norman ships landed at Cape Mount. In the following year they sailed farther along the Liberian coast to Grand Bassa. Small settlements were established at these points and the Normans carried on trade with the "Grain (or "Pepper") Coast," as Liberia was then named, until the early part of the fifteenth century.

Portuguese penetration of the West African Coast began in the early 1400's. The famed Prince Henry the Navigator decided to investigate tales spread by Moorish traders from North Africa of a vast "river of gold" located somewhere south of the Sahara. However, at the time of the prince's death, explorations had reached no farther than present-day Senegal. King Alfonso V, realizing the importance of Henry's efforts to extend Portuguese influence over this fertile area, commissioned Pedro de Sintra to chart the Guinea coastline and beyond.

Leaving Lisbon in the early part of 1461, De Sintra landed on Liberian shores at Cape Mount and at Cape Mesurado in late autumn of the same year. At the latter point, now the site of Monrovia, one of the local tribesmen (probably Vai) was captured in accordance with the king's order that a man from the last country visited be brought to Lisbon "by force or by love." It is said that, despite the fact that a woman slave was able to interpret the tribesman's dialect, all Alfonso apparently was able to learn was that "unicorns" were part of the country's fauna. After taking his reluctant guest on a tour of Lisbon, Alfonso loaded him with presents and sent him home the following year on De Sintra's second voyage.[12]

The Portuguese maintained a monopoly on West African trade for nearly a century, and not without benefits for Liberia. The Portuguese settlers, though not many in number, did introduce to the primitive economy the orange, pineapple, coconut, tobacco, hog, Muscovy duck, and European ox. In addition, the coastal peoples became familiar with a European language and the ways of the white man, with whom contact has continued unbroken to the present day. Using the pretext of Spain's absorption of Portugal, the English, Dutch, and French began in 1600 to snatch West African territories from Portuguese hands. By the twentieth century, all that remained, and still remains, of Portuguese influence in West Africa are the nomenclature and the tiny enclave of Portuguese Guinea.

English interest in West Africa was aroused in the fifteenth century by pepper, "the grains of paradise." Since the Portuguese monopolized West African trade, they cornered the market and drove up the price of pepper, which was then the rage of Europe. (It was even used in brewing beer.) In 1482, Edward IV of England enjoined two Englishmen from journeying to the Grain Coast in response to the Portuguese king's demand that his country's trade restrictions be respected. Eventually, an Englishman who got a job on a Portuguese ship voyaging to West Africa[13] uncovered the secret Portuguese route. Captain Windham was empowered to carry out the expedition and in the fall of 1553 the crews of the *Primrose* and the *Lion* disembarked onto Liberian shores. The next year, the *Trinity*, the *Bartholomew*, and the *John Evangelist* landed near Cape Mesurado on December 21.

In 1555, Captain William Towerson described the Liberian coast as "full of woods and great rocks aboard the shore, and the billows beating so sore that the seas brake upon the shore as white as snow, and the water mounted so high that a man might easily discern it four leagues off."[14] Farther along the coast they "met with divers boats of the country, small, long, and narrow; and in every boat one man and no more. We gave them bread which they did eat and were very glad." Describing the port-like entrance of the Sino River, he wrote: "Directly before the mouth of it there lieth a ledge of rocks

. . . so that a boat must run in along the shore a good way between the rocks and the shore before it come to the mouth of the river; and being within it, it is a great river, and . . . divers other rivers fall into it: the going into it is somewhat ill, because that at the entering seas do go somewhat high; but being once within, it is as calm as the Thames."

Of the natives, he said:

> they are mighty big men, and go all naked except something before their privy parts, which is like a clout about a quarter of a yard long, made of the bark of trees, and yet it is like cloth. . . . Some of them also wear the like upon their heads, being painted with divers colors; but the most part of them go bareheaded, and their heads are clipped and shorn of divers sorts, and the most of them have the skin of their bodies traced with divers works in the manner of a leather jerkin. The men and women go so alike that one cannot know a man from a woman but by their breasts. . . .

Dutch ventures in West Africa coincided in time with those of the English. Their gains were stripped away, however, by French plundering in the latter half of the seventeenth century. Levinus Hulsius, a German geographer, compiled a definitive account of Dutch navigation during the first half of the seventeenth century. He published an account of the voyages of Samuel Braun to West Africa in 1626. Braun called at the Grain Coast to purchase pepper and rice with iron bars and beads. Knowledge of the coastal tribes acquired by the Dutch adventurers is summarized by Dr. O. Dapper in a work published at Amsterdam in 1686. Many of the observations and classifications appearing in his study are still valid. According to Dapper, dysentery was unknown to the natives until the arrival of the white man. It spread to plague proportions in the early part of the seventeenth century and a great majority of the coastal peoples died or fled into the hinterland.

The tribal ruler at that time was a Mandingo called Mendi

Manou, more commonly referred to as King of Manu. Dapper suggests that Islam had already established itself with the Vai peoples of the interior. The Karou tribe, under the leadership of Sokwalla and his son Flonikerri, subdued the Vai and later settled near the present site of Monrovia. Conquering the Gora, Folgia, Gibi, Dogo, and Kwoya tribes, Karou gained control as far west as Sherbro Island. By the eighteenth century relations between the white man and the coastal tribes were so cordial that the chiefs were beginning to bear European names. The slave trade had already begun and victorious chiefs were always ready to sell their prisoners to the highest bidder.

Following the era of wars under Louis XIV, the French and the Dutch joined in an informal alliance aimed at systematizing the slave trade and colonizing tropical areas of Africa and Latin America. In 1725, the Chevalier des Marchais was sent to investigate the trading potential of West Africa and Guiana. Describing his visit to the Grain Coast he wrote:

> Almost every vessel, after leaving Cape Mount, touches at Cape Mesurado. They are obliged to call at this last cape for wood and water, to serve them while they remain at the factory of Fida where the water is indifferent and difficult of access. Another reason is that the natives of Fida, looking upon trees of every kind as species of divinities, will neither cut them down themselves nor allow other people to do so. In the third place rice, maize, or Indian corn, fowls, sheep, goats, and even oxen are in greater plenty at Mesurado than at Fida. . . . The course from Cape Mount to Cape Mesurado is southeast; the distance eighteen leagues. The coast is clear, and the anchorage is everywhere good. If the wind be contrary it will be proper to anchor; if there be a calm, for security against the currents, you must also put out your anchors.

Marchais also journeyed into the interior via the Mesurado River, and reported the existence of flourishing "nations" whose prosperity was made possible by trade in gold, ivory, and slaves. He wrote: "The Mesurado runs through fine countries, but is so rapid that those who have labored three months in ascending it may return in eighteen days. The Negroes call the rich country . . . Alam, that is, the country of gold."

His impressions of Liberian life were recorded as follows:

The religion of the natives . . . is a kind of idolatry, ill understood, and blended with a number of superstitions to which, however, few of them are bigoted. They easily change the object of their worship, and consider their fetishes only as a kind of household furniture. The sun is the most general object of their adoration; but it is a voluntary worship, and attended with no magnificent ceremonies.

In the space of a few leagues are . . . villages swarming with children. They practice polygamy, and their women are very prolific. Besides, as those people deal no further in slaves than by selling their . . . criminals to the Europeans, the country is not depopulated like those in which the princes continually traffic in their subjects. The purity of the air, the goodness of the water, and the abundance of every necessary of life all contribute to people in this country.

The natives are of large size, strong and well-proportioned. Their mien is bold and martial, and their neighbors have often experienced their intrepidity, as well as those Europeans who attempted to injure them. They possess genius, think justly, speak correctly, perfectly know their own interests, and, like their ancient friends the Normans, recommend themselves with address and even with politeness. Their lands are carefully cultivated, they do everything with order and regularity, and they labor vigorously when they choose, which, unfortunately, is not so often as could be wished. Interest stimulates them strongly, and they are fond of gain without appearing so. Their friendship is constant; yet their friends must beware of making free with their wives, of whom they are very jealous. But they are not so jealous with respect to their daughters, who have an unbounded liberty, which is so far from impeding their marriage that a man is pleased at finding that a woman has given proofs of fertility, especially as the presents of her lovers make some amends for that which he is obliged to give her parents when he marries her. They tenderly love their children, and a sure and quick way to gain their friendship is to caress their little ones and to make them trifling presents.

Their houses are very neat. Their kitchens are somewhat elevated above ground, and of a square or oblong figure; three sides are walled up, and the fourth side is left open, being that from which the wind does not commonly blow. They place their posts in a row, and cement them together with a kind of fat, red clay, which, without any mixture of lime, makes a strong and durable mortar. Their bedchambers are raised three feet above the ground. This would seem to indicate that the country is marshy or sometimes inundated. But this is by no means the case. The soil is dry, and they take care to build their houses beyond the reach of the greatest floods. But experience has taught them that this elevation contributes to health, by securing them from the damps caused by the copious dews.

The whole country is extremely fertile. The natives have gold among them; but whether found in this country or brought thither in the course of trade is not precisely known. The country produces fine redwood, and a quantity of other beautiful and valuable woods. Sugar canes, indigo, and cotton grow without cultivation. The tobacco would be excellent if the Negroes were skillful in curing it. Elephants, and consequently ivory, are more numerous than the natives wish; for those cumbrous animals very much injure their cornfields. . . . The frequent attacks of lions and tigers [leopards?] hinder not their cattle from multiplying rapidly; and their trees are laden with fruit. . . . In a word, it is a rich and plentiful country, and well situated for commerce, which might be carried on here to any extent by a nation beloved like the French; for no nation must think of establishing themselves here by force.[15]

His statement about the French being "beloved" was not merely flag-waving. The tribes along the Grain Coast exchanged hostages and took every possible precaution when dealing with English and Dutch traders, but not with the French. The natives would board the French ships unarmed and the French in turn did not fear to enter tribal villages with goods in hand. In fact, King Peter, a local chieftain, gave Bushrod Island, located at the mouth of the St. Paul River, to the French in the hope that they would settle there. But for a decision of the Senegal Company to base its operations farther up the coast at Dakar, the whole history of Liberia might have been changed drastically.

However, by 1730 the only Europeans traveling Liberian shores were English and Spanish pirates. The English and Dutch had unsuccessfully tried to capture slaves instead of buying them and this had unified the coastal tribes in their hostility toward the white man. White traders along the entire Grain Coast were either killed or forced to leave. Not until Ulrik Nordenskiold, a Swede, visited Liberia late in the eighteenth century did any European nation again seriously consider colonizing the area. Although colonization by the Swedes never materialized, they have played a significant role in the country's development.

Independence Out of Slavery

The roots of Liberian independence are imbedded in the aftermath of the slave traffic that once flourished on its shores. The emergence of Liberia as an independent republic involved a complicated process that developed partly out of the antislavery movement, but more significantly from the problems of freed slaves.

The dissent of Lord Mansfield in the Somerset Case of 1772 was a landmark in the historical prelude. The case involved an American Negro slave, James Somerset, who traveled to Great Britain with his master and promptly declared himself free by virtue of his presence on British soil. A majority decision denied his petition, but Lord Chief Justice Mansfield wrote the dissenting minority opinion. His opinion was that English Common Law guaranteed freedom to all men. The tenet set forth by Mansfield soon became law through the efforts of such eminent figures of the time as Granville Sharpe, Thomas Clarkson, and William Wilberforce. Thus, in 1772,

England became the first country to abolish slavery. Early in the nineteenth century the slave trade was proscribed, and by 1840 slavery was entirely abolished within the British Empire.

During the American Revolution, many Negroes had sided with their Loyalist masters in exchange for their freedom. After the war, these and other slaves who had been given or had bought their freedom made their way to England via Nova Scotia. However, they felt just as much out of place on the streets of London as they did in the cities and towns of the southeastern United States. The free blacks did not live on easy terms of equality with the whites, and their very presence was viewed by many as an embarrassment and a threat to the established institutions and mores. While undoubtedly some proposals for the repatriation of Poor Blacks, as they were called, were truly humanitarian and philanthropic in character, for the most part the repatriation movement was fostered by vested interests or fanatics. In 1787, Granville Sharpe, one of the few nonutopians of the movement, led a group of Negroes to Sierra Leone in West Africa under the auspices of the British Government. Here they founded the settlement of Freetown.

In 1794, the United States Congress passed a bill forbidding Americans to participate in the slave trade; by 1808 all importation of African slaves had ceased. Soon the number of free blacks in the United States made up 10 per cent of the total 2 million Negro population. The successful British experiment in Sierra Leone, which had by now received the status of Crown Colony, was looked on as the solution for the American dilemma and became the model for various colonization schemes advocated in the United States. Governor James Monroe was instructed by the Virginia Legislature to sound out President Jefferson about the possibilities of purchasing a tract of land outside of Virginia where "persons obnoxious to the laws or dangerous to the peace of society" could be located. Jefferson's inaction on the proposal killed it.

Later the Legislature explicitly cited Africa as the most suitable place.

Since federal participation was not forthcoming, the colonization concept was pursued by private persons and societies. For instance, in 1815 a wealthy Negro from Massachusetts, Captain Paul Cuffee, outfitted at his own expense an expedition of about thirty free Negroes and sent them to Sierra Leone. But individual efforts could not hope to conquer the tremendous undertaking. Thus, on December 4, 1816, at a meeting in Washington, D.C., Elijah Caldwell and Dr. Robert Finley outlined their proposal for the establishment of the American Society for the Colonization of Free People of Color of the United States. On January 1, 1817, the Society was founded with Bushrod Washington as President,[16] Robert Finley and Francis Scott Key as Vice-Presidents, and Elijah Caldwell as Secretary. It was explained in the constitution that the Society's purpose was to "promote and execute a plan for colonizing with their consent the free people of color residing in our country, in Africa, or such other place as Congress shall deem most expedient."

However, the view that the free Negro had no place in the American polity was not passively accepted. On January 16, 1817, a group of Negroes released the following statement:

> Our ancestors were, though not from choice, the first cultivators of the wilds of America, and we, their descendants, claim a right to share in the blessings of her luxuriant soil which their blood and sweat manured. We read with deep abhorrence the unmerited stigma, attempted to be cast on the free people of color, that "they are a dangerous and useless part of the community." We declare that we shall be never separated from the slave population of this country; that to thrust the free people of color into the wilds of Africa without a knowledge of the arts and sciences, and without a government of any kind, is to send them into perpetual bondage.[17]

But such protests lacked influential backing. The Congressional Committee on the Slave Trade, whose members

were close political and personal friends of the founders and
officers of the American Colonization Society, endorsed the
colonization concept. Congress passed a measure on March 3,
1819, which secured the support of the Federal Government,
although not in the form of a subvention or charter, as the
Society's supporters wanted. The act gave the President broad
powers to remove slaves captured at sea to Africa, and appropriated $100,000 for this purpose. While the Society was
not given the charter, for all practical purposes its efforts represented the policy of the United States Government. But
the Society was so indignant at not having its own way with
Congress that no expression of gratitude was offered and the
public's impression that colonization was the exclusive doing
of the Society was allowed to go uncorrected.[18]

It was generally thought that the Negroes should be delivered to Sierra Leone, and a "mission of inquiry" headed by
Samuel J. Mills and Ebenezer Burgess in 1818 found the
tribal chiefs on Sherbro Island of Sierra Leone willing to sell
them land. On the basis of these findings, the Board of Directors of the Society voted to dispatch the first group of emi-
grants. In 1820, eighty-eight Negroes under the leadership of
three whites (two of whom were appointed by President
Monroe) set sail for Freetown backed by $33,000 from the
Federal Government. When the good ship *Elizabeth* put into
port at Freetown, Charles Macarthy, the British governor of
Sierra Leone, refused the foreigners settling rights, thinking
that the journey was prompted by other than philanthropic
motives. More or less anticipating this cool reception, they
sailed immediately down the coast to Sherbro Island, but
again they were unwelcome. The chiefs reneged on their offer
to sell land and negotiations lasted several weeks to no avail.
Stricken with malaria and yellow fever, all of the whites and
twenty-two of the Negroes died. Daniel Coker and Elijah
Johnson led the heartbroken survivors to Freetown where
they recuperated while waiting to hear from the Society.

Early in 1821, Ephraim Bacon sailed from New York on

the Navy brig *Nautilus,* commanded by Captain Stockton. Stopping first at Freetown to help his fellow colonists, he sailed directly to Cape Mesurado to inspect the area and, hopefully, to purchase land. His mission also failed and broken health forced his return. Stockton saw promising signs in Bacon's initial approach and, accompanied by Dr. Eli Ayres, he made another try on December 11, 1821. With the help of a mulatto trader, John Mill, a bargain was struck with Chiefs Peter, Yoda, Long Peter, and George. The Society was given a coastal strip of land 140 miles long and 40 wide in exchange for six muskets, one barrel of powder, six iron bars, ten pots, some beads, two casks of tobacco, twelve sets of silverware, tobacco pipes, three mirrors, and an assortment of other items with a total value of about $300.

Because the chiefs did not have sufficient command of the English language to grasp the terms of the contract in full, each side ended up claiming rightful ownership of the land. The determined settlers on Bushrod Island tried to explain to the local natives that the land they lived on was no longer theirs. But the even more determined natives proved their point by driving the settlers off the fertile tract and onto a marshy little island in the Mesurado Lagoon, today called Providence Island.

The colonists braved rampant fever and native sniping for many weeks until the American brig *Strong,* carrying fifty-three new colonists, saved them on August 8, 1822. Jehudi Ashmun, the newly appointed director of the colony and the man most responsible for its success, arrived on this voyage.[19] His first act was to mobilize the resources and men of the settlement. His determined leadership gave the pioneers fresh energy and morale.

On November 11, the native chiefs ordered an attack at dawn. Armed with munitions from Spanish and Cuban slavers, the attackers drove the settlers into the surrounding woods. However, instead of chasing them, the savages busied themselves plundering the goods of the village. Ashmun quickly regrouped his men, who, by firing simultaneous rounds, routed the surprised natives.

But the victory was not permanent. The attacks continued and on December 1 over 1,000 natives attacked at once. The day was saved when Matilda Newport, a widowed pioneer from Georgia, ignited an old cannon with the coals of her pipe. The enemy retreated, "leaving behind them over six hundred souls dead or wounded."[20] (Since then, December 1 has been a national holiday bearing the heroine's name.) Shortly thereafter, the *Prince Regent,* a British war vessel, arrived. Seeing the precarious position of the settlers, a midshipman named Gordon and eleven sailors volunteered to remain behind to lend them a hand. Unfortunately, within a month all but three, including Gordon, died of a virulent fever. Finally, however, help did come from America. The warship *Cyane* brought over 100 colonists, munitions, and six new cannons.

By the following year the settlement was relatively secure and the number of colonists had increased fivefold. Ralph Gurley, representing the Society, together with Ashmun, drew up a constitution christening the colony "Liberia" and the settlement on the Mesurado promontory "Monrovia" in honor of the President of the United States. The constitution and the names were ratified by both the Society and the Senate in February, 1825.

With the restoration of peace, Ashmun, now holding the formal title of Governor, negotiated with the chiefs for more land and succeeded in concluding several important treaties. On October 27, 1825, Chief Freeman granted the colony right of access over a tract of land south of present-day Grand Bassa, which was then the headquarters of Theodore Canot, a Cuban slave trader. Ashmun was actually carrying on a personal campaign to end slave trading on the Grain Coast. Each treaty contained a provision by which the local chiefs would prohibit the sale of humans.

Curiously, the "philanthropists" of the American Colonization Society tried to stop Ashmun from entering such agreements. They seemed to have qualms of conscience about the free but not the slave; they wanted to make amends but not erase the evil. Nevertheless, he would not compromise his convictions and, on April 12, 1826, he bought a strip of land entirely surrounding the Cape Mount area, thus striking at the heart of the Spanish slave operations along the Liberian coast. He was soon referred to by slavers as the "white American devil." By October, Ashmun had control of the entire coast between Cape Mount and Grand Bassa. However, the most important land deal was the last. On March 14, 1828, King Boatswain ceded vast areas of the interior to the colony.

Suffering from a serious wound received while leading his colonial army against pirate slave traders, Ashmun died at his home town of New Haven, Connecticut, where he returned for treatment on August 25, 1828. In the six years of his administration, he left an imprint upon Liberia that still survives. For example, his land treaties usually contained the provision that the lands would never be resold to foreign governments or subjects. Accordingly, Article V, Section XIII, of Liberia's constitution states: "The great object of forming these colonies being to provide a home for the dispersed and oppressed children of Africa and to regenerate and enlighten this benighted continent, none but Negroes or persons of Negro descent shall be admitted to citizenship of this republic." Further, the constitution provides that only citizens can own land.

Ashmun also deserves a large part of the credit for Liberia's becoming the first independent Negro republic on the continent of Africa. A few days before his death, he urged the American Colonization Society to make all offices in the colony, except that of Director, elective, with the vote being reserved for loyal Negro males. His proposal went into effect two months after his death.

Up until 1831, the American Colonization Society was the only group actively engaged in the process of repatriation.

However, in the 1831–32 assembly of the Maryland Legislature, the Maryland Colonization Society, previously loosely
associated with the parent organization in Washington, was
incorporated as a distinct body, and $200,000 was appropri-
ated for its use. At the same time, the Legislature passed an
"Act Relating to Free Negroes and Slaves" which prohibited
anyone of Negro blood from settling in the state. Robert S.
Finley was appointed Colonial Agent and plans were completed to ship the first group of volunteers on the *Lafayette* as
soon as possible. Since previous attempts to procure land
within the limits of the Liberian colony failed, a white man,
Dr. James Hall of Baltimore, led the 146 passengers to Cape
Palmas, southwest of Monrovia, where they purchased land
from Chief Freeman. The colony was given the name Maryland, and the town Harper. Hall was installed as Governor
and he proved himself an able administrator.

A market was quickly established, labor pooled in the construction of houses, and currency issued. The door was
opened to native participation and enterprise. This was a
striking contrast to the disorganization and strife seen at the
birth of Liberia. When Dr. Hall returned to his native state
in 1836, he was made secretary of the Maryland Society. His
successor, Governor Russwurm, also a vigorous and enterprising individual, effectively led "Maryland in Liberia" for
fifteen years. During this time New York, Pennsylvania, Loui-
siana, Mississippi, Georgia, and other states, using Maryland as
a model, set up their own societies and colonies along the
Grain Coast.[21]

While relations between the various state societies and the
parent organization were not the most cordial, their purposes
were the same. Separate rule was chiefly a matter of prestige,
interdependence of the settlements actually being natural and
necessary in view of their common motivation and obstacles.
In 1839, all of the settlements except Maryland merged to
form the "Commonwealth of Liberia," and a new constitution drawn up by Professor James Greenleaf of Harvard Uni-

versity was unanimously ratified by the respective directors. According to the stipulations of the Constitution, executive power rested with a governor, assisted by a vice-governor. Thomas Buchanan, a cousin of James Buchanan, was elected by the franchised adult male population to the first post, and Joseph Jenkins Roberts, later the first President of the republic, became vice-governor.

In 1841, Roberts, an octoroon, succeeded Buchanan as governor upon the latter's death, becoming the first leader of Liberia with Negro blood. Despite the fact that Maryland refused to join the Commonwealth, Roberts and Russwurm agreed that a common policy on customs tariffs would serve the best interests of both colonies, and an import duty of 6 per cent ad valorem was accordingly fixed.

The British created a crisis by defying the levy, citing the ill-defined legal status of the colonies. In 1845, Liberia impounded the *Little Ben,* a ship belonging to a Sierra Leonean, for nonpayment of harbor dues. The British retaliated by sending a warship into the port of Grand Bassa and seizing a Liberian-owned freighter on the charge that the owner was suspected of slave trading. Roberts turned to the American Colonization Society, which appealed to the United States Government for advice. While the Government seemed to have little interest in the incident, as a matter of procedure it requested an explanation from Great Britain. The British Government replied it would not accept a private commercial enterprise as a sovereign government. The United States was not willing to go so far as to declare Liberia an American colony. Independence was the only solution.

In January of 1846, the Board of Directors of the American Colonization Society announced that it was then "expedient for the people of the Commonwealth of Liberia to take into their own hands the whole work of self-government, including the management of all their foreign relations." On October 7, 1846, the Colonial Council approved the move unanimously. On May 8, 1847, the Maryland settlers voted to pursue inde-

pendence also. On July 26, 1847, the Liberian Commonwealth issued its Declaration of Independence, drafting a
constitution almost identical to that of the United States.

In 1857, after three years of independence, Maryland in
Liberia found itself on the brink of economic and political collapse because of an outbreak of hostilities with the
natives, and appealed to the Republic of Liberia to admit it
as an integral part. Up to the present day it is known as
"Maryland County of the Republic of Liberia." Ironically,
Great Britain was first of the leading powers to extend the
Republic diplomatic relations, and the United States was the
last to do so. That was in 1862, the second year of the American Civil War.

A CENTURY OF INDEPENDENCE

Just as free Negroes were considered dangerous to the institution of slavery, the existence of a Negro Republic was
viewed by the colonial powers as a menace to their continued
occupation of Black Africa. Since the young Republic had
very limited natural resources, it thus became engaged on two
fronts. It struggled to attain economic viability while at the
same time defending itself against those who sought its dis-
memberment both from within and without. One hundred
and fifteen years of this political and economic survival have
produced a nation unique in Africa. In the economic realm,
Liberia is a "newly emerging" and developing country, but
its political dialogue with the developed nations is one of
equality and respect, rather than of tutelage or condescend-
ing benevolence.

When the nineteenth-century rape of Africa was at its
height, President J. J. Roberts spoke to the Legislature of the
threat it posed to Liberian sovereignty in the following terms:

For when it is remembered that . . . Liberia has been established upon principles recognized by the whole civilized world
—the suppression of the African slave trade, the civilization

and Christianization of Africa, and the establishment of a sovereign and independent government, composed of people of color from the United States and elsewhere; and when it is remembered that in view of this, thousands of our brethren, now fellow citizens, bade adieu to all that was dear to them in America, left their native land, determined to brave the dangers of an African climate, endure the hardships consequent upon settling any new and unbroken country, to build up a government here that will some day bring them into respectable connection with the nations of the earth. And now that we have overcome most of the difficulties that have arisen in our way, and beginning to realize fully the practicability of the plan of colonization, is the door of our hope to be closed? God Forbid!"[22]

Despite great financial and international difficulties, Roberts, by skillful diplomacy, preserved his country's autonomy. During his first four terms in office (1848–56), he successfully consolidated and extended Ashmun's land agreements and completely suppressed the slave trade both along the coast and in the hinterland. Sixteen years later, the "Father of Liberia" returned to office for two terms (1872–76) in order to save the country from the near bankruptcy resulting from the administration of Liberia's only impeached President, Edward J. Roye.

During the interim between Roberts' two administrations, four Presidents were elected. Under Stephen Allen Benson (1856–64), a Grebo uprising in Maryland County was successfully quelled, and Liberia College was established with a total faculty of three. The terms of Daniel Bashiel Warner (1864–68) and James Spriggs Payne (1868–70 and 1876–78) were relatively uneventful. Prior to the election of Edward James Roye in 1870 (he served until October of the following year), the country was steadily gaining some degree of stability. Roye decided that Liberia, "now an independent State of twenty years existence . . . should imitate all the other independent States of the world and have a loan and a public debt."[23]

Roye negotiated a loan of £100,000 with London banks at usurious terms. Cash in hand, after deducting a prepaid fifteen-year interest charge, amounted to less than half of the total loan. This caused much discontent at home, and Roye became concerned about his chances in the coming election. He canceled the election and announced that he would automatically succeed himself for another two years. It is generally held that this provoked the citizenry to send a cannonball through the executive residence and imprison Roye. The night before he was to be tried by the Supreme Court he escaped with the loan money, mostly in gold and silver coins, tied securely around his waist. It is said that he drowned when the dugout in which he was attempting to reach an English ship capsized.[24]

The Roye affair cost Liberia more than a public debt and loss of prestige. At the same time that Roye was in London negotiating the loan, the British offered to end the long-standing dispute over the Sierra Leone–Liberia border by recognizing the territorial rights of Liberia over the area east of the Sherbro River. Roye accepted the proposal but Roberts, who was subsequently re-elected under regular constitutional procedure, vetoed it before it went into effect merely because it was Roye who approved it. Had this plan been ratified by Roberts and the Legislature, Liberia would have lost only about one-tenth of the land it was eventually forced to cede.[25]

In 1878, the matter was brought up again by the Governor of Sierra Leone, who charged that the Liberian Government was incapable of keeping the tribes peaceful west of the Mano River, Liberia's present western boundary. He placed the area under the protection of the British Government and demanded an indemnity of £8,500. A joint commission was set up to arrive at an amicable solution of the frontier question and to discuss payment for damages suffered by British traders from native attacks. At the end of several months, negotiations broke down and four gunboats were sent to Monrovia. Liberia yielded to British demands at first but reneged after the ships sailed.

President Anthony William Gardiner (1878–83) held the view that if, as the British asserted, the land legally belonged to them, then why should the Liberian Government have to pay for damages done by the inhabitants of that land? On the other hand, if Liberia did pay the indemnity and thus admit its responsibility for keeping order in the area, why should it be deprived of the land? Unimpressed by this line of reasoning, the British took possession of the area up to the Mano River without Liberian approval in March, 1883.

President Gardiner resigned because of ill health in the last year of his term and Vice-President A. F. Russell served until the inauguration of Hilary Richard Wright Johnson (1884–92). On November 11, 1885, President Johnson signed a treaty with Britain accepting the new boundary in return for a guarantee against further encroachments and a reimbursement of some £5,000 for the amount paid in the original purchases dating back to Liberia's founding; virtually an admission of the illegitimacy of British claims.

About this same time, the French were dreaming seriously of an African Empire. They dug up vague historical evidence supporting their claim to almost all of the Liberian coast and large tracts in the hinterland. In fact, they went so far as to announce their intention of declaring Liberia a protectorate, and they probably would have succeeded in this aim had it not been for an unofficial expression of concern on the part of the United States over "threats to Liberian independence." As it was, the French took a little less than half of Liberia's territory, pushing the boundary back to the Cavalla River on the north and east. Powerless to do otherwise, President Joseph J. Cheeseman's (1892–96) government agreed to this usurpation in a treaty with France signed on December 2, 1892.

Following the ominous Roye loan in 1870, which took over

three decades to repay, no President seriously suggested securing another foreign loan until the term of Arthur Barclay
(1904–12). In his Inaugural Address he said:

> Money is one of the great sources of political power, and a
> means of territorial aggrandizement. Show me a State at the
> zenith of power and prosperity and I shall be able to point to a
> properly conducted and well-ordered financial management.
> Among millions of men there will be only a few who can strike
> the rock of national finance with success and effect.[26]

Serving for a time as General Treasurer of the powerful True
Whig Party and later as Secretary of the Treasury, Barclay
considered himself to be one of the few who could "strike the
rock of national finance with success and effect."

In 1906, he went off to London in search of half a million
dollars. The loan was eventually secured by the Liberian Development Company, headed by Sir Harry Johnston,[27] in the
name of the Republic. The total was to be apportioned in the
following manner: (1) $25,000 to meet pressing liabilities;
(2) $35,000 for operating expenses of the Liberian Develop-
ment Company; (3) $125,000 for payment of internal debts;
(4) the remaining $315,000 to be used by the Company for
unspecified "banking and road" projects. The brokers accepted the country's customs revenues as security, with the
condition that their representatives be given direct control
of the entire customs operation. In addition to this infringement of Liberia's sovereignty, it was stipulated that the Republic would pay $15,000 biannually as interest until the full
amount of the loan was repaid. Within two years, "the Liberian Development Company constructed fifteen miles of
automobile road in the Careysburg district, bought a small
steam launch for the St. Paul River, and purchased two auto-
mobiles; it then announced that its road fund was completely
exhausted, after having spent, on an ordinary dirt road, about
$163,882."[28] Once again, the Liberian Government found it-
self financially threadbare and humiliated.

President Barclay requested Johnston's Company to make an accounting for nearly $200,000. Johnston refused with no small amount of impertinence, saying that "the President should have required the company to furnish a statement of accounts." The Company's charter was immediately revoked, along with its mining and minerals concessions, but what became of the $200,000 remains a mystery. Liberia then assumed direct responsibility to the London brokers, Erlander and Company, for the full amount of the loan.

In 1909, by which time the Republic had been whittled to less than a quarter of its original size and was hopelessly in debt, the United States Department of State sent out a commission to investigate conditions at first hand. The commission report, written by Dr. Samuel J. Scott of Howard University, stated that "an empty treasury is so frequent as to be almost the rule." Of its several recommendations, the most urgent was for money. In 1912, a loan of $1.7 million was secured from American banks, the major part of which was to be used to settle domestic and foreign liabilities amounting to $1.3 million. As was the case in the 1906 loan, Liberia had to put up its customs revenue as collateral and a general receiver was to be appointed by the President of the United States. The latter was to have three assistants appointed by the governments of Great Britain, Germany, and France, respectively. In view of the fact that these governments no longer had a financial hold on Liberia as a result of the American loan, the purpose of their presence is not clear.

The loan saved the government from bankruptcy, and at the time Liberian officials heralded it as the prime factor in preventing the nation's annexation by one of its powerful colonial neighbors. Later judgments were not so kind. One Liberian writer in a recent book considered the terms of the loan "more favorable to Liberia than the other two" but felt that "there were several weak and dangerous points in the whole plan which are too glaring to be enumerated herein." He went on to say:

But before passing, it would not be amiss to mention that as ultimate results of this loan . . . , Liberia for many years, was under an American receivership with white officials at the head of its financial institutions. These officials drew high salaries which were incompatible with the wage scale of the country and far beyond the capacity of the receipts and revenues of the country.[29]

A. Doris Banks Henries, wife of the present Speaker of the House of Representatives and a popular Liberian historian, charges:

Liberia, once more, was in the clutches of foreign powers. This loan was not advantageous to Liberia because much of the money went for salaries of officials from foreign countries and the rate of interest was exorbitant.[30]

In domestic affairs the Barclay administration concentrated on incorporating the natives into the nation. From the time of its founding, the Republic had been almost continuously torn by internecine tribal warfare. On many occasions this warfare was directed against the settler or "Americo-Liberian" element, but, since intertribal jealousies were too bitter to be overcome by such resentment, the attacks were never unified. In 1908, President Barclay signed the Frontier Force into existence. Krus, Vais, Grebos and others were dealt with one by one, and their secret societies either abolished or limited; the government's authority was accepted within the span of a few years. Since the Force was made up of the most warlike natives, its methods "did not always conform to some of our rather strained and artificial ideas of 'civilized' warfare . . . but today Liberia's Frontier Force,[31] which is really its Army, is an organization of which the Republic is rightly proud. Brave, well-officered, and well-trained, it is an alert and efficient instrument of the Government, making for law and order and noted for its vigor in action."[32]

Barclay was succeeded by President Daniel Edward Howard (1912–20), under whose administration the finances of the Republic reached their lowest ebb. A year or so after he took office, the $1.7 million loan was used up; the government borrowed again and issued about $200,000 in 3 per cent bonds, and a series of paper pledges was authorized. Corruption and mismanagement put the government on the verge of bankruptcy. By 1917, the country's aggregate income could not even maintain interest payments and the United States suggested a series of internal reforms. In the next year, Liberia instituted the "suggested" measures and petitioned the United States for a $5 million loan. The American Secretary of State asked Congress to approve the sum with the argument that the United States had a "moral obligation" to Liberia resulting from historic ties and the latter's declaration of war on the Central Powers. Congress refused the appropriation mainly because it was not convinced that the government had reformed sufficiently to prevent a repetition of past failures. However, forces were at work which were soon to change Liberia's economic history dramatically.

The Stevenson Restriction Act (or Rubber Plantation Act), which went into effect on November 1, 1922, was part of a plan fostered by Winston Churchill to make "the rubber industry pay off the British World War I debt to the United States through abnormal profits obtained at America's expense, thus paying Paul by robbing Paul, not Peter."[33] In effect, since the British had all but a monopoly on the world's crude rubber production and the American consumer used over half of that production in the form of tires, the idea was simply to push the price up and collect the difference. Almost overnight the price of rubber jumped from $.14 to $1.23 per pound. The additional cost to American buyers amounted to more than $250 million a year.

In the meantime, Harvey S. Firestone was searching for ways to break the cartel. His first attempts to set up large-scale plantations—in Mexico and the Philippines—were complete failures. In 1923, he sent a group of experts to Liberia. They found the soil and climate ideal for extensive and high yield cultivation of the *Hevea brasiliensis*, or rubber tree. He promptly sent his oldest son, Harvey S. Firestone, Jr., to negotiate a land concession with President Charles D. B. King (1920–30). In November, 1926, the Firestone Plantations Company was given a ninety-nine-year lease[34] on a million-acre tract at 6 cents per acre annually. In addition, Liberia was to receive an export allowance of 1 per cent of the world market price. While this agreement in a sense guaranteed that Liberia would receive long-range benefits, Firestone's presence was felt in a more immediate way.

On July 1, 1927, Liberia obtained a $5 million loan from the Finance Corporation of America, a subsidiary of the Firestone Rubber Company expressly created for the purpose.[35] The country began to stabilize and the government gained in self-confidence only to be rocked by a twofold crisis: the Great Depression and threats to Liberia's sovereignty by the League of Nations. Production of the new crop fell drastically short of initial expectations and national finances returned to their sad state. President Edwin Barclay, (nephew of former President Arthur Barclay), King's successor and heir to a sizable national debt, dealt with the entire loan fiasco in his Inaugural Address, when he said:

> Our experience with loans whether advanced under the auspices of government or privately, teach a lesson of caution, and upon my administration this lesson will not be lost. Loans are shackles, and limit, by virtue of the obligations incurred under them, the independent functioning of the government. And where they are floated merely for the purpose of refunding indebtedness, they are most pernicious in their effect both upon governmental freedom of action, untrammeled national independence and the economy of the state. Through them the wedge of impertinent foreign control is let into the structure of our sovereignty, and he who has borrowed becomes in actual fact the slave of the lender. My administration, therefore, will be definitely committed to the policy of no more loans for debt refunding, and only such loans as may be utilized for purposes

which are almost immediately productive will be given a cautious acceptance.[36]

During the 1920's, in addition to financial difficulties, rumors began to circulate about slavery in the Black Republic. They were based on the government's tacit approval of a labor agreement under which certain Liberians "recruited" laborers for the Spanish-owned Sindicato Agricola, which operated vast cacao plantations on the islands of Santa Isabel and Fernando Po. The agreement, first signed during the last term of Arthur Barclay's administration, was later canceled because of the ill-treatment of workers on these islands. This crippled the Spanish cacao industry, faced with severe competition from growers on the Gold Coast who had a more than adequate labor force. By 1928, the Sindicato was desperate. It approached the Liberian Government with a new proposal guaranteeing better treatment for workers. The ban was lifted by President King and a new agreement was entered into. (See 1928 Labor Agreement in the Appendix.)

In 1927, Thomas J. R. Faulkner, defeated presidential candidate of the People's Party, went to the United States. While there, he charged the King administration with rigging the recent election and accused Vice-President Allen N. Yancy of participating in compulsory recruitment of natives with the assistance of the Frontier Force. In a formal note to the Liberian Government on June 8, 1929, the United States expressed its concern over these reports, indicating that "existing conditions incident to the so-called 'export' of labor from Liberia to Fernando Po have resulted in the development of a system which seems hardly distinguishable from organized slave trade, and that in the enforcement of this system the services of the Liberian Frontier Force and the services and influences of certain high Government officials are constantly and systematically used."

In the face of mounting criticism, Liberia proposed that the League of Nations appoint a Commission of Inquiry made up of a League representative, an American, and a Liberian. The proposal was adopted by the League, which appointed Dr. Cuthbert Christy, a British dentist, as chairman; the other members were Dr. Charles S. Johnson, an American; and former President Arthur Barclay for Liberia. Investigations began on April 7, 1930, and, after five months of hearings, the Commission concluded that slavery in the classic sense did not exist in the Republic, but that a system of forced labor "hardly distinguishable" from slavery did in fact exist.

The Commission's main recommendations were: (1) removal of barriers preventing assimilation of the natives; (2) greater equality of educational opportunities; (3) outlawing of the system of pawning, practiced widely in the hinterland; (4) more stringent control of the Frontier Force. In December, 1930, the President encouraged the Legislature to enact these suggestions. There was an immediate storm of protest by the Americo-Liberians since it appeared as if King's administration had thus abandoned the country's sovereignty. King and Yancy were forced to resign and Secretary of State Edwin Barclay, became chief executive in the absence of any rule of succession beyond the Vice-Presidency in the Liberian Constitution.[37]

Despite popular opposition, Barclay signed the reforms into law within one month of his inauguration on December 3, 1930. A few days after the laws went into effect, the British announced their desire to have the Republic placed under a Governing Commission controlled by the League of Nations; Britain wanted the Government of Liberia itself to request implementation of the plan. In other words, Liberia should voluntarily give up its independence. In addition, Britain suggested that Liberia apply to the League for a loan. Mr. R. Earle Anderson, writing about this latter proposal, points out:

> The Liberian Government must ask to be put into an international receivership, or else! . . . Furthermore, strong pressure was to be exerted to induce Liberia to violate its agree-

ment with the Firestone interests by agreeing to a loan that would in effect give the League, and thus probably the British, the powerful position of a creditor. With Liberia facing the possibility of financial as well as political bankruptcy, such a loan might be the lethal weapon to end the Republic.[38]

In 1931, there was an outbreak of fighting along the coast, quickly labeled by the British the "Kru War." It was charged that the Frontier Force was being used to take reprisals on the Kru tribe for cooperating with the Christy Commission. This was used as further evidence of the government's inability to maintain domestic peace. In February, 1932, the British, with the support of France and Germany, demanded that Barclay and his administration cease to govern. While there is no doubt that a few high government officials were actually participating in and profiting from what amounted to slavery, one must seriously question the true motivation of Britain and France, who together controlled three-quarters of the African continent and whose possessions surrounded Liberia on all sides. Certainly the slave trade was deplorable, particularly so in view of Liberia's heritage, and drastic reforms were necessary. But it also appears that the colonialists were overanxious to see Africa's only black republic reduced to a dependency. A surrender of national sovereignty was, as far as the Liberians were concerned, too great a penalty to pay for the crimes of several of their officials, no matter how high or important those officials were; especially in view of the fact that the actions of these officials were in no way sanctioned by Liberian law. (This observation was also made in the report of the Commission of Inquiry.)

Facing formidable world opponents, President Barclay informed the League that his government accepted in principle the British proposal that Liberia be assisted in effecting the reforms recommended by the League. He applied to the League for a loan and requested that a "plan of assistance" be drawn up by the League for Liberia's consideration. However, he made it clear that this action did not imply that Liberia was willing to give up its sovereignty when he said:

> Every state, whatever its powers, extent or wealth, possesses certain unconditional prerogatives, which no other state may infringe without violating the fundamental canons of international society. Among these are the right to select its administrative personnel. These are the basic criteria of an independent national existence.[39]

Referring to Liberia's relations with the four big powers after they had called for an end to the Barclay administration, he said:

> Being, as it is, a member of the community of nations, the Republic of Liberia has encouraged and will continue to encourage and gratefully to acknowledge the closest possible relations and cooperation with every friendly member of that community. Its government cannot, however, be expected to permit its national life to be stultified because any nation, however powerful and wealthy, exercises its prerogative of non-intercourse. Nor should our people permit themselves to be misled as to the legitimacy of any constitutional act of theirs because it should chance to be unacceptable to those whose friendship we do now, and have always, considered as valuable and whose assistance and cooperation we have always sought and appreciated.[40]

The League of Nations Committee on Liberia shortly afterwards submitted its "plan of assistance" to President Barclay. Its two most significant aspects were: (1) the proposed appointment of a Chief Adviser who in effect would dictate major policies of the country; (2) the suggestion that, since the treasury was broke again, Firestone should agree to a moratorium and reduction of interest payments due its subsidiary (Finance Corporation of America), increase the amount of its loan, and raise the rental payments on its million-acre tract from 6 cents to about 50 cents per acre. President Barclay wrote the Finance Corporation of America requesting a deferment of the payment date of interest and amortization until such payment could be met. The Finance Corporation refused.

To enable the President to cope with the situation, the Legislature approved a Moratorium Act on January 12, 1934. Under its provisions, the President was "empowered to pay from time to time annually against interest and or sinking fund due the said Finance Corporation of America such sums from public money which may be available out of surpluses or otherwise remaining over and above the cost of administration as fixed by the Budget."[41] Although Firestone was not happy with the arrangement, the moratorium was effected. Liberia made its last payment to the Finance Corporation of America in 1952, fifteen years in advance of its due date.

As for the first and most threatening part of the plan, it was skillfully sidestepped and finally killed. Liberian Secretary of State Louis A. Grimes,[42] whose diplomatic ability and stratagems won him international fame, completely frustrated the workings of the League Committee by proposing revision after revision and engaging leading world statesmen in endless debate. Meanwhile the Liberian Legislature passed a resolution along with the above mentioned Moratorium Act which authorized the President to complete negotiations on the plan provided that "no power be granted to any advisor appointed under the Plan which would be in derogation of the powers and authority of the President, Legislature, or courts constitutionally established." Further, "no question affecting the interest of the State shall be subject to the decision of any outside or alien authority. . . ."[43] The League backed down and withdrew its Plan of Assistance.

The Barclay administration brought Liberia's first century of independence to a close on an optimistic note.[44] It had been an era of protracted financial, internal, and international conflict. Of course, all of the country's problems were not solved, nor did President Barclay entertain any unrealistic hopes in this regard. In his Inaugural Address of 1932 he stated:

I shall content myself merely with limited objectives . . .
—The re-establishment of law and order with the Republic;
—The rehabilitation of the country's international reputation;
—The laying down of the basis for economic independence;
—The securing of some measure of financial freedom for Government; and
—The initiation of works of social welfare.[45]

Within this framework, his administration must be assessed as successful, since each objective was fulfilled. Over and above his declared aims, Barclay gave Liberia a new spirit and courage, thus laying the foundation for the new Liberia, a nation struggling to meet the challenge of progress, not survival.

2

The Republic's Turning Point

In the past two decades, as an ambitious structure of economic and social development has moved from drawing board toward realization, a single architect of progress has dominated the Liberian scene. President since 1944, William Vacanarat Shadrach Tubman has, in the opinion of this writer, directed the Republic through a period of astonishing progress. Prophet of unification, promoter of an economic Open Door Policy, "dean of African statesmen," Tubman has dominated the transformation of his country. Its turning point as a nation both on the African and the world scene came with the administration of Liberia's eighteenth president. His family background reaches deeply into Liberian history and his career of public service epitomizes the New Liberia.

The Tubman story begins in 1834 when his paternal grandparents, William Shadrach and Sylvia Tubman, migrated to the Colony of Maryland under the sponsorship of the State of Maryland Colonization Society. Before being freed when their master died, they had lived in Augusta, Georgia. Upon landing at Cape Palmas, they settled in a section of East Harper which later became known as Tubman Town. Here the young couple tilled the soil and raised three sons, Alexander, William Shadrach, and John Hilary. The senior William

Shadrach, President Tubman's grandfather, at the age of thirty-four was fatally beaten by a group of Grebo tribesmen angered because he kicked over a pot of sassywood about to be used in a traditional trial by ordeal.

Alexander, the President's father, became a mason after finishing Mount Vaughn Episcopal School. After serving out his apprenticeship at Tubman Town, he moved to the more prosperous Harper City, where he started his own business. Several years later, he was converted to the Methodist Church by a famous Liberian evangelist, Amanda Smith, and entered the ministry. His preaching and missionary work eventually led him into politics. During three decades of public life he served in the House of Representatives, rising to the position of Speaker, and in the Senate.

President Tubman's mother, Elizabeth Rebecca Barnes, left Atlanta, Georgia, with her parents, Martha Anne and Nathan, and arrived in Liberia in 1872. They landed at Harper City but moved inland to join some friends and settled at a small town called Philadelphia. In 1875, when the Grebo tribe rose against the National Government over a decision concerning an intertribal boundary dispute, Philadelphia was one of the towns plundered and razed. Elizabeth and her parents managed to reach the protection of Harper City, where they were taken in by the Reverend and Mrs. Anthony Woods, fellow Methodists.

In December, 1894, Alexander Tubman and Elizabeth Barnes were married in the Methodist Church at Cape Palmas; on November 29 of the following year, William Shadrach, the future President of the Republic, was born. Of the other seven Tubman children, only Alexander, the President's younger brother, survives. William, called Shad by his friends, entered the three-year Government Elementary School in 1903 and completed his formal education at the Methodist Seminary in Cape Palmas. The philosophy of education in those days was to use, not spare, the rod, and the President recalls vividly the whippings he received from his elementary school teacher, Miss Agnes Thompson, for consistently misspelling the word "water" with two t's.

At home, things were no easier. The President's father was a fervent and very strict Christian. At four o'clock every morning, he rang a bell for the family to gather for prayers. After this, the boys tended their gardens of okra, cabbage, beans, tomatoes, and lettuce, then washed, ate breakfast, and were in school at 9:00 A.M. No tobacco in any form or alcoholic beverages were permitted in the house. The children were provided with only one pair of shoes each, which could be worn only on Sundays. The rest of the week they went barefoot, using only palm oil for protection against drying and cracking of the skin. They were not allowed to use mattresses, in the belief that they made a person soft and lazy; bamboo reeds, palm leaves, and a bed sheet sufficed. Belts were also forbidden in order to prevent deformation of the body. But this really made little difference since the boys wore only shorts. It was their father's idea that if a lad was man enough to want long trousers, he should also be man enough either to purchase or to make them. Shad chose the latter alternative. He took a part-time job as a tailor's apprentice and at the age of fifteen made his own.

After graduating from the seminary (high school) in 1913, Shad continued his studies under the private tutorship of Professor George W. Hutchins, a Liberian scholar, and Dr. Joseph C. Sherrill, an American missionary. The latter wanted to take the young man to the United States for higher education but Shad's father refused, saying "no son of mine is going to any country for the cold to kill." This made little difference to Shad, who by this time was already teaching in the Cape Palmas Seminary and aspiring to become a lay minister in the Methodist Church. But Alexander Tubman had other ideas about his son's future. He wanted him to enter the legal profession.

When his father suggested a law career, Shad was surprised, because his father had often condemned lawyers for taking merciless advantage of people. In addition, Christ had denounced the profession in the Bible. Shad asked his father why, of all professions, he should study this one. Alexander replied that Liberia needed good lawyers in order to keep the others honest, pointing out that Christ also pronounced at least six woes on the preachers in the twenty-third chapter of Matthew. So Shad began reading for the law and in 1916 he passed the bar examination.

However, political considerations caused the bar committee to balk at recommending his admission to the bar. A year earlier, Shad had formed a small political organization which opposed the powerful True Whig Party in the Harper City elections. Though the True Whigs won by a wide margin, Tubman and his Young Men's Political Association represented opposition. After several months of inaction by the bar committee, Shad appealed to the local judge, asking that the court request the committe's decision, pro or con. Again no action was taken.

In the early part of 1917, when Judge Henry Page of Bassa County was assigned to Harper, Shad went to the Judge and explained his situation. Page sent for Counselor Stevens, the chairman of the committee, and ordered that the committee report to him at two o'clock that afternoon. Shad and the Judge waited in the courtroom until three and, when the committee did not present itself, Page turned to the young man and said, "Mr. Tubman, by my authority you are hereby eligible to take your oath." Judge Page then administered the oath and Shad became a member of the bar. Soon afterward he added the name Vacanarat to his original name and thus became known as William V. S. Tubman.

This was a turning point in the life of Shad Tubman. As a lawyer, he fought for right and justice even though most of the time he knew his clients were too poor to pay even his expenses. Unlike most of his colleagues, he seemed to enjoy opposing those in power, especially if the case concerned basic principles. His personal courage and dedication were already evident when at the age of fourteen he joined the Government forces fighting to put down the Sasstown Uprising of 1910. He also fought in the Bolobo Expedition under Captain Esau Carr in 1915, and two years later in the Glaro Expedition under Captain Hawkins, a United States Army officer. During his time in the Army, he rose from the rank of private to that of colonel.

His career of nearly half a century in government service began in 1916, when President Howard appointed him Recorder in the Monthly and Probate Court at Harper City. He served until he was admitted to the bar, at which time he was commissioned Collector of Internal Revenues for Maryland County. Shad's honesty, efficiency, and zeal led to his promotion to the post of County Attorney in 1919. Four years later, Maryland County elected him to the Senate at the age of twenty-eight, making him the youngest senator in Liberian history. With his sharp mind, quick wit, and pleasing personality, he served brilliantly in this post for fourteen years. While it has not been until recent years that records of the debates and proceedings in the National Legislature have been kept, old-timers say that it was a rare instance when a bill supported by Tubman did not pass.

By 1937, Tubman was one of the most popular and promising Presidential possibilities. But he had alienated the highly conservative Liberian elite, who regarded him as a dangerous revolutionary, particularly for his advocacy of friendly rapprochement with foreign business interests. In those days, the conservatives had virtually a free hand in running the country and a politician defied them at his own peril. But Tubman, true to the pattern that had become well established in his career, became involved in several bitter encounters with the old guard.

Since Tubman was too popular to be beaten at the polls, he was kicked upstairs to the post of Associate Justice of the Supreme Court by President Barclay at the urging of the True Whig leadership. An astute politician, Tubman turned the appointment into a steppingstone to the Presidency. Although he could no longer campaign publicly for his policies, his new job kept him in Monrovia, the seat of the national government and headquarters of the True Whig Party. He became active in party organization. By securing the support of many tribal leaders for the True Whigs, he became an important force in the party. He was also careful not to embarrass the old guard on economic matters. Consequently, in 1943 the party asked him to seek the Presidential nomination.

Realizing that he needed the support of the conservative faction, he included in his policy proposals only one passing reference to the question of natural resources development. This assured the old guard that he had given up his ideas about internal development and they gave him the nomination. But they soon were accusing President-elect Tubman of being "ungrateful" after he requested U.S. President Roosevelt to send in a geological survey team—in effect a tip-off of his true intentions.

But Tubman still had to go slow. The conservatives were still a significant factor, and he needed them to keep the government functioning. He also knew the ruthless tactics that they would use if he completely ignored them. Thus, his first term was used to survey Liberia's minerals, study development plans, and win as much support from the conservative faction as he could.

Despite his efforts, some conservatives would not yield on their outmoded views, and over the years, this group has periodically plotted to assassinate the President, or at least to remove him from office. However, such attempts have been abortive for various reasons, mainly because no one could sway any significant amount of popular sympathy. Looking at it from the people's side, it is understandable that the overwhelming majority stand with Tubman. For the first time in their lives, indeed for the first time in the history of the Republic, change has literally been visible.

Tubman enjoys the power and glory that goes with being

President William V. S. Tubman with his first Cabinet in 1944. Seated from left to right are Former President Edwin Barclay, Vice President Clarence L. Simpson, President Tubman, Chief Justice Louis Arthur Grimes, and Former President C. B. D. King.

President William V. S. Tubman

President and is reluctant to delegate his authority to subordinates. For this reason, his work schedule is unbelievably heavy for a man of sixty-eight. There is virtually no major item of business—private or governmental—on which the "old man" is not consulted. It is said that his last opponent (1959) in a Presidential election received Tubman's permission to have his name placed on the ballot. Tubman won by a landslide at that time, and in the 1963 election there was not even token opposition. But even if there had been, it is generally conceded that Tubman would still have won easily. No other person in all of Liberia can claim even a fraction of the President's widespread popularity. He is an astute politician who knows and looks after his people. The people are satisfied and will probably continue to be so as long as Tubman is.

THE PURSUIT OF UNITY

In his first campaign for the Presidency, Tubman addressed himself to the most difficult and most persistent internal problem that has plagued Liberia throughout its history. This was the highly explosive problem of incorporating the native population into the political, economic, and social life of the nation. The problem had cast a shadow over the country from the first arrival of the settlers. It had only one acceptable solution: the pursuit of unity.

But a history of tense relations and of bloodshed had to be overcome. From the time of the land purchase of 1821, the natives had resisted dispossession by the newly arrived settlers, and though the question of land ownership was resolved, it was replaced by intense social and cultural conflict. The natives and the Americoes were worlds apart. The latter brought much of the U.S. South with them—government, religion, language, customs, and an appetite for aristocratic ways which they wanted to satisfy. It was the only way of life they knew and it was their view of how they would bring civilization to Africa. They shared the cultural blindness of any other group of African settlers.

But the indigenous people did not understand the approach of the Americoes, and because the latter made little effort to adjust their institutions to ancient tribal law and custom, open hostilities were frequent. The outnumbered settlers were not pushed into the sea only because the natives had intertribal jealousies and hatreds which were older and deeper than their quarrel with the Americoes. The attacks, therefore, came from only one tribe at a time and were for a time easily defeated by the well-armed Monrovia Government. However, the colonialists were quick to furnish dissident natives with modern weapons. Thus the Americoes never won what could be considered an overwhelming victory, and the quarrel extended, in one way or another, over a century. This kept the issues alive and also made them more deeply felt.

Charles Henry Huberich, a famed international lawyer, best presented the issue involved when in his work on Liberia he wrote:

> It is a serious defect in the Constitution that no provision was made regarding the government of the native tribes, leaving all questions to be determined by general legislation subject to the limitations imposed by a Constitution framed for the government of an entirely different population.
>
> Entirely different problems of administration and law necessarily arise in the two grand Administrative Subdivisions into which the country is divided. The area of County Jurisdiction is inhabited by a small population that has grown up in surroundings of a Christian Western civilization, in large part descended from emigrants from the United States and the British West Indies, with a common language and common system of laws and customs, and governmental institutions and a political philosophy based on American traditions, with a just pride in their political and cultural achievements in the century and a quarter of the existence of their State.[1]

Every president of Liberia has in some way attempted to make the Liberian people one under the law and in spirit. In

1866, President Danial B. Warner said in his Annual Message to the National Legislature:

I have for a long time thought that the native tribes residing within the near jurisdiction of the Republic could be brought into closer relationship with us, by being required to contribute to the support of the Government, and by being allowed such a representation in our National Council as will easily commend itself to their comprehension. Such a measure inaugurated among these, will induce those tribes more remote to seek to sustain similar relations to us. No desire to exterminate these people and aggrandize their territory brought us here. They are our brethren, deluded though they often appear; and our Constitution expressly declares that their improvement is a cherished object of this Government. The Government, then, being for mutual advantage, is one that calls for mutual support. The aborigines should assist in the great work we have to perform. Like the civilized population, they should give something in return for the protection and redress which our courts always, and our armies often, are required to render them. And I doubt not that many are now willing to assist; and when they shall have been convinced that the civilization of which the Republic is the nucleus must spread far and wide over this continent, enlightening and refining its inhabitants, and raising them in the scale of being; that it is a work designed by the Almighty himself, and cannot be stayed,—I am sure they will become willing coadjutors. . . .

There are in these forests men of royal blood, and of minds susceptible of the most exalted ideas of systematic and well-balanced government; and, by a proper appreciation of them, they could be made to sustain to us a much nearer and dearer relation than that of being mere contributors to our treasury.[2]

Two years later the Interior Department was created under the administration of Warner's successor, James S. Payne. During the next three-quarters of a century, there were two main developments favoring the native populations. The first was the appointment of "native referees" who would attend the sessions of the National Legislature and advise the representatives on issues affecting their respective tribes. The second was the initiation of national conferences, under President Arthur Barclay's administration, which provided the chiefs with an opportunity to consult directly with the chief executive of the National Government. These conferences were continued under the King administration and by President Edwin Barclay. Although these efforts were at the time significant, it was not until the Tubman administration that the theory of unification became a reality and the process of integration became a national policy.

As a candidate for the Presidency, Tubman stressed "oneness" as Liberia's only hope for progress worthy of the name and promised "to strive with all our might to agglutinate and unify our populations."[3] He proposed to accomplish this by "educating the population in these regions into citizens, who are one people with us all, having equality of rights and privileges, and deriving identical responsibilities, benefits and protection; hence . . . that they receive the training that will inspire in them the principles of devotion to one authority, to their only native land, Liberia. . . ."[4]

In his first Inaugural Address he announced that, in accordance with his campaign promises, the spirit of his administration would be one of "No Reprisals; No Pay-Backs; No Get-Even-With; but let the dead past bury its dead."[5] In the same speech he expounded his philosophy of government:

> This government, in my opinion, must be in the hands of the people. They must be faithful and able depositaries of that trust. The people of Liberia must therefore be educated in these principles, and they must be intelligent, independent and virtuous.
>
> . . . The people of Liberia should . . . fear no man, honor and respect lawful and constituted authority, yield a cheerful obedience to and live within the law. Mark you well—I do not advocate license, nor will any such attitude be tolerated. But I advocate fearlessness and stamina in our people in acquiring

and possessing property, in exercising and pursuing peace, happiness and the enjoyment of life as vitally essential to national peace, prosperity and security.

. . . It is only when the people are ignorant and corrupt, when they degenerate into a serfage populace, that they are incapable of exercising their sovereignty. Usurpation becomes then an easy attainment, and the people themselves become the willing instrument of their own debasement and ruin.

Then, for the first time in the history of Liberia, a policy of goodwill and equality for the indigenous people was promulgated:

To effect this, we shall engage in and strive at the assimilation and unification of our various populations composing the body politic. . . . Liberia must be a place for all Liberians to live in alike—all to stand equally privileged, responsible and protected by like administration of law.

All classes of our people must be made to fuse and coalesce into a solid whole. This we think may be effected by a faithful and an ardent adherence to the fundamental individual values guaranteed by our Constitution. . . .[6]

Getting down to specifics, he said:

In the administration of our population inhabiting the Hinterland, our aim and purpose shall be to educate them into good and useful citizens, capable of knowing their duty, status and rights as citizens, and competent of exerting, enjoying and asserting them; to have them love their native land and feel proud to be called Liberians.

The customary tribal laws so far as they are humane and reasonable shall be adhered to in the administration of the tribes for the benefit of their tribesmen . . . where they do not abrogate or conflict with the Constitution or other Statute Laws.

Due regard for the Tribal Authority shall be insisted upon and cases of malfeasance and misfeasance by officials charged with the administration of Hinterland Districts shall be dealt with specially rigidly and effectively. Penalties shall extend beyond removal from office.

We shall insist upon and see to it that complaints from these less-favored citizens receive careful attention and prompt disposition. They shall receive in all matters, fair and humane treatment. . . . In the meantime, firmness of judgment and prompt enforcement of law will be the attitude of the administration. Rigid correctives will be administered to willful and recalcitrant characters in particular.

On July 24, 1944, President Tubman convoked a special meeting of leaders in government to discuss measures to be taken to carry out his Unification Policy as quickly and as effectively as possible. His ideas were openly opposed by a group of reactionaries who felt that Tubman was "selling out" the country economically and socially. They were protecting their own class interests. The open door to foreign capital meant the end of their economic strangulation of the country and the open door to the tribal population clearly endangered their political and social monopoly. The President stressed his position that "national consciousness must replace reactionary greed" and asked "all those who consider themselves Liberians" to assist him in carrying out the program.

Despite the active opposition by arch-conservatives, Tubman instituted sweeping reforms during the first few years of his administration. The vote was extended to all citizens throughout the country and, for the first time in the history of the Republic, to women. All constitutional rights, plus the right to bear arms, were restored to the tribal people and the Constitution itself was amended to give them representation in the House of Representatives (today they have more than one-third of the total). By executive power he put a stop to all abuses and exploitation of the tribal people by government authorities and appointed personal representatives (Provincial Commissioners) in each province to ensure that the order was obeyed. He recommended (and the Legislature approved) the introduction of the secret ballot for all elections.

More important than the enactment and enforcement of more equitable laws is the President's total personal commitment to the spirit of unification. During the early years of his administration, he traveled thousands of miles throughout the interior by jeep, on foot, and even in dugouts in order to meet his people and hear their grievances. He lived with them, shared their food, learned their languages, and danced their dances. And whenever a tribal elder went to Monrovia the President greeted him as an old friend and would see to it that he was treated in a manner befitting his standing. With his untiring efforts, Tubman won the hearts of the tribal people. By the end of his first term, century-old suspicions and fears were being erased from the pages of Liberian history. The people were ready to follow Tubman's vision of a New Liberia.

In his Second Inaugural Address (1952) he announced the second stage of the unification process, that of integration. He said:

> With firm and unswerving faith and complete belief in the principles of freedom, equality and justice for all . . . and with the ardent and ultimate hope that the blessings, privileges, rights and benefits of sovereignty and independence shall be our prized possession and that of our posterity . . . *we deem it to be of the highest national importance and most appropriate at this time to call for national unity and solidarity.*
>
> We have consistently and insistently pursued the policy of unification and agglutination, so that the whole body of the people of this Nation may be *integrated and fused together* in the common patriotic endeavor of preserving, developing and defending this sacred heritage.
>
> In strict accord with our inherent detestation, denunciation and complete disbelief in the pernicious policy of "Divide and Rule," we shall as in the past, with unrelenting zeal, renewed vigor, and all the powers at our command, continue to oppose this policy, for in such opposition lie all of our hopes for permanent and enduring national peace, happiness and prosperity.[7]

To carry out this stage, the President initiated a series of National Unification Councils to provide an opportunity to review the program's development. The Councils are attended by all Paramount and Clan Chiefs and elders from every province, district, chiefdom, and tribe of the hinterland. Thousands of people attend these meetings to present grievances to the President. At the first Council, held at Harper City in 1954, there were nearly 500 representatives of the tribes flown in at government expense. In his keynote address to the delegates at that time, President Tubman said:

> It has been proved in our own lifetime that the civilized population cannot get along without the uncivilized; neither can the uncivilized population get along without the civilized; that neither element can exterminate the other.
>
> We must now destroy all ideologies that tend to divide us. Americo-Liberianism must be forgotten and all of us must register a new era of justice, equality, fair dealing and equal opportunities for every one from every part of the country, regardless of tribe, clan, section, element, creed or economic status.
>
> For the past ten years we have been working hard for the unification of the people; and thus far the results have been favorable and encouraging. But there are still a few die-hards on both sides opposing the Unification Program in the hope that one element will overcome or exterminate the other. This is a fallacy. No such thing will ever happen.
>
> If any person, civilized or uncivilized, opposes the unification of this nation, he is an enemy of the State, a confirmed political lunatic and should not be followed.
>
> Let us resolve at this . . . Council for ourselves here present, our constituents and our posterity to make our country a United Nation under God with liberty and justice for all. This is the principal reason for this convocation.[8]

For the next six weeks the President heard complaints ranging from boundary disputes to a need for more doctors. Upon hearing a report that the people of the Pleebo District were indifferent to the government agricultural program, he rebuked the chiefs of that district in the following terms:

The Government has employed an agricultural expert for you, as it has done for the other provinces, and sent him here to teach you and your people how to plant cocoa, coffee, oil palms and rubber. Government has not required you to buy the seeds and seedlings. They are furnished you free of cost and you can get as many as you wish.

When you plant them, they become your personal property. Within five or six years, you will begin to reap the rewards of your labor. You can then use your money to buy cars, or trucks or anything you want. You can build better homes and furnish them. You can buy food and clothing for your wives, your children and yourselves. But you have to work to earn money.

I think your greatest trouble is that you are too contented with your present condition. You have to become dissatisfied with your present way of living. Can't you see that everybody else is working? Can't you see that people with rubber, coffee, cocoa and oil palm farms are building new homes, living more comfortably and spending more money? Can't you see that everything is changing and improving fast in the country?

You have to improve your living conditions, and this cannot be done unless you work. Supposing all the people in the world were satisfied with their conditions. Would we have ships plying the oceans, or planes flying in the air, or radios, telephones, refrigerators and cars today? We would have none of these things. But you cannot get these things unless you have money. And you can't have money unless you work for it.

You do not have to go to school and "know book." You do not have to wear extraordinary clothes. You do not have to wear shoes or be civilized before you can work to earn money and improve things. No matter who you are or where you are, you can get land enough to plant anything you want. [The President makes reference to the fact that every Liberian is entitled to at least twenty-five acres of land for agricultural purposes.]

The Government is trying to help you by opening ways and means for you to make money. And you appear to be too lazy to work. You seem to believe that if you plant your crops you will be dead before they mature and your children will enjoy the results of your labors; so rather than work you live poverty-stricken.

If that is what you think, that is shortsightedness. You have to look to the future. A poverty-stricken people make a poverty-stricken nation.[9]

It is apparent from this and other public speeches of the President that he feels the fastest way to end the ethnic differences among the Liberian peoples is by closing up the economic gap between the few and the many. Better standards of living lead to better educational opportunities, which in turn create increased social and political mobility. For this reason, the Open Door Policy and the Unification Policy are so mutually complementary that they are almost one. As President Tubman himself pointed out at the 1963 Unification Council:

This policy could not have been successful without the Open Door Policy and vice versa the Open Door Policy could not have succeeded without the Unification Policy. The Open Door Policy brought about better and numerous roads to almost every part of the country, airfields and other means of communication and transportation which made the remotest parts of the country accessible to traders and businessmen and thereby activated development in these areas, as well as affording to the people in different sections of the country the means whereby they could communicate with, visit and get to know more about each other. The Open Door Policy has also brought greater advantages in education, health, social and other benefits to the citizens of the country. It made possible the coming to various concessions such as the mining and agricultural concessions which enable more of our people to be gainfully employed and to receive practical on-the-job training, higher wages and other benefits.

Moreover, we felt that not only should the Government and the concessionaires share in the profits of these concessions but that the people themselves should also obtain direct benefits therefrom. In this connection we enunciated the policy that whenever possible Liberian citizens, without regard to station, tribe or clan inhabiting the littoral or the hinterland, be offered the privilege to purchase stocks in these concessions. Many of the chiefs and the citizens living in their chiefdoms are holders of share certificates in one or more concessions.

The purpose for all of these has been our wish to raise the standard of living of the people of the nation and to develop a middle class which is so necessary in a democracy and free enterprise system of government.[10]

Has the Unification Policy really been effective? Has it really improved the lot of the tribal people? Has it really brought a change in the attitudes of the Americo-Liberians toward their tribal countrymen? Based upon several months of research and firsthand observation, this writer must reply in the affirmative. The advances that have been made in the fields of health and education since 1944, as was seen in an earlier chapter, have been dramatic. The economic boom resulting from the Open Door Policy has placed the tribal man in a promising position by creating new demands for his products and labor. He is, in effect, being pulled into the money economy and the modern social system. And it is this factor which has made unification successful.

As for Americo-Liberianism itself, it has in actual fact all but disappeared. Prior to 1944 Liberians in government or business would hide any "tribal blood." Today, tribal background presents no problems for success. (In fact, the vogue now is to stress one's tribal background.) Many cabinet members and leading government officials during the Tubman administration have tribal backgrounds. The tribal people now believe that ability will lead to success. But those with highly placed friends still rise more rapidly—as in any society.

Summing up the social progress resulting from two decades of unification, President Tubman told the National Unification Council at Kolahun on February 14, 1963:

We feel gratified that all sections of the country, and the people have cooperated in making the Unification Policy a success. During the last twenty years there have been no intertribal wars. All tribes, segments and elements of the country have stood together in support of the nation and the Unification Policy. . . .

There is no question that the Unification Policy has been successful and that it has brought manifold benefits to the nation. This gives much satisfaction to all those who had anything to do with the inauguration, the shaping and execution of the policy as well as to every citizen who has cooperated in making the practical application of the policy a reality.[11]

THE OPEN DOOR POLICY

In 1955, President Tubman made the following statement to his people:

Seeing that we have been seriously handicapped by a closed door policy, and wishing to bring to fruition the dream of our fathers . . . , we have, since the beginning of this administration, enunciated and vigorously fostered an Open Door Policy. Because of this policy, thousands . . . have come . . . in search of a land where they can be helpful in securing themselves and our citizens against the curse of ignorance, poverty and disease; where . . . business of every kind and profitable investments on a basis of mutuality can be established.[12]

These words summarize Tubman's program, for the radical improvements that have touched virtually all aspects of Liberian life have been made possible by the success of his economic Open Door Policy. From early in his career, Tubman has consistently advocated partnerships with responsible foreign interests on the premise that Liberia lacked the necessary capital and technical know-how to develop itself. While he was still in the Senate, it was his introduction of the bill and his behind-the-scenes politicking that made it possible for Firestone to enter the country in 1926. This was the first and only large-scale foreign enterprise ever to operate in Liberia prior to the Tubman administration.

Senator Tubman's argument on the Firestone bill was clear-

cut: it was a matter of swim or sink for the Republic. In subsequent floor debates he continued to expound his economic
philosophy. One of his most frequent themes was that riches
buried in the ground are valueless to an owner who cannot
afford to buy a shovel. In his public speeches he stressed the
view that it was the responsibility of the National Government to promote the survey and development of these riches
in the interest of the general welfare. His ideas rapidly gained
currency among the people as his homespun logic translated
them into popular terms. Besides, Tubman was one of the
few men in Liberian history who, after carving out a successful political career, did not forget the little man. The riches
belong to the nation and the people are the nation; that was
and still is his credo of economic development.

This Tubman formula, which earned the enmity of the old
guard during his senatorial years, could not be implemented
as quickly as he wished when he became President. But he
laid the groundwork during the early years of his administration. He concentrated on transportation facilities, which are
a prelude to economic development; Liberia needed roads,
good port facilities, airfields, utilities. During World War II,
he capitalized on the opportunities presented by his country's
strategic position. Roberts Field was already an international
crossroads for U.S. military air transport, but President Barclay was reluctant to align Liberia fully with the Allied war
effort. Tubman rejected such reluctance when he came to
office.

President Tubman's first actions were to move Liberia out
of the sterling zone, making the U.S. dollar the official currency, and to declare war formally on Germany and Japan.
The latter action made Liberia eligible for Lend-Lease funds,
which built the $22 million Free Port of Monrovia.[13] Tub-
man's uncompromising wartime support of the United States
paid even bigger dividends in peacetime. When President
Truman of the United States announced the Point Four Program in 1949, Liberia applied for and received $40 million

for public construction. The Joint Liberian–United States Commission for Economic Development, which was set up as part of this program, still exists in cooperation with the U.S. Agency for International Development. It apportions, according to priorities, U.S. funds appropriated for Liberia's internal development. In 1962, the United States gave Liberia nearly $11 million in aid, plus a $4.8 million long-term loan. During the Tubman administration, U.S. assistance altogether has amounted to more than $150 million.

In addition, Tubman did a remarkable job of cleaning up the mess he inherited after decades of negligence under previous administrations. He streamlined the hopelessly bureaucratic government departments and procedures, put through a series of excise and personal tax measures, made the government the exclusive purchaser of gold, encouraged the banks of the country to endorse long-term loans for private Liberian enterprises, and saw to it that the laws relating to corporations were drawn up so as to create a favorable climate for business. The result was an increase in national revenue from $1.5 million to $12.8 million during his first term. He put Liberia on a pay-as-you-go financial footing.

Perhaps the crowning achievement of this early period was the government's repayment in full of the $5 million Firestone loan of 1926. This was historic, for it made Liberia free of all external debts for the first time since 1871. To mark the event, the National Legislature passed a bill for the erection of a monument that now stands on a meticulously kept plot of land in front of the University of Liberia campus.

The President did not pursue fully his Open Door Policy until his election to a second term in May, 1951. His landslide victory at the polls convinced him that the arch-conservatives no longer constituted an imminent danger. His success in implementing his policy has not only transformed Liberia, but influenced all of Black Africa, for, according to United Nations statistics, he built the fastest-growing economy in the world.

The lesson of Liberia was important to the Free World and to Africa. At a time when various African countries were courting the Communist powers, Liberia made an economic breakthrough by depending on Western support and using democratic methods. On the one hand, Liberia demonstrated that successful aid from the West can be free of exploitation; this was a lesson for Africa. On the other hand, Liberia demonstrated that Africa was ready to move ahead free of Communist domination and in cooperation with the West; this was a lesson for the Free World. In this writer's view, the Open Door Policy is an important model for the continent-wide progress of emerging Africa.

In his Second Inaugural Address on January 7, 1952, President Tubman summarized what the Open Door Policy meant:

> We shall encourage foreign investments and the granting of foreign concessions where Liberians have not reached the position where they are capable and competent to explore and exploit the potential resources of the country. We shall continue to guarantee protection to investors and concessionaires of all investments and concessions. All concessions, I stress again, must be on a basis of mutuality.

When he spoke spontaneously on this subject, he made his points more dramatically:

> I stand for free trade and the Open Door Policy. I believe in protective tariffs and measures in favor of Liberians when they have developed and presented what should and can be protected and to assist them to develop their trade. But I am not in favor of, and I am diametrically opposed to, and do not subscribe to, pursuing protective measures and tariffs after phantoms or oases of the desert.

He said of the closed-door policy of his conservative predecessors:

> I will never subscribe to such a supercilious, shortsighted, contracted and phobic policy that paralysed industry and in-

vestment and kept the nation in poverty, suspicion, despair, commotion and turmoil. . . .[14]

And so, with total conviction and complete confidence in himself and his people, Tubman threw his program into high gear. The period of hesitation was over.

All of the thirty-eight major foreign concerns now operating in the country, representing a combined investment of nearly three-quarters of a billion dollars, have come in under Tubman. All but three signed agreements with the government after the President's second inauguration. Liberia Mining Company entered in 1946 but did not begin exporting ore until late 1951. The Liberia (Rubber) Company (1947) had not yet begun production. The only concession of the three that contributed to the national revenue was Liberia's pioneer concessionaire, Firestone. Therefore, the policy enunciated during Tubman's first term did not make its impact until the 1950's.

According to J. Milton Weeks, Director-General of the Office of National Planning, "the economic growth of the Liberian economy has been unsurpassed in performance by any other country during the last decade preceding 1961." He cites the following:

> Gross domestic money income more than quadrupled between 1950 and 1961, government revenues increased more than eightfold, tonnage of goods imported nearly quadrupled, rubber exports rose by nearly a third from an already large base, iron ore exports increased from nothing to over three million long tons per year, the money sector labor force nearly tripled, net money income of tribal households more than quadrupled, mileage of all weather roads was multiplied by a factor of four. There was unprecedented expansion in all areas of the economic life of the nation.[15]

Foreign capital has been pouring into the economy at an average annual rate of $75 million. Over-all economic expansion during this period averaged 15 per cent annually, and the $50 million budget approved by the Legislature for the fiscal year 1963 represents a 1200 per cent increase over the 1950 figure.[16]

In his Third Inaugural Address (1956), the President gave this progress report on the Open Door Policy:

> Our aim has . . . been to cooperate with honest and reasonable foreign capital and technical knowledge in the economic exploitation of our wealth. By removing hampering restrictions, by developing a fair tax structure and maintaining a stable government we believe the atmosphere has been created which has proven favorable not only for foreign capital operating alone, but has also served as an inducement to joint enterprises.
>
> Today, all major exploitations of Liberian mineral resources are being conducted on a joint-partnership basis. Furthermore, the confidence and mutual trust thus inspired have manifested themselves by cooperation between foreign and Liberian private capital.

It is true, of course, that the economy is dominated by foreign private capital and will be for the next several decades. But the benefits have been tremendous for the country and its citizens. Schools and hospitals are being built on an unprecedented scale. New ports, roads, airfields, and railroads are opening up the entire country; all of this will stimulate local agriculture, industry, and trade. During the past two decades of the Tubman Era all sectors of the economy have undergone great changes. This is forcefully demonstrated by the rise in the government budget from $750,000 in 1943 to $50 million in 1963.

There is every reason to believe that the future will even be brighter. For example, iron ore alone will add about $20 million to the national revenue within the next few years. George Blowers, a former director of the Export-Import Bank in Washington, predicts that "Liberia in the next decade will experience one of the most rapid increases of gross national product in the world." As far as President Tubman is concerned, "the cooperation of foreign capital in the exploitation of our natural resources has proven mutually beneficial and has enabled us to avoid the pitfalls of extremist nationalist policies."[17]

Now that Liberia is on the move, the President is anxious about one thing: to make certain that Liberians take full advantage of the opportunities presented to them. During 1962 and 1963 he went on the campaign trail selling iron-ore stocks on a long-term, no-interest basis. He made radio broadcasts to the nation, called special meetings and even traveled the interior bush country. His sales talk went something like this:

> You know how it is when you trade. You buy some small-small things. Then you sell those things one-one and you make small profit on the things you sell. Then you buy more again and sell more and sometimes you can make good money by trading.
>
> Or you buy a cup of peanuts and plant them. And when the peanuts are full you get four cups of peanuts or more from that one cup of peanuts. And so you have made a profit. The same is true of rubber or cocoa or coffee. When you plant rubber, however, you do not see any money coming in from the money you have spent for maybe five years. Then after five years time, you can see profit.
>
> In this iron matter, it is like this: It takes plenty money to start this thing. They must buy machines to build roads, to make houses for the workers to live in, to dig the iron itself. All this takes money. Someone must have faith to believe that when all this is done and the iron is dug out, the iron itself will make money to pay for all these machines. Those people are called a company. No one person has enough money to pay for all this. It must be many people who pay for it. And it is good that many people can help because then the profit comes to many people and not to just one person.[18]

3

The State of the Republic

Health

Until recent years West Africa, including Liberia, was known as the "white man's grave"; but the African also faced an early grave in the tropical climate with its threat of disease and sickness. The African was resigned. His recourse was a visit from the medicine man who chased away evil spirits, provided psychological relief, and often became a carrier of the disease himself.

However, the African traditionally has followed some elementary sanitation practices, partly out of superstition, but also out of a sense of personal and community cleanliness. In the tribal villages, to give a few examples: trenches were dug to serve as the village latrine; refuse was deposited at one particular point and periodically burned or buried; the hut and belongings of a member who died after a long illness and suffering were burned; those sharing food from a common bowl had to wash their hands before eating. Many other examples could be cited to show that communal cleanliness was in practice before the white civilizers arrived.

Public health efforts in Liberia began in 1928 when President C. D. B. King set up a Bureau of Public Health. This was transformed by President Edwin Barclay, in 1930, into the Bureau of Health and Sanitation, with a staff composed of the country's three doctors. The Bureau's effect on the country was negligible. It was only a spare-time effort by the doctors, who would not give up their private practices, and the Barclay administration failed to give more than verbal support. Moreover, it was made clear at the time of its creation that the Bureau's services were to be limited to the Monrovia area.

When President Tubman took office in 1944, the Bureau underwent dramatic improvements. In his first year in office, he did more for the health of the Liberian people than all previous presidents combined. Three full-time doctors were appointed and a five-year development plan in public health was drawn up with the assistance of a group of American experts headed by Dr. J. B. West. President Roosevelt himself appointed the advisory group upon the request of the Liberian Government, and, later, approved the plan. Within three years, there were doctors, trained technicians, and nurses in every county and province of Liberia. The Bureau was elevated to a Department in 1950 and today only Sweden spends more than Liberia on public health relative to national income. Some Liberians have charged that the outlay, which amounted to slightly more than $2 million for the fiscal year 1962, is too extravagant. The President, who remains firm in his policy, has stated:

> I cannot compromise with any opinion, no matter how forcefully expressed, which holds that funds used for public health and sanitation are wasted. I am convinced that the progress of any nation is measured in terms of the progress and prosperity of its individual citizens; and if that citizenry is poverty-stricken, disease-ridden, unhealthy and illiterate, that nation is bound for failure, retrogression and eventual disintegration. If we create the opportunities, make available the possibilities, I firmly believe that the people will utilize them to their best advantage.[1]

The National Public Health Service, headed by Director-General Edwin M. Barclay,[2] has carried on a vigorous program in the last few years. The Service operates eight general hospitals and five specialized hospitals at various points in the country. Together they have a total of 729 beds, 33 full-time doctors,[3] and 1,064 employees. The two largest hospitals are situated in Monrovia; namely the Liberian Government Hospital, with 180 beds and 10 physicians, and the Maternity Center, with 120 beds and 8 physicians. In addition to the Maternity Center, the other specialized institutions are two tuberculosis annexes at Monrovia, the Mental Rehabilitation Center at Paynesville, and the Eye Clinic at Monrovia.

The interior is served by over a hundred small clinics supported partly by private missionary and other groups. The Service also has a mobile dental unit which periodically visits the interior. Private firms operate five hospitals which provide free medical care primarily for their employees but accept all emergency cases.[4] Protestant missionaries operate another three,[5] and the Roman Catholic mission will have a modern 150-bed general hospital in the Monrovia area by 1965. The latter is being completely financed and staffed by a Spanish order of priests and brothers, St. John of God. Liberia also boasts the only Research Institute of Tropical Medicine in West Africa.[6]

Liberia, thanks to the assistance of the World Health Organization (WHO), the United Nations Children's Fund (UNICEF), and the U.S. Agency for International Development (AID), has had remarkable success in controlling communicable diseases. For example, in 1954, the total prevalence rate of yaws was estimated at 19 per cent, with 2 per cent in the infectious stage. By 1961, these figures were reduced to 0.74 per cent and 0.17 per cent, respectively. With the greatest part of the job completed, the yaws campaign has entered a second phase, that of surveillance and regular treatment, a long-term effort aimed at total eradication.

A WHO advisory team made a survey of the leprosy problem in September–December, 1960. They found a prevalence rate of 2.2 per cent among the general population. Of the total found infected, 7 per cent were lepromatous, 62 per cent were tuberculoid, and over 50 per cent showed some disability. In 1961, a program was initiated by the Service, in cooperation with UNICEF and WHO, which will treat all leprosy cases over a ten-year period. The first two years are being devoted to the establishment of a pilot project in the Central Province and the training of aides. The plan calls for extensive use of several mobile units and teams by 1964. In addition to rendering medical treatment, they will attempt to educate the people on how leprosy is spread and how to avoid it.

In the area of smallpox control, the Service estimates that 95 per cent of the population will have received vaccinations by 1965. In February and March of 1962, a group of volunteer physicians from the United States known as the Brother's Brother gave smallpox vaccinations to slightly more than 200,000 persons. They trained Liberian aides in the use of multijet inoculators and the campaign has been carried into the interior. Figures released by the National Public Health Service show that 750,000 persons had received protection by the end of 1962.

One disease seriously underestimated by the government in the past has been tuberculosis. Although it has been known for many years that pulmonary tuberculosis has been on the increase, the full magnitude of the problem did not come to light until WHO made a prevalence survey in 1960. According to their findings, 70 to 80 per cent of the population over the age of thirty is infected.[7] The Monrovia area is said to have the highest percentage of infected persons while the interior has the lowest.

Director-General Edwin M. Barclay notes in his 1962 Annual Report to the President that, although "tuberculosis infection does not necessarily coincide with tuberculosis disease, it would be unjustified to assume that any substantial improvement will evolve in the absence of large-scale tuberculosis control measures."[8] He went on to suggest that "the T.B. Annex is a dilapidated temporary structure, a fit object for abandonment to be substituted by a construction for 100 patients near the site of the Congotown unit."[9] This disease seems to be replacing malaria as the country's number one health problem. However, for the moment, malaria takes the greatest toll of the Liberian population, both in the number of deaths and in reducing work efficiency.

In 1953, a WHO–UNICEF team began studying the possibility of employing large-scale spraying of insecticides to control malaria. In Liberia they set up their headquarters at Kpain and their experiments covered roughly one-third of the country. For the first four years they used dieldrin and benzine hexachloride in spraying selected villages once a year. At the end of 1957, it was discovered that transmission interruption was only temporary and that the mosquitoes could develop a resistance to the chemicals. The following year, DDT was used and it proved completely successful.

However, it was estimated that the annual cost of DDT would be roughly $1.50 per capita, which made it impossible to implement the plan immediately. In 1962, WHO agreed to assist those governments interested, providing advisers, equipment, and supplies for a two-year training operation so that technicians would be available when the country could afford a total eradication program.[10] The Liberian Government has allocated $200,000 of the 1963 budget for this pre-eradication training program. According to a projection made by the National Public Health Service, total eradication will be effected by 1970.

In the field of medical education there is still a big job ahead. The government-sponsored Tubman National Institute of Medical Arts, organized in 1946 for the training of paramedical workers, has suffered from a lack of qualified teachers. From the time of its founding until 1961, a total of 108 professional nurses, 49 practical nurses, and 41 midwives graduated from the Institute. A school of sanitation was added in 1961, graduating nine of the first fourteen students who enrolled. Aware of the need for better organization and administration, the goverment has recently made arrangements with the University of Cincinnati to run the Institute. In addition to specialized training, general health courses are included at all levels of education. Annual physical examinations, vaccinations, and medical treatments are provided without charge for all full-time students.[11]

Education

President Tubman has said:

> Education is an essential and indispensable element in the life and progress of a nation. It is one of the safeguards of the liberties of a people and the index finger pointing to the future prospect of the continued survival, progress and life of any nation. Within the context, I feel very strongly that an assessment of the educational system of the country is highly desirable and essential as it will determine the basis of our national outlook, efficiency and preparedness. . . .[12]

Largely as a result of this, developments in education have been extensive. The number of schools has increased from 240 in 1944 to 841 in 1962; classrooms from 720 to 2,424; and students from 10,200 to 80,321.[13] Annual expenditures have multiplied some thirty times to a 1962 high of $2,935,000, about 8 per cent of Liberia's national budget. This included $917,000 spent on 559 government-sponsored scholarships awarded to students studying locally and abroad.[14] Considering the country's limitations, both in economic and human resources, the record is remarkable.

The barriers to educational opportunity included also linguistic and psychological problems. Before 1944, mass education was unknown in Liberia and the population spoke over twenty different dialects. Anyone traveling in the interior either had to speak the local dialect or hire an interpreter, if one could be found. There were no roads, railroads, or airfields. Qualified teachers could be counted on one hand, including missionaries! And, perhaps worst of all, the tribal man was reluctant to release his children from their herding or farming chores to obtain the kind of education which had no practical bearing on life in the hinterland. In the tribal context, a successful man was one who could plant a good crop of rice, not write a 500-word composition.

Although progress has been made in spite of these barriers, the President does not hide his concern. In a 1957 speech, he said:

> While there may be several reasons that could be assigned for this slow progress, there are . . . two that strike me forcibly and which I regard as extremely important. First and foremost is the lack of technically-trained citizens, and secondly, the lack of capital. I have intentionally placed capital last because without the skill and adeptness to administer it, capital can be easily wasted.[15]

In the short run, economic progress has outstripped education. With President Tubman's Open Door economic policy, national income has more than tripled, but the shortage of qualified Liberians has required the importation of thousands of trained foreigners.[16] An acute shortage of masons, carpenters, electricians, mechanics, and the like has forced every major firm in the country to hire foreign labor at extraordinarily high wages. This drives operating costs up at the expense of the Liberian consumer without direct benefit to Liberian employes. Foreign employes remain only a few years, save as much as possible, and spend most of their Liberian earnings at home. In an effort to limit this drain on the economy, fourteen junior and senior high schools have introduced elective vocational programs. The International Labor Organization (ILO) has agreed to help Liberia by making available $1 million to build a large vocational training center. Germany, Switzerland, and Sweden have agreed to help Liberia with various vocational training schemes which will add 300 skilled workers to the labor force by 1966.

has plans to erect a new multi-million dollar campus on a 5,000-acre plot eighteen miles outside of Monrovia at Johnsonville.[20]

In the area of international technical assistance, the United States Government is by far the largest contributor. In 1962, of the $10.6 million granted to Liberia for development, $4.3 million, or 41 per cent was allocated for education. The funds were administered by AID to build twenty-two new schools, to supply over a hundred teachers for Liberian schools at all levels, and to provide eighty-five full and partial scholarships to Liberian students for training in the United States. On August 24, 1962, ninety-six teachers of the U.S. Peace Corps arrived to take up posts in elementary and secondary schools throughout the country. Indications are that their number will triple in the next few years. Secretary Mitchell calls them a "boon to the educational program in Liberia."

U.S. Government efforts are supplemented by several American volunteer programs. Cooperative American Relief for Everywhere (CARE) gives teacher-aid kits and free history books to the Education Department for distribution. In 1962, CARE initiated a school-lunch program in Monrovia which, it is hoped, will be eventually extended to cover all schools. In mid-September, 1962, over 200,000 textbooks were donated to the Liberian school system by the California Board of Education as part of a privately sponsored "Books from America" program. Each summer about forty American teachers are sent to Liberia by a group known as "Crossroads Africa." They hold a series of seminars to train Liberian teachers in the latest pedagogical methods. The American community in Liberia also has several volunteer programs. One of these is the American Women's Assistance to Rural Education (AWARE) which is made up of the wives of American officials and privately employed Americans. They give one day per week to the preparation of educational aids for use in the schools of the interior.

While assistance from other foreign governments and international agencies (e.g., UNESCO and ILO) is increasing, their combined efforts, both in terms of money and personnel, are still a small fraction of those of the United States. UNESCO provides six scholarships and eight teachers for the University of Liberia. Five Liberian students are currently studying in Germany on Pax Romana Scholarships sponsored by the Roman Catholic Church. Others are offered by the German, Swiss, and Swedish governments, but the language problems leave most of these unfilled.

THE ECONOMY

Although Liberia is the oldest Negro republic in Africa, its economy is still young and growing. The road of independence has been uphill, lonely, and difficult. During Liberia's early decades of independence, the British and French were antagonistic toward what they considered a threat to their colonial ambitions as well as a refutation of the assumption that the black African was incapable of self-government. Across the Atlantic, Liberia's unofficial mother country, the United States, was still in the isolationist period of its history; its gestures of friendship were few and cautious. Nor did Liberia have easy-term foreign-aid programs to provide quick remedies for financial crises. Pleas for aid fell upon the ears of unsympathetic bankers. For the first eighty years or more, each of Liberia's several loans was used to repay the last. The battle was for survival, leaving little opportunity for development.

When outside funds finally became more available, the Liberian Government was distrustful. All foreign capital was kept out in the belief that this was the only way to safeguard the nation's sovereignty. As a result, in 1943, after ninety-six years as an independent republic, Liberia had a national revenue of only $1.5 million and its entire economy was dependent on one crop and one company, the Firestone Rubber

Plantations Company. And even the latter had been allowed to enter Liberia only on condition that it guarantee a desperately needed $5-million loan.

In 1944 Tubman forced the closed door open. His invitation to foreign enterprise and his relentless promotion put Liberia and the Liberians on the move. National income soared from the 1943 figure of $1.5 million to $36.1 million in 1962. The May, 1962, issue of the *United Nations Monthly Statistical Bulletin* reports that, in the 1950's, Liberia had the greatest percentage increase in per capita gross national product in the world and was exceeded only by Japan in real GNP growth for the same period. But this is only the beginning; the full effect of the Open Door Policy has not yet been felt. Conservative estimates place the revenue figure for the year 1970 at $100 million.

Agriculture

At present, agriculture is the bedrock of the national economy, with over 90 per cent of the Liberian labor force directly engaged in agricultural production. In order of their importance, the principal crops consumed domestically are rice, yams, okra, cabbage, cassava, corn, peppers, beans, peas, plantains, bananas, peanuts, pineapples, oranges, grapefruit, coconuts, guavas, limes, mangoes, and pumpkins. As already pointed out, agricultural methods are generally crude, except on the large-scale rubber plantations. The great majority of the crops consumed domestically grow wild. If the natives could be taught how to cultivate them, the surplus could be used for export. There are now five export crops; ranked in order of their dollar value, they are rubber, palm kernels, coffee, cacao, and piassava.

Rubber. Rubber growing in Liberia has served the strategic interests of the United States from its inception. In the mid-1920's, Harvey S. Firestone used it to break the rubber cartels which were keeping the world price at an artificially high level. Later, during World War II, the Japanese captured

the major sources of rubber in the Far East; Liberia, geo-
graphically closer and safer, supplied a quarter of the natural
rubber needed in the Allied war effort. Productive capacity
had doubled to nearly 45 million pounds when the war ended.
Planting continued in the postwar years, and in 1961 rubber
was still Liberia's largest export crop by a very great margin.[21]

However, the future of Liberian rubber is not promising.
Synthetics are replacing natural rubber while, at the same
time, other areas of the world are competing for the rapidly
shrinking world market. For more than a decade, over-all
world production of natural rubber has been increasing at a
rate almost double that of demand; the world price has fallen
drastically, particularly since the 1958 recession. In a ten-
month period during 1961, the price dropped 25 per cent to
an all-time low of 28 cents per pound. Since then, there have
been no significant upward movements and from all indications there will be none in the near future.

The Firestone plantation, the largest in the world, produces
nearly 90 per cent of the country's rubber, with about 1,900
independent growers accounting for the remainder. Firestone
and the five new rubber concessionaires[22] have already begun
planting the higher-yielding variety of rubber tree in order to
meet the competition with more and better natural rubber.
By 1970 their combined production figure will be 50 per cent
higher than the 130 million pounds achieved in 1961, although the total number of acres under cultivation will have
fallen by a quarter. Their world position will be relatively
secure if their present plans are carried out.

However, the independent growers, almost all of them
Liberians, will suffer. Most sell their latex to Firestone, which
buys it at substantially less than the world market price.[23]
Their trees are generally old, low-yielding and no longer
economically competitive. The Rubber Advisory Service of
the government has reported that, unless the old trees are re
placed immediately with higher-yielding clones, the position

of the independent growers will become critical before 1970. They are faced with falling profit margins due to lower prices and increasing labor and equipment costs. Firestone has been furnishing the new clones from its nursery free of charge, but the cost of clearing new land and carrying through the replacement is still prohibitive. Barring some unexpected turn of events, many of the small farms will go out of business in the 1970's. Nonetheless, Liberia will remain a major world rubber producer until at least the end of this century.

Other Agricultural Exports. Other agricultural exports, in order of dollar value, include palm products, coffee, cacao, and piassava. Their combined value makes up about 4 per cent of the Liberia's foreign trade. The largest single item among these is the palm kernel, which has an export value of more than a million dollars annually. The product's principal use is in the manufacture of soap, although Liberia loses much of this market to other areas of the world where the palm tree is cultivated on a large scale. The kernels are picked by hand and taken to markets across the country, where they are bought by local dealers. About 30 million pounds of kernels are gathered and sold in this way annually.

Coffee was Liberia's leading export crop in the latter half of the nineteenth century, but the market was largely taken over by Brazil at the turn of the century. Today, coffee grows wild for the most part, but plantations of the *robusta* species are being developed. Production of the *liberica* species still dominates the local market and restaurants throughout the country take great pride in serving espresso-like "Liberian Coffee." Each year about 2.2 million pounds are exported, but value has dropped by more than half in recent years to a low of $360,000 in 1961. The instability of market prices precludes any large-scale development of this product in the near future.

Annual exports of cacao and piassava fluctuate widely in volume and value. Due to a fall in world demand, exports of these products were valued at $368,000 in 1961, or roughly a third of the total for the previous year. Until stability is brought about in these markets, extensive cultivation will not be initiated.

Natural Resources

Timber. Liberia is the only country in West Africa which has high evergreen forests covering more than 85 per cent of its total land area.[24] These forests, representing one of the greatest timber reserves on the continent, contain more than 235 species of trees.[25] Utility tests made at the Yale University School of Forestry reveal that twenty-one of these could be used for furniture and interior trim, twenty for heavy construction, twenty-seven for general carpentry purposes, sixteen for the manufacture of various tools, and twenty for wood pulp. According to a report by a U.S. Forestry Mission, there are 8.7 million acres of commercially usable timber which, if operated on a sustained yield basis, could produce 2 billion board feet of usable boards yearly without depleting the standing volume, which is currently estimated at nearly 140 billion board feet.

However, two factors limit the development of this resource. One is transportation. Few of Liberia's rivers could carry the timber more than a couple of miles. Roads through the interior, while increasing in number and quality, are still inadequate for heavy transport. The railroads that do exist lead to iron-ore deposits, and none of the six timber concessions[26] now in Liberia are near enough to these lines to take advantage of them.

The other factor is the type of forests found in the country. In West African forests the trees are not predominantly of a single species, as is the case in the major forests of North America. Instead, there may be a hundred or more different species on each acre, of which the company may be interested in felling only one or two. In each instance, a road must be cut to the tree to bring in the heavy equipment for sawing and removal. Only highly experienced outfits can make the proposition profitable.

Consequently, Liberia's timber industry is developing more slowly than would be expected at first glance. In 1962, timber exports amounted to not quite 10 million board feet, or less than 0.1 per cent of the estimated potential. With the development of transportation in the country's interior and the adaptation of lumbering techniques to overcome the obstacles of African forests, the industry will grow. But it will take time.

In the meantime, preparations are under way. Surveys of the major forest areas are being carried out through the Department of Agriculture and Commerce in order to facilitate future development. The timber concessions presently operating in the country are required to apply certain conservation measures that are not unduly restrictive on normal activities. Also, the government has set aside 4 million acres of virgin high forests in National Forest Reserves[27] which will be preserved for more efficient exploitation by future generations.

Iron Ore. Liberia has the richest iron-ore deposits in the world. At least 635 million tons of proven high-grade ore are located within its borders, with a content of between 66 and 70 per cent—greater than that of Swedish ore, which previously held the record, and about 20 per cent higher than that of the Lake Superior (Mesabi) deposits. In 1961, iron ore became Liberia's chief dollar-value export,[28] and it will continue to be so for many years to come. The development of these deposits, the greatest success of Tubman's Open Door Policy, has placed the economy in a boom situation seldom achieved on the continent of Africa.

Application of what businessmen refer to as the "Tubman Formula" (the arrangement whereby the government receives 50 per cent of the profits) guarantees that the Liberians will benefit directly. Moreover, Liberia is the only country in Black Africa where the citizens can buy shares in the various companies involved. For example, Liberian Iron Ore, Ltd., offered capital stocks to Liberian citizens at 80 per cent of the market quotation (or about $12 per share); they were given three years to pay, without interest.

Liberia's economic transition from a sea of rubber to a mountain of iron is an exciting story. Virtually from the time of Liberia's founding there had been stories and tribal legends about the vast riches of its upland stretches. Nothing was ever done about it, however, as the Liberians feared that foreign big business would quickly plunder and cheat the country of its only promise for the future. Their fear had some validity in the days when underdeveloped areas were exploited and the survival of the Republic itself was touch and go. By the time both of these factors began to be less important, jealous protectionism and economic isolation had become a way of life for the Liberians.

In 1943, when President Barclay and President-elect Tubman visited President Franklin D. Roosevelt in the United States, Tubman asked President Roosevelt to send a geological survey team to Liberia, much to the surprise of Barclay and the others in the delegation. It was this team which first confirmed the commercial possibilities of Liberian iron ore. At the time they made specific reference to the deposits at Bomi Hills, which they estimated held 200 million tons of ore with a metal content of 56 per cent. Today this is considered one of the smaller deposits.

In 1954, Mt. Nimba (4,600 feet above sea level) was discovered to contain iron ore. Subsequent assays placed the tonnage (proven) at 300 million, with a metallic purity of as high as 70.4 per cent. This estimate is based on exploratory drillings on less than a quarter of the mountain; the actual tonnage may be much more. An adjoining reserve, Mt. Bahm, is estimated to hold another 225 million tons with between 55 and 60 per cent iron content. About nine other mountains in this area, known collectively as the Nimba Range, are believed to hold similar deposits.[29] One expert, Fred Ryan of LAMCO, called the Mt. Nimba deposit "unquestionably the greatest and richest iron ore reserve in the world." With only a foot or two of soil, overburden is negligible, and because of the high metal content no benefication (crushing and separation) is necessary. Other deposits currently known to exist in the country are located in the Bassa Hills, Putu, the Mano River area, and the Bong Hills. It is considered probable that more deposits of commercial quantity and quality remain to be discovered.

At present there are four major iron-mining operations in Liberia. The largest of these, and the largest private enterprise on the African continent,[30] is the LAMCO Joint Venture Enterprise at Nimba. The project began in September, 1953, when the Government of Liberia awarded the International African-American Corporation (IAAC) a mineral concession over a total area of 500 square miles. The greatest part of the concession covered most of the untested Sanniquellie District, at the northern tip of the Central Province, but also included were two known iron deposits at Bassa Hills (60 miles southeast of Monrovia) and Putu (in the Eastern Province).

IAAC had initially planned to develop the Bassa Hills deposit, because of its proximity to the Port of Monrovia. However, when explorations in the Sanniquellie District uncovered the vast riches of Nimba, these plans were temporarily scrapped. As news of the find spread, steel companies from all over the world began competing for an interest in its exploitation. Since IAAC was itself too small to undertake a project of such scope, a complex financial structure known as the LAMCO Joint Venture Enterprise was drawn up in 1960. The partners are the Liberian American-Swedish Minerals Company (LAMCO), which owns 75 per cent, and the Bethlehem Steel Corporation, which has the remaining 25 per cent. LAMCO ownership is divided between the Republic of Liberia (50 per cent) and Liberian Iron Ore, Ltd. (50 per cent).

The latter in turn is owned by the original concessionaire, IAAC, and the Swedish LAMCO Syndicate, which hold shares in the proportion of 40 per cent and 60 per cent, respectively.[31]

The Joint Venture expects ultimately to invest slightly more than $200 million.[32] It is building a 165-mile railroad (Nimba-Buchanan) and a deep-water harbor at Buchanan to accommodate 45,000 ton ore ships at all levels of tide. The harbor will have complete loading and storage facilities. Full production is scheduled to begin by 1965, when the Venture will be exporting between 7 and 8 million long tons annually. By 1971, it is expected that 12 million long tons could be exported without major changeovers. The concession agreement (signed April 28, 1960) covers a seventy-year period. Development of the Bassa Hills and Putu deposits is still on the drawing boards. With major harbor and railroad facilities already complete, this will be a relatively routine task. Depending on world demand, these projects will be started probably in the early 1980's.

The first commercial iron-ore mine in Liberia, and in fact in all of Black Africa, is located at Bomi Hills, 45 miles northwest of Monrovia. It is being exploited by the Liberia Mining Company,[33] which entered into an eighty-year mining concession agreement with the government on January 22, 1946. The mine commenced production in 1951, and since 1957 annual exports have averaged slightly less than 3 million long tons, with a value of about $30 million. The company's total investment is $37 million, most of which was spent on the Bomi-Monrovia railroad, an ore-loading finger pier at the Free Port of Monrovia, and a $12 million benefication plant to crush and separate crude ore. In addition it has its own water-pumping and electric power plants and saw mill.

Since LMC was the first concession to enter Liberia under the Open Door Policy, the government's original share in the profits was quite small. Liberia was to receive only a royalty of 5 cents per ton. However, when it became clear that profits were to be greater than initially anticipated, the company took the lead in negotiating a more equitable arrangement. Today the government receives 35 per cent of the company's net earnings; this will be increased to 50 per cent by no later than 1968. Legally, the company did not have to renegotiate. It has been this type of fair dealing that has borne out President Tubman's faith in the free-enterprise system and has kept the open door from swinging shut.

The second largest ore project in Liberia with respect to size of total investment ($100 million) will be that of the German-Liberian Mining Company (DELIMCO)[34] in the Bong Range. A seventy-year concession agreement dating from 1958 gives the company mining rights over 300 square miles located 50 miles northeast of Monrovia. The management, financing, and operation of the concession has been subcontracted by DELIMCO to the Bong Mining Company.[35] The latter estimates the reserve at 200 million tons of crude (35 per cent iron content) ore. A benefication plant, presently under construction, will concentrate the ore to 65 per cent purity for export. Production will begin in 1965, and by 1967 the company will export about 5 million tons annually. A 60-mile railroad and a loading pier at the Free Port of Monrovia are also being built.

Iron ore has put much of the previously idle Liberian capital back into the economy. Ninety per cent of the National Iron Ore Company, Ltd., is controlled directly or indirectly by Liberians.[36] A 1958 (eighty-year) concession agreement gives the company rights over the Mano River and Bie Range deposits, located near the Sierra Leonean border. The operation is being handled by Mine Management Associates, Ltd.,[37] another Liberian corporation. The Mano River deposit is already in production and a capacity of 4 million tons (55 per cent iron content) will be exported each year beginning in 1965. Surveys of the Bie Range are not yet complete, but there are over 65 million tons of proven reserves. A 52-mile railroad spur has been built linking up with LMC's

Bomi-Monrovia line. Existing facilities at the Free Port of Monrovia are being used. Power and benefication plants have been built at the Mano River site.

Other Minerals. Other minerals known to exist in the country are diamonds, gold, manganese, columbite, bauxite, tantalite, corundum, graphite, copper, mica, mercury, and zinc. The extent and quality of these deposits have not yet been determined. However, diamonds and gold are being developed commercially on a small scale. There are indications that alluvial diamond deposits along the Lofa River and in the Sanniquellie District are large.

Their discovery in 1957 caused a diamond rush of Olympic proportions as workers from all over the country left their jobs. Firestone and other rubber plantations were crippled. The government was finally forced to close off the diamond areas in order to return the country to a state of normality. But stories are still frequently told about native boys who lived like millionaires on proceeds from one or two stones they found before the government stepped in. And even today, Mandingo traders who can afford the necessary license fees periodically come into Monrovia with small bags of stones worth $100,000 or more.

At present, the only diamond concessionaire in the country is the Liberian-Swiss Mining Corporation. Organized in 1962 to develop a small area around the Lofa River, it will not begin production until 1965. In addition, there are a few small diamond dealers and brokers who exported about a million carats of gem and industrial stones in 1962. There is no doubt that mining and export of diamonds will expand significantly within the next few years.

Some small-scale gold mining is going on, but all the gold must be sold to the government-backed Bank of Monrovia at a price slightly lower than that on the world market. In 1962, the bank purchased 2,184.368 ounces. It does not appear likely that this figure will grow substantially unless new discoveries are made.

4

On the African and World Stage

LIBERIA IN AFRICAN AFFAIRS

In the history of this new Africa which has just come to the world, Liberia has a preeminent place because she has been for each one of our peoples the living proof that our liberty was possible and nobody can ignore the fact that the star which marks the Liberian National Emblem has been hanging more than a century—the sole star which illuminated our night of dominated peoples.[1]

—President Sékou Touré

Both psychologically and politically, Liberia has played a special role in the emergence of Black Africa. From 1820, when the first pioneers from America were prevented by the British from settling in Sierra Leone, until Ghana's achievement of independence on March 6, 1957, Liberia represented the aspirations of Black Africa to self-determination and independence. Though not the only independent African nation during this period, Liberia was more than any other free country linked by color, location, and tradition to Black Africa. Playing an important part in the League of Nations and later in the United Nations, Liberia has been a voice of Africa. It has shared its victories and its defeats with a continent that until 1957 saw freedom only as a distant goal on the horizon.

At the League of Nations, of which Liberia was a charter member, its representatives consistently defended the cause of African self-government. The defeat in 1934 of the controversial Plan of Assistance that would have undermined Liberian independence was regarded as a victory for African nationalism. It was a fitting prelude to President Tubman's leadership in a policy of total African liberation. In Liberia, almost every aspiring African nationalist has found support for his cause, including financial aid. Other Africans have been prepared for independence by the education they received in Liberia or from scholarships provided for study abroad.

In the United Nations, Liberia has distinguished itself in the cause of African freedom and has also served the larger purposes of world peacemaking. The Liberian record in the United Nations reflects favorably on all African nations in their pursuit of diplomatic maturity. While acting as a leader of African aspirations, Liberia has stressed constructive proposals and has shunned extremist approaches to African and world problems.

On December 20, 1960, Liberia became the first country of Black Africa to be elected to the Security Council. The term from January 1 to December 31, 1961, was particularly involved with African problems. These included revolution in Angola, the Algerian war, the Bizerte incident, chaos in the Congo, and racial oppression in South Africa. Liberia's permanent representative to the United Nations, Ambassador Nathan Barnes, was president of the Security Council during the critical days after Secretary-General Dag Hammarskjöld's death. With Ambassador Mongi Slim of Tunisia, then president of the General Assembly, Barnes represented the world organization at Hammarskjöld's funeral in Uppsala, Sweden, and later was instrumental in helping to defeat the "troika" doctrine and electing U Thant to fill Hammarskjöld's unexpired term. Liberian representatives have also been active on all the main U.N. committees, where their reputation for doing their "homework" has in several instances led to election as chairmen or to other leadership positions.

During the Sixteenth General Assembly Session, Liberia's Assistant Secretary of State, Miss Angie Brooks, was chairman of the Fourth (Trusteeship) Committee, a committee with which she has worked during most of her nine years with the Liberian mission. Miss Brooks is considered the U.N.'s outstanding woman diplomat and is credited with helping to make Africa's transition to independence more peaceful and orderly than was expected even by the optimists. African delegates refer to her as "the first lady of African independence."

In its African policy, Liberia has combined moderation with anticolonialism and thereby helped to steer other African nations toward constructive approaches to world problems. In 1960, when the newly independent African nations were beginning to flock to their seats as members of the U.N., President Tubman sounded a note of caution:

> In the hour of our triumph we Africans must remember that what we seek is justice and not revenge. There is no time for us to brood over the grievances and the sufferings of the past. We look to the future—a future which we hope to see cleansed of the racial hatred which brought such misfortune upon our own people. We must extend to the white man the hand of forgiveness and fellowship. We must invite him to join us in burying misunderstandings and in working for a better and happier world.[2]

Referring to this statement and to Liberia's position on the issues before the U.N., W. Averell Harriman, in a letter to the editor of the *New York Times* (October 6, 1960), wrote:

> It is a pity that these displays of moderation, good sense and good will seldom make the headlines. They deserve to be applauded for what they are—courageous attempts to inch the violent passions of our time a little way over in the direction of sanity.

With this in mind, Liberia's recent activities as spokesman for Africa can be examined in detail in regard to Angola, South Africa, South West Africa, and the Congo crisis.

Angola

Liberia first drew attention to the Angolan situation on February 15, 1961, when it brought the matter before the Security Council[3] only three days after fighting broke out. In the first few days after the Luanda uprising of February 12, hundreds of Africans were killed by the indiscriminate fire of Portuguese police. The Angolans were led by Holden Roberto, head of the Union of Angolan Peoples (UPA) and Prime Minister of the Government-in-Exile of Angola.

The Liberian delegate argued that the Angolan situation merited immediate consideration under Article 34 of the United Nations Charter, which empowers the Council to investigate any dispute "likely to endanger the maintenance of international peace and security." On February 20, the Liberian Government addressed a formal letter to the president of the Security Council requesting that the matter be placed on the agenda forthwith and urging positive action to put a stop to the "further deterioration and abuse of human rights and privileges in Angola."

On March 10, when the Council met to consider the question, the meeting began with the reading of a letter signed by thirty-four nations praising and supporting the Liberian initiative. The Liberian representative then submitted a resolution co-sponsored by Liberia, the United Arab Republic, and Ceylon, calling on Portugal to introduce reforms in Angola and requesting the Council to set up a subcommittee to examine the situation. However, the resolution failed to carry the required majority (the vote was 5 affirmative and 6 abstentions) at the end of debate on March 15, when some nations remained unconvinced that there was an imminent threat to peace.

The Liberian delegation, disappointed at the failure of the

Council to act, worked for the support of forty Afro-Asian members and forced the issue to a debate on the floor of the General Assembly. On April 20, Liberia introduced the resolution again, substituting the words "General Assembly" for "Security Council." In a roll-call vote, it was adopted by an overwhelming 73 to 2 (with Spain and the Republic of South Africa against). The preamble to this resolution, 1603 (XV), viewed the situation as "likely to endanger the maintenance of international peace and security," thus serving notice to the Security Council that its decision the month before did not represent the opinion of the great majority. This particular sentence received 67 affirmative votes. The operative part of the resolution reads as follows:

The General Assembly,

. . . .

1. Calls upon the Government of Portugal to consider urgently the introduction of measures and reforms in Angola for the purpose of the implementation of General Assembly resolution 1514 (XV), with due respect for human rights and fundamental freedoms and in accordance with the Charter of the United Nations;

2. Decides to appoint a sub-committee consisting of five members to be appointed by the President of the General Assembly concerning Angola, to receive further statements and documents, to conduct such inquiries as it may deem necessary and to report to the Assembly as soon as possible.

The General Assembly resolution 1514 (XV) is cited in all resolutions pertaining to Angola. Its wording is largely the work of Angie Brooks. Its operative part reads as follows:

The General Assembly,

. . . .

Declares that:

1. The subjection of peoples to alien subjugation, domination and exploitation constitutes a denial of fundamental human rights, is contrary to the Charter of the United Nations

and is an impediment to the promotion of world peace and co-operation.

2. All peoples have the right to self-determination; by virtue of that right they freely determine their political status and freely pursue their economic, social and cultural development.

3. Inadequacy of political, economic, social or educational preparedness should never serve as a pretext for delaying independence.

4. All armed action or repressive measures of all kinds directed against dependent peoples shall cease in order to enable them to exercise peacefully and freely their right to complete independence, and the integrity of their national territory shall be respected.

5. Immediate steps shall be taken, in Trust and Non-Self-Governing Territories of all other territories which have not yet attained independence, to transfer all powers to the peoples of those territories, without any conditions or reservations, in accordance with their freely expressed will and desire, without any distinction as to race, creed or color, in order to enable them to enjoy complete independence and freedom.

6. Any attempt aimed at the partial or total disruption of the national unity and the territorial integrity of a country is incompatible with the purposes and principles of the Charter of the United Nations.

7. All States shall observe faithfully and strictly the provisions of the Charter of the United Nations, the Universal Declaration of Human Rights and the present Declaration on the basis of equality, non-interference in the internal affairs of all States, and respect for the sovereign rights of all peoples and their territorial integrity.

Soon after the adoption of 1514 (XV), the Assembly adopted resolution 1524 (XV) which placed Portugal under obligation to transmit information on its territories to the Fourth Committee in accordance with Chapter XI of the Charter.

Thus the attitude of the overwhelming majority of the General Assembly was clearly set forth when the situation became increasingly dangerous in Angola in the spring of 1961.

A May 25, 1961, article in the *Times* (London) was typical of the reports reaching the United Nations:

> About fifty armed Portuguese are reported to have forced 1,800 Africans to leave their village in the Enclave of Cabinda. The assailants are said also to have forced the villagers in the Luali sector of Cabinda to abandon their villages under threat of death or mutilation. One man of those who escaped reached the frontier with his ears cut off.

These and other reports created a general fear that widespread bloodshed was imminent. Within a few days, eighty Protestant and Catholic leaders—from both the clergy and the laity—in Canada and the United States sent an urgent appeal to President Americo Tomas of Portugal asking his government to take into consideration the "legitimate and just aspirations" of the Angolese. They concluded by suggesting to him that "this is an opportunity for the Portuguese people to rise to greatness and to meet with the appropriate leaders of the Angolan people in an atmosphere of mutual trust and determination to effect a solution that is just for all concerned."[4] However, Portugal ignored this suggestion and refused to comply with any of the above U.N. resolutions.

Again, a forty-two-nation joint letter was sent to the Council President. This letter, to which Liberia was a signatory, complained that "the armed suppression of the Angolan people and the denial of political rights and self-determination to them are in contravention of the Charter and of the General Assembly's resolution on Angola and constitute a serious threat to international peace and security."[5] When the matter was debated in the Council from June 6 to June 9, Ambassador Nathan Barnes said in the opening speech:

> On 26 May the village of Quipaku was bombarded by three Portuguese Air Force aircraft, killing thirty-one and seriously wounding twenty-two others, and in that bombardment twenty-five houses were completely destroyed.
>
> We are reliably informed that the defenseless civilian popu-

lation is constantly under heavy Portuguese military aerial bombing, while the Portuguese Navy is shelling the entire Angolan coast, that the number of inhabitants killed and missing has now reached 30,000 and that the number of Angolan refugees in the Congo has now reached 80,000. The Portuguese are setting fire to plantations and crops by air to deprive the population of food, thus forcing them to surrender.

It is reported from reliable sources that a large-scale epidemic is threatening the country, with several thousand bodies being left unburied in abandoned villages, that entire villages have been burnt to the ground and the villagers ordered into the center of town and shot. Missionaries, African pastors and other religious leaders have been brutally slaughtered. Further incidents in Luanda, apart from the massacres in February of this year, occur every day and include detentions and killings of people who try to assert their aspirations to the right of independence or the right to be treated like human beings and who protest against racial discrimination.[6]

In the same speech he said:

I must tell you that no fewer than 100 million Africans, represented by their leaders at the Monrovia Conference, have recognized the situation in Angola as a threat to world peace and stability; have pledged whole-heartedly their material and moral support to the Africans in Angola in their struggle for fundamental freedoms; and have appealed to the universal conscience against the atrocities and the bloody repression of the Angolan people.

He concluded by introducing his government's draft resolution (with the co-sponsorship of Ceylon and the United Arab Republic). The resolution, with two amendments by Chile that did not affect its substance, was adopted by a vote of 9 affirmative, no negative, and 2 abstentions. Accordingly, the Council affirmed the previous action of the General Assembly and called on Portugal to "desist forthwith from repressive measures and further to extend every facility to the subcommittee to enable it to perform its task expeditiously.

On September 27, Secretary of State J. Rudolph Grimes, son of the famous Liberian diplomat, Louis Arthur Grimes, told the General Assembly:

> The Portuguese Government defiantly refused to permit the United Nations Commission to enter Angola to make the necessary inquiry. . . . I do not think it is necessary to go into the details of whether the territory is indeed a province of Portugal or not, for the overwhelming majority of the members of the United Nations wisely rejected that contention. Until August 28th, 1961 in the so-called "province of Angola," with a population of four and a half million Africans, only about thirty thousand have been assimilated and this after five hundred years of Portuguese civilization. But the announcement of August 28th by the Portuguese Minister of Overseas Provinces that the Angolans were then full citizens of Portugal and "are subject to a law which is the same for everyone, with no distinction of race, religion or culture" is in our opinion an admission that nothing other than a repressive colonial regime continues to exist in that territory.
>
> A dangerous practice seems to be developing on part of some countries to ignore decisions taken by this organization and we have to be careful not to tolerate or permit it to go unchallenged. It is hoped that the Commission will make a full report.
>
> It is reported that arms allegedly supplied by NATO to Portugal are being used to carry out these repressive measures. NATO countries contend that arms supplied for defence are not provided for such military purposes, but the fact remains that some of those self-same arms are being used to repress the legitimate aspirations of the indigenous people. My delegation will therefore propose at this session that an arms embargo be imposed against Portugal.

On December 19 the Fourth Committee, under the chairmanship of Angie Brooks, put through the Assembly a resolution requesting member states "to deny Portugal any support and assistance which it may use for the suppression of the peoples of its non-self-governing territories." In compliance with the spirit of this resolution, NATO countries put pressure on Portugal to discontinue use of NATO arms in Angola. In a subsequent statement, the Portuguese government announced that it would respect the wishes of its partners. A few weeks later, these arms were replaced with war surplus equipment, or at least so the Portuguese claim.

Because of Liberia's uncompromising position on Angola, Portugal attempted to embarrass Liberia diplomatically. In mid-1962, its representative to the International Labor Organization at The Hague brought a complaint concerning the use of forced labor against Liberia; the charges were dismissed by a commission of inquiry on the grounds that the Portuguese move was prompted by political considerations. (But Liberia was found guilty of not having submitted annual reports as required by the ILO.) Moreover, Liberian officials who, in their travels to various conferences, must change planes at Lisbon have been detained by Portuguese police and sent back on the next flight.

In a statement to the Seventeenth Session of the General Assembly (September 26, 1962), Secretary Grimes announced:

> My Government will . . . join in any reasonable action designed to persuade and coerce Portugal to see the error of its ways and to conform to the principles of the Charter. I desire to emphasize, however, that continued defiance of United Nations decisions is not compatible with membership in the United Nations.

And he reminded the Portuguese that "we are not the enemy of Portugal. The real enemy of Portugal is Portugal itself."

South Africa

In the long-simmering controversy over South Africa's racial policies, Liberia has played an increasingly important part in applying diplomatic pressure. Liberia was instrumental in stage-managing a flamboyant gesture in the United Nations General Assembly in 1961 and has on other occasions expressed the outrage of independent African nations.

As an issue, South Africa's race policy has plagued the United Nations since 1952. The persistent refusal of South Africa to relent on its "apartheid" policy has survived repeated pleas and demands, but with the emergence of African representation at the U.N., the diplomatic pressure has been intensified. After the Sharpsville riots of March, 1960, in which hundreds of unarmed Africans were slaughtered, the Security Council passed a resolution on April 1 recognizing that the situation in South Africa was a threat to the peace. The Council once again called on the government of South Africa to comply with past U.N. resolutions. As usual, South Africa ignored the resolution.

On October 11, 1961, when Eric Louw, South African Minister of Foreign Affairs, made his annual speech refusing to acknowledge the merits of complaints about his country's race policy, Liberia created a sensation in the General Assembly. Before Louw could leave the podium after delivering his speech, Henry Ford Cooper, the fiery vice-chairman of the Liberian delegation, raised a point of order that touched off a heated protest against South Africa by Afro-Asian representatives. Cooper said:

> As the General Assembly is master of its rules, I move that the whole speech of the representative of South Africa be deleted from the official records of this Assembly. It is an insult to every African here, and not only to every African, but to every man of intelligence. The whole speech is fictitious, and for him to come here and say that the Bantu tribe . . . approves of everything the South African Government does is beyond human reason.[7]

While Liberia's motion did not pass, it received strong support from the newly independent nations. Liberia had made its point. (Louw later expressed surprise that "inferiors" had so much power.) A few days later, South Africa received an overwhelming vote of censure—a rarity in U.N. history. This episode, incidentally, occurred a few weeks after South Africa had left the British Commonwealth, thereby increasing its diplomatic isolation. Spain and Portugal remain today its only supporters.

On October 30, 1961, shortly after the censure vote, Ambassador Nathan Barnes made a statement before the Special Political Committee. He said in part:

> This censure should be such a drastic shock to South Africa that its Government must begin to heed cumulative United Nations resolutions and the entire force of world public opinion which demands an end to apartheid, and coming on top of South Africa's break with the British Commonwealth, has now virtually isolated the South African Government from the rest of the world community.
>
> There are certainly few if any precedents in modern history where a government has so persistently pursued a wholly immoral, impractical policy in the face of total condemnation by the rest of the world. . . . This frustrating anomaly has quite naturally led to strong movements within the United Nations for the employment of political and economic sanctions against . . . South Africa, and even for its expulsion from the United Nations.

He then went on to explain the reasons for his government's concern:

> Our purpose has been four-fold: First, to alleviate abysmal conditions under which our brothers on the African Continent live; second, to help bring about a change in the attitudes of the white South Africans; third, to focus world attention on this most unhappy spectacle of human behavior so that the world will long remember with dismay and disgust the things they have seen through our eyes; and, fourth, to help the United Nations translate its high principles into living realities in South Africa and throughout the world.

He concluded with a plea for more forceful measures:

> We just cannot go on from year to year passing resolutions requesting the South African Government to modify its policies and sit idly by while this Member State flouts these resolutions

in addition to its own Charter obligations. It is imperative now
that we find some more effective means of bringing the South
African Government to its senses and providing creditable support for our resolutions.

The Ambassador's closing remarks reflect the Liberian Government's growing impatience with the South African problem.

South West Africa

Besides its campaign against apartheid within the Republic
of South Africa, Liberia is doing more than any nation to
combat the illegal extension of this system into South West
Africa. After years of unsuccessful attempts to settle the mandate dispute by means of negotiation through the various
agencies and committees of the United Nations, Liberia filed
its application instituting contentious proceedings against
South Africa before the International Court of Justice on
November 4, 1960. Ethiopia joined Liberia in the proceedings, since it, too, was a member of the League of Nations at
the time of its dissolution.

The history of the case dates back to May 7, 1919, when the
Allied Powers Supreme Council assigned the mandate over
the former German protectorate of South West Africa to the
King of England. The Union of South Africa was in turn
designated by Britain to administer the mandate.[8] Under the
terms of the Mandate Agreement signed on December 17,
1920, the Union of South Africa was to "promote to the
utmost the material and moral well-being and the social
progress of the inhabitants of the territory. . . ."[9] The underlying premise of the entire mandate system was of course
eventual independence, but since the League was controlled
by the colonial powers, it was left to the mandatory power to
decide when a territory was ready for independence. Moreover, there was no specific provision for termination of the
mandate agreement. Thus, not one African mandate territory

became independent during the time of the League's existence.

During the interwar years, the Union submitted annual reports on the territory and apparently fulfilled its obligations.[10] On April 18, 1946, the Assembly of the League met to consider the future of the mandate territories and adopted a resolution that they would continue to be administered "in accordance with the obligations in the respective mandates" until "other arrangements could be established." In the same year, South Africa proposed to the first session of the General Assembly that it permit South West Africa to be merged as an integral part of the Union. The South African petition was based on a referendum held by the government in which the people of the territory chose annexation. The Assembly doubted this claim and suggested that South Africa follow the policy of all other mandatory powers by placing the territory under U.N. trusteeship. In the following session, the Union Government announced that it would not release the territory to the U.N., but neither would it formally annex it.

In 1949, the white population of South West Africa was given representation in the Union Parliament, implying that the territory was being incorporated into the Union. This caused the Fourth Session of the General Assembly to request an advisory opinion from the International Court of Justice on the territory's legal standing. On July 11, 1950, the court opinion rejected the contention that the mandate ceased with the League's demise by pointing out: "If the mandate lapsed, as the Union Government contends, the latter's authority would equally have lapsed." While it held that the Union was not obliged under law to place the territory under the U.N., it also maintained that the Union could not unilaterally change the territory's status (as it had in fact done). The court also considered the U.N. as legal heir to the League in this matter. In other words, the U.N. has the right to supervise the handling of the territory's welfare. But the decision also made it clear that the degree of supervision could not exceed that of the Mandates Commission.[11]

Since an advisory opinion is not binding, the General Assembly set up an Ad Hoc Committee on South West Africa to negotiate with South Africa on carrying out the court's decision. After three years of talks got nowhere, the Eighth Assembly established a Permanent Committee on South West Africa. The committee has submitted annual reports to the Assembly, but it did not succeed in obtaining the cooperation of the South African Government. In 1958, the committee reported that "the existing conditions in the territory represent a situation contrary to the Mandates system, the Charter of the United Nations and the Universal Declaration of Human Rights." During its Fourteenth Session in 1959, the General Assembly adopted a resolution (1361) which called attention to the special report of the Committee on South West Africa concerning the legal action open to the member states in the mandate dispute. In the meantime, Ambassador George A. Padmore, the Liberian envoy in Washington, was commissioned by his government to employ the services of Ernest A. Gross, a highly respected international lawyer, to investigate the technicalities of the case and to submit the results of his study to the Liberian Government for examination. At the Second Conference of Independent African States, held at Addis Ababa in June, 1960, Liberia and Ethiopia jointly announced their intention of instituting contentious proceedings against the Union of South Africa.

In its Application Instituting Proceedings, Liberia states:

A dispute has continuously existed during more than ten years . . . between Liberia and the Union regarding the interpretation and application of the Mandate. The subject of the dispute is the following:

(1) Liberia has contended that, as established by the Advisory Opinion of the International Court of Justice rendered July 11, 1950, the Mandate continues to exist and the Union continues to have the international obligations set forth in . . .

the Covenant, in the Mandate, and in the decisions and rules of the Council of the League of Nations. Liberia has likewise contended that . . . the supervisory functions over the Mandate are to be exercised by the United Nations, to which annual reports and petitions should be submitted in accordance with the Mandate. The Union has continuously denied and disputed these contentions, insisting that the Mandate has lapsed and the Union has no duties thereunder.

(2) Liberia has likewise continuously sought to assert and protect its legal interest in the proper exercise of the Mandate by disputing and protesting the violation by the Union of its duties as Mandatory. . . . Liberia has contended and now contends that existing conditions in the Territory of South West Africa and the trend of administration by the Union represent a situation not in accord with the Mandate system, as the said system must be interpreted in the light of current international standards. . . . The Union has continuously disputed the foregoing contentions and has contended that its duties under the Mandate have lapsed.

. . . .

In order to protect the legal interest of Liberia in the proper exercise of the Mandate, as well as that of other States similarly situated, and taking cognizance of the fact that Liberia was a member of the League of Nations at the time of the League's dissolution, that it has a dispute with the Union relating to the interpretation and application of the Mandate, and that such dispute cannot be settled by negotiations, Liberia . . . has instituted these proceedings.

In supporting its allegations, Liberia cites (among others) the following instances:

The Union, by law and practice, distinguishes as to race, color, national and tribal origin in establishing the rights and duties of the peoples of South West Africa. This official practice is referred to as "apartheid."

The Union, in administering the Territory, has adopted and applied legislation, regulations, proclamations and administrative decrees which are by their terms and in their application arbitrary, unreasonable, unjust and detrimental to human dignity.

The Union . . . has . . . suppressed rights and liberties of inhabitants of the Territory essential to their orderly evolution toward self-government.

The International Court of Justice commenced hearings on the Liberian complaint in September, 1962, and they were still in process late in 1963. Liberia is represented by Assistant Attorney-General Edward R. Moore, who had handled the successful Liberian defense before the ILO against forced labor charges (discussed earlier). Secretary of State Grimes expressed Liberia's confidence and determination in the case:

The story of South Africa . . . is one of extreme sadness. Perhaps we should pity those people in their incredible actions. But the continued defiance of the resolutions of the United Nations, the pursuit of the iniquitous policy of apartheid and the enactment of more stringent laws which deny the Africans all fundamental rights require . . . action.

· One can understand the reluctance of the non-African communities of Central and Southern Africa to give up the special privileges which they now enjoy. One cannot understand their failure to realize that, in their own interest, this reluctance must be overcome. Have they read nothing of recent history? Can they not realize that of the long succession of Colonialist wars fought since 1945, not one has ended with a victory for the moribund Colonial cause? Six and a half years of struggle in Algeria have just ended with the now familiar denouement —the triumph of nationalism. Those non-Africans who will dream of clinging to power in Africa can hope for no more success than was achieved in Algeria. All they can hope to do is to prolong a battle which they are bound to lose and which will grow more and more bitter, more and more futile, as the months and years are allowed to pass and the last opportunities for conciliation are frittered away.[12]

The Congo Crisis

During the Congo crisis, which threatened the existence of the United Nations, Liberia stood firmly behind the international organization. In its emphatic commitment to the U.N., Liberia made an important contribution during a crisis which began with Congo's achievement of independence on June 30, 1960, and lasted until the end of Katanga's secession in January, 1963.

From the beginning of the Congo crisis, Liberia maintained a consistent policy of restraint. Soon after the Congo was plunged into chaos and anarchy, Moise Tshombe, leader of the Katangan secession, appealed to President Tubman for diplomatic recognition "without delay." In his reply, the President set down his government's position:

> While my Government is ever ready and willing to give support to peoples striving for, and demanding self-determination and independence, your case presents a situation which . . . is somewhat complicated, since your territory and people were originally a part of the Republic of the Congo which was recently declared independent. To set up an independent State would mean secession from the Government of the Republic of the Congo and secession is generally regarded with disfavor by the Liberian Government. Therefore, at this stage of the matter, having already recognized the . . . Congo Republic which included the Katanga Province and territory, I would be placed in an embarrassing position to comply with your request. While the question of the declaration of your territory as an independent state is purely and entirely a domestic matter, if you and the leaders of Mr. Lumumba's Government would permit, my Government would suggest and offer its good offices to activate a movement aimed at trying to resolve the differences and restoring peace and unity. Furthermore, the whole question of the disturbance in the Congo is being presently handled by the United Nations and it may be best not to press for secession while the issue is in the process of consideration. . . .

A few weeks later, the late Secretary-General Dag Hammerskjöld requested the Liberian Government's assistance in restoring peace. In his reply the President suggested to him that a "representative delegation might precede military force . . . to appeal to all sections and elements of the Congolese people to stop the conflict . . . but the troops will proceed so as to be at hand." Though a delegation was not sent, Liberia kept its troops in the Congo until their mission was complete. One of the most heroic episodes in the Congo crisis was the feat of 300 Liberian soldiers who stopped 5,000 armed Baluba tribesmen led by European mercenaries. The troops were honored for their heroism by President Tubman at homecoming ceremonies.

At the Fifteenth General Assembly Session in 1960, Liberia demonstrated its policy of restraint and moderation in the face of a movement to place the U.N. military effort in the Congo under an African command. The Casablanca Powers, which were making this demand, also talked of sending African troops into the Congo independently of the U.N. operation. At this crucial point, Secretary Grimes told the General Assembly:

> The Liberian Delegation regrets the state of affairs in the Congo but is unable to endorse the suggestion of a purely African command over the United Nations Forces in the Congo. This suggestion, in our opinion, appears to violate the fundamental principles of the United Nations which should operate without regard to race, color or creed. Moreover it would establish a precedent which might undermine future effectiveness of the United Nations.[13]

In expressing his government's opposition to the concept of an African army independent of the U.N., he said:

> It is our opinion that no useful purpose would be served by nations and particularly the underdeveloped nations in attempting to by-pass the United Nations or to flout its authority. The United Nations supports the independence and defends the sovereignty of all nations and, as many states are gaining independence today and especially the African states, it is the organization to which we look for protection and defense in times of crisis.

In line with this policy, Liberia sponsored and put through a resolution which "forbids unilateral action to be taken by any nation in the present situation in the Congo for the purpose of exploiting an unfortunate situation for selfish ends."[14] This resolution countered all threats—African, Russian, or Belgian—of military action independent of the U.N., and no doubt helped to save the Congo from even greater chaos and bloodshed.

On the question of the "troika" doctrine which was precipitated by events in the Congo, Liberia took this stand:

> Any revision of the Charter which abolishes the position of the Secretary General for an executive triumvirate that would operate on the basis of unanimity or which would be predicated on regional alignments or blocs would only contribute to the total and complete destruction of the United Nations and would be a travesty of the principles on which the United Nations was founded.
>
> Instead of creating new blocs . . . we should strive to do away with all blocs and seek to create one brotherhood among men.[15]

Again on September 26, 1962, Secretary Grimes spoke out strongly on this subject in an address before the General Assembly:

> Once the principle of dividing up the Secretariat among the different groupings in the Assembly is accepted, we may find ourselves urged in a year or two to advance from the "troika" to the "four in hand," in order to recognize the rights of some newly-organized bloc of delegations. Before long, indeed, the Secretary General might find himself trying to control with one rein a whole regiment of cavalry. He would then be able to match the feat of the Stephen Leacock character who leapt upon his steed and rode madly off in all directions.

During the two and a half years of turmoil created by the Congo crisis, Liberia remained steadfast in its commitment to support and strengthen the effectiveness of the United Nations. It was the first member state to pay its share of the costs of the Congo operation. When other nations refused to pay their share, Liberia requested the International Court of Justice to render an advisory opinion regarding the obligations of these nations. The Court advised that all members were obliged to pay their share of the costs whether they agreed with the U.N. action or not.

Basically, the dynamic role Liberia has played in the United Nations on behalf of Africa and world peace has been developed by its chief policymaker, William V. S. Tubman. In his address before the General Assembly on October 23, 1961, he summed up the reason for Liberia's policy:

> It is only in such an atmosphere of faith and dedication to the ideals to which we have subscribed by our membership in this world body that mankind can face the future fearlessly and bravely and work reassuringly so that, eventually, right may triumph over might, justice overshadow oppression, reason replace irrationality, the blessings of liberty obliterate the tyranny of domination and human welfare transcend race-centeredness. These are the ideals to which we have dedicated ourselves, and we stand committed to them in the critical days which face us.

TUBMAN ON AFRICAN UNITY

Liberia's role in Africa in shifting from leadership in the struggle for independence to pursuit of cooperation and unity on the African continent. This changing role conforms to historical necessity, as independence, largely achieved, must be followed by cooperation and unity, largely unrealized. In economic, social, and political terms, the approach toward unity has been complicated and handicapped by the arbitrary boundaries of the new states, which were drawn with a view toward colonial administration, not eventual independence. The resulting fragmentation of tribes, disregard of economic requirements, and multiplicity of political entities have thoroughly Balkanized the continent.

In their early independence period, the African nations are

attempting to counter this Balkanization with joint effort and combined activity. Inevitably, a variety of approaches have emerged in the search for unity; as might be expected from his past leadership, President Tubman, the "Dean of African Statesmen," is playing an important part in the search. His formula for Africa-wide unity, which opposes blocs and supports a program combining independence and cooperation, has had considerable impact and shows signs of surviving the more extreme views, with their overtones of dominance of some African nations over others. President Tubman described his approach in 1957:

> The question of leadership of Africa . . . is being skillfully maneuvered deliberately at this time to separate and weaken the ties of friendship which should exist among African States, and have the African States leave the proverbial substance for the shadow.
>
> In this connection I have observed that there seem to be three schools of thought on this subject. There are those who feel that Liberia should assume leadership based on the fact that she is the oldest African Republic and is riper in political experience; but it will require more than age and political experience to assume leadership of Africa.
>
> There are others who hold that Ghana should assume that role because she is physically more developed and embraces larger territories. It will require more than development and larger territory to assume leadership of Africa.
>
> And there are yet those who opine that Egypt with its rich traditions dating back to the remotest antiquity should assume leadership. It will require more than rich traditions of antiquity. It will require, in my opinion, the aggregate of all three of these and more besides. It will require the aggregate of the best of all that Liberia, Ghana, Egypt, Tunisia, Ethiopia, the Sudan, Morocco, Nigeria . . . and all other African territories and states possess, moulded together, to assume the leadership of Africa, compounded in such a manner as to represent the divisibility of Africa indivisible.
>
> I am inclined to the view that each African State must re-

main independent, entering, of course, into pacts, treaties or international agreements, naturally so as to strengthen and accelerate mutual intercourse and reliable ties of friendship among them, which will be beneficial to themselves and the world. Now, more than ever before, it should be our concerted effort to repel and subdue any and all doctrines or ideologies which would tend to divert us from the path of human dignity and the rights of the individual, and particularly those that envisage national disintegration and enslavement by stealthy artifice and subversive actions.[16]

On January 26, 1959, the Liberian Government published an *Official Gazette Extraordinary* by order of its President, expressing its views on the best means of achieving African unity—views which influenced the historic movements now taking place on the continent. The section proposing "The Associated States of Africa" set down a concrete program (the complete document appears in Appendix 7):

Hence, taking into consideration differing economic systems, differing political allegiances and preferences, differing cultural backgrounds and differing social customs; and not wishing to superimpose any artificial unity upon these differences, it is the opinion of the Liberian Government that the peoples of Africa should resolve to achieve close association and cooperation, without prejudice to their national or international identities, in the following or some similar manner:

1. That a single Convention which would provide for a permanent organization to be known as The Associated States of Africa, be concluded among the independent African nations and those which have fixed dates upon which they shall achieve independence, with the understanding that other non-independent countries of Africa shall have the right to join the organization upon attaining independence.

2. That the Associated States of Africa provide for continuing consultation on problems of common interest and for the peaceful solution of all disputes which may arise among its members.

3. That, within said organization, Regional Associations be

recognized where they already exist or be organized to develop closer unity and provide uniform and common solution to specific problems in certain areas. For instance, it is suggested that in West Africa:

a. A regional health authority should be created which would concentrate on the eradication of diseases common to the area.

b. An agency should be developed to direct regional scientific research and training projects.

c. A common cultural institute for the region should be developed.

d. A uniform reduction of tariffs and a Customs Convention should be undertaken.[17]

It is significant that, while many African governments subsequently took similar positions, Liberia was the originator of this approach.

The Sanniquellie Summit (July, 1959)

On April 7, 1959, several weeks after Liberia put forth this proposal, President Tubman wrote to Prime Minister Kwame Nkrumah of Ghana and President Sékou Touré of Guinea suggesting a meeting to discuss "matters of interest to our respective countries and the unity of the continent of Africa." Kwame Nkrumah replied on April 20 that he would "discuss the matter with President Touré," realizing that Tubman's idea of "association and cooperation, without prejudice to . . . national or international identities" was a threat to the Nkrumah approach of one great African state headed by Nkrumah. In an attempt to outflank Tubman's move, Nkrumah paid a brief visit to Touré in Conakry, and on May 1 they announced their intention to form the "Union of African States." In their joint declaration they stated that membership in the Union "shall be open to all independent African States or Federations adhering to the principles on which the Union is based." Nkrumah apparently felt that he had outmaneuvered President Tubman. An interesting exchange of correspondence among the three heads of state followed.[18]

On May 4, President Touré wrote to President Tubman, inviting him to join the Union. He said: [translation]

> As your vast experience permits you to know, this Union, which you also have been advocating on several occasions, is destined to play an important role in the life of our Continent. . . .
>
> I am personally convinced that you would be willing to accept the role of "Dean" of the Independent African States, so that rapidly, the hopes which have come into existence in the various African Territories by the birth of this Union should be fulfilled and thus we engage ourselves resolutely on the basis of achievements thus far realized in an Inter-African cooperative movement on the one hand and between Africa and the world on the other. . . .

In a letter to Touré dated May 27, President Tubman replied:

> Your advocacy of the President of Liberia as the Dean of the Independent African States seems plausible; but how can that be considered practicable when Guinea and Ghana have already for themselves, developed a Constitution and a Flag for the African Independent States without reference to or consultation with the Government of Liberia?

Meanwhile, Nkrumah, had responded—on May 15—to President Tubman's proposal for a meeting of the three heads of state. Nkrumah wrote:

> I am happy to be able to say that President Touré agrees with me that a meeting between the three of us will be most useful.
>
> . . . .
>
> It is my view also that the meeting should be held in Liberia, provided that you are willing to act as host. Further, I consider that we should, if possible, keep private those meetings at which serious discussions will take place. The great importance

of our deliberations to our respective countries and to Africa will require that our discussions are held in an atmosphere of complete frankness and calm. For that reason, if you agree, it may be convenient for the serious discussions to take place outside Monrovia City itself. A statement can be issued to the public at the conclusion of our discussions.

I trust that you will find my proposal regarding this conference acceptable and that you will let me know as early as possible what your final proposals are as regards the time and place.

President Tubman answered the letter on May 24:

It is with pleasure that I acknowledge the receipt of your letter of May 15, in which you refer to my letter of April 7, regarding my proposal for a conference to be held between President Sékou Touré, you and me. . . .

.   .   .   .

You suggest that the meeting be held in Liberia provided I am willing to act as host. Since you recommend the meeting to take place in Liberia, it follows as a normal sequence that I will in that case become host.

I am in agreement that some of the discussions which we expect to have should be kept private and also welcome your suggestion that these discussions should be held in an atmosphere of complete frankness and calm. I have always advocated and practiced frankness, calm and poise in all deliberations; hence I heartily concur with your suggestion.

When the three met on July 15–19, 1959, in Sanniquellie, a small town in Liberia's Central Province, President Tubman was at a disadvantage. Ghana and Guinea had an organization already formulated; Liberia had none. Nkrumah and Touré knew that if they got Tubman to put his "African and international authority and weight" behind their Union, it might be the signal for the rest of Africa to follow suit.

What emerged at the conference was a confrontation between the Nkrumah view of unity achieved by immediate political union and the Tubman view that unity must begin with cooperation on matters of mutual interest. For Nkrumah it was politics before practical steps; for Tubman it was practical steps before politics. President Tubman set forth the underlying theme of his position in the following words:

> It is my opinion that a practical approach to a mutually acceptable formula should take full account of all the essential elements which make for mutual confidence, oneness of purpose and willingness to participate in joint actions for our common good. Mutual confidence in international relations is absolutely necessary, but it can only be obtained in a climate of mutual trust, candor and honesty. There must be a willingness to meet and negotiate on a basis of reciprocal respect coupled with a conscientious willingness to make wise and judicious compromises in the larger interest of the millions of our continent who are yet being deprived of their liberties and of their sovereign rights.
>
> . . . .
>
> To generate that needed and essential incentive in us all towards our determined goal of African unity and solidarity, we need first of all to create a spirit of mutual confidence devoid of personal ambitions and aspirations either as individuals or as nations. We need to strive to be understanding and understandable in our ideals, policies and programs and make it clear that we aim at the triumph of principles.[19]

During the course of their "full and frank" discussions of the next three days, the three heads of state reviewed the two basic positions as contained in the Conakry Declaration and the Liberian *Official Gazette Extraordinary.* In arguing that unity had to be achieved through immediate political union, Nkrumah sought unity from the top down. Tubman maintained that this would only create an artificial unity and that it would be more realistic to begin by cooperating on practical matters of common interest until a solid foundation was established for political union. At the beginning of the talks, Touré supported the Nkrumah view, but by the third day he had almost completely abandoned it in favor of the Tubman position.

At the end of the conference, the three nations issued the Sanniquellie Declaration,[20] a statement of principles concerning a proposed *Community* of Independent African States. The concept of *Community,* as opposed to *Union,* represented a turning point in Pan-Africanism and a significant victory for Tubman. This was particularly evident in the third and most important principle of the Declaration:

> Each State or Federation, which is a member of the Community, shall maintain its own national identity and constitutional structure. The Community is being formed with a view to achieving unity among independent African States. It is not designed to prejudice the present or future international policies, relations and obligations of the States involved.

The three leaders further agreed on "holding . . . a Special Conference in 1960 of all independent States of Africa, as well as non-independent States which have fixed dates on which they will achieve independence, to discuss and work out a Charter which will achieve their goal of unity between independent African States." However, the "spirit of mutual confidence devoid of personal ambitions" that President Tubman urged in his opening speech was not achieved and this special Conference was never called.

In fact, soon after the Sanniquellie meeting, the hardening of the two opposing approaches became in itself a stumbling block to unity. This was illustrated on August 4, only a few weeks after the declaration was signed. At the Conference of Independent African States[21] held in Monrovia, Ghanaian Foreign Affairs Minister Ako Adjei avoided any reference to the Sanniquellie Declaration and, except for mentioning that he had accompanied his Prime Minister to Liberia a few weeks earlier, completely ignored the fact that there had been a Sanniquellie Conference. But Ghana did not officially repudiate the Sanniquellie Declaration until the Second Regular Conference of Independent African States in June, 1960.[22] In his opening address, Mr. Adjei completely twisted the meaning of the Declaration when he said:

> The unity which the three leaders discussed and agreed upon was intended to be a real political unity of independent African States, and not merely a system of economic cooperation. The three leaders signed a joint declaration in which they proclaimed to the whole world the principles upon which the Union of African States shall be based.

He then went on to read the Declaration of Principles to the delegates and added:

> It is clear from this declaration of principles that the Union of African States, which the three leaders discussed and agreed upon, is intended to be a political Union. Such a political Union, in their view, will provide the framework within which any plans for economic, social and cultural cooperation can, in fact, operate to the best advantage of all.
>
> As I have already indicated, the Sanniquellie Declaration was made in Liberia in July, 1959—barely a year ago. And the Delegation of Ghana has no reason to think that the three leaders have modified their views or changed their position since they signed this declaration.[23]

President Tubman chose his Fourth Inaugural Address (1960) to spell out in detail his views on how to implement the Sanniquellie Declaration, underlying the differences on unity:

> As a means of cultivating stronger ties of friendship between Africans, we envisage an accelerated program of cultural and economic exchange between African States as a basis of lasting and fruitful co-operation. We now advance the proposals of regional economic and trade councils with a view to:
>
> 1. Negotiating and concluding treaties and instruments of friendship, commerce and navigation.
> 2. Opening doors for multinational investment in enterprises

which require greater funds, greater markets, greater resources than would be available in any one state.

3. Investigating and presenting proposals for regional marketing programs of products of regional importance on the assumption that even the largest and strongest unit would benefit from additional size and strength through association with its neighbors.

4. Studying, adapting, rejecting or adopting experience in regional economic cooperation amassed elsewhere.

5. Training a sufficient number of persons and even more to man governments, businesses, schools and hospitals as well as other enterprises in Africa as there is no need in Africa at the present time as great, pressing and important as the need for trained people. With a need so great African nations could use the greatest imagination, show the greatest flexibility in finding ways to fill this void.

We propose a detailed survey of the resources for education, training and research which exist in African states and we suggest the pooling of those resources so that each nation might have access to existing institutions of education and training and contribute to their support, enlargement and improvement in proportion to its size and ability to use such an institution. For example, Nigeria has the Medical School at Ibadan; Ghana, the new business administration course at its university; Liberia, the new Forestry School and Guinea, the Mali Federation and other African states with such specialized institutions as they may have. Without committing any unit to refrain from establishing such schools for themselves later (the need will increase with time for more and more schools, so this seems inevitable), the purpose would be to enlarge and make widely available the facilities which now exist.

The Monrovia Conference (May, 1961)

Liberia called the Monrovia Conference of May, 1961, in an attempt to end the drift toward disunity in Africa as national interests and rivalries led to formation of blocs. During the previous year, twelve French-speaking African countries had met in the Ivory Coast to discuss the future of the French

Community and means of coordinating their policies. They supported Mauritanian independence and Algerian self-determination as well as U.N. efforts in the Congo and called for negotiations to end the Algerian hostilities. They agreed to meet in the Congo (Brazzaville) in December to formally join an association based upon their "oneness of culture and community of interests." They named their association the Union Africaine et Malgache (U.A.M.)—although they are more commonly referred to as the Brazzaville Twelve[24]—and announced that their aim was "to affirm their political independence through the economic and social advance of their populations."

The formation of the U.A.M. upset King Mohammed V of Morocco. On the basis of some vague historical claims, he had long considered Mauritania to be part of Morocco, and the Brazzaville group's support for Mauritanian independence undermined his claim. Thereupon, the King decided to call his own conference. As in Brazzaville, there was no intention to represent all Africa: A bloc was sought to serve national interests and ambitions. Because of the prestige he would bring to the conference, President Tubman's participation was sought. On December 14, King Mohammed cabled Tubman suggesting a conference of African chiefs of state to consider "primarily" the deteriorating situation in the Congo. In a telegram two days later, Tubman replied:

> I am in favor of the proposed conference and am willing to cooperate but . . . I note that other African states such as Nigeria, Senegal and Tunisia whose interest in normalization of the situation in the Congo is no less than ours have not been invited. In my opinion such an act will cause a further breach in the unity of Africa and I am not willing to contribute to it. I therefore suggest that all African states with troops in the Congo be invited to attend the conference. If this is done you can depend on my cooperation. However I may mention that it will be impracticable for me to leave Liberia before the end of January 1961 as the legislature is in session at the present

time and I am presently engaged with the budget for 1961. Any other date after January will be convenient to me.

But the King ignored Tubman's suggestion, and the meeting was held on January 3–7, 1961, resulting in the formation of a six-nation group known as the Casablanca Powers.[25] Each member gained something by joining: The United Arab Republic obtained a resolution condemning Israel as an imperialist base; Algeria received sympathy and promises of material aid; the Union of African States (Ghana, Guinea, and—the latest addition—Mali) obtained support for political union; and Morocco received encouragement in its efforts to annex Mauritania. As it turned out, the situation in the Congo, the stated reason for the conference, was the last item discussed, and the participants failed to agree on whether or not to support the U.N. operation!

The creation of the Brazzaville and Casablanca blocs within a period of a few weeks established a tendency to label African nations as members of a bloc or as "uncommitted." President Tubman, who felt strongly that bloc politics obstructed solution of the continent's pressing social and economic problems, moved to arrest this trend. He made plans for a conference to take place in Monrovia on May 8–12, 1961.[26] The heads of state of all independent African nations except South Africa were invited; and the original list of sponsors included members of the various alignments: Guinea and Mali of the Casablanca Powers, Ivory Coast and Cameroon of the Brazzaville Twelve, and the uncommitted states of Togo and Nigeria as well as Liberia.

A few days before the conference, the Casablanca Powers met in Accra and, in an abortive attempt to sabotage the meeting, announced that they would not go to Monrovia "at this time." Accordingly, Guinea and Mali withdrew themselves as co-sponsors. As the conference hung in the balance, Tubman promptly announced that while he regretted the Casablanca decision the conference would be held as scheduled "so that

Africans can make a start in the reconstruction of their continent." This announcement undoubtedly saved the conference, especially in view of the fact that several states had received messages from the Casablanca states to the effect that the Monrovia Conference was postponed.

Despite this setback, the first conference session on May 8 was historic in two respects: It was the first attempt to bridge the gap between French-speaking and English-speaking Africa, and it was the largest convocation of African heads of state ever held. A total of twenty states were represented, including all of the Brazzaville states, Liberia, Togo, Ethiopia, Somalia, Sierra Leone, Nigeria, Libya, and Tunisia.[27] In his opening speech, President Tubman dealt frankly with African political developments and expressed what, in his opinion, should be the spirit of the Monrovia deliberations (the full text of this speech is given in Appendix 12):

> We do not want our endeavours to be construed in the light of personal rivalries or ambition for recognition or leadership. We have no desire to seek fame for ourselves, nor is this conference intended to undermine the conclusions of previous conferences; nor will we fail to endorse and support such decisions of other conferences which we know to be in the best interest of Africa and the World. Rather, all that we seek to achieve is to bring all African leaders to reason together towards determining a consensus in the interest of peace and better understanding and to endeavour to provide a climate in which large as well as small states will participate as equal partners in building a New Africa and a new world order.
>
> . . . .
>
> It should be crystal clear to every leader that Africans cannot live in isolation if they expect to allay suspicion, fear and tension. The idea of *primus inter pares,* first among equals, is destructive to African Unity and Peace. Tolerance, good faith, honour, good neighbourliness, justice, equality and mutual respect are the most vital constituents of Unity and Solidarity.
>
> . . . .

History has clearly demonstrated that Political Union as opposed to Political Domination can be more rapidly achieved where there is a community of economic interest, cultural cross-fertilization as well as free social intercourse and association.

It would probably be unreasonable to expect that we can at this Conference work out a complete pattern of mutual action in this respect. However, we trust that agreement can be reached on the guiding principles which would enable technical experts representing us to concretize proposals for economic cooperation and collaboration as well as the establishment of common identities toward which we may strive in the immediate future. In this way we believe steps can be taken now to reach goals which will enable each member country to make a distinctive contribution to lasting, natural unity in Africa.

After unanimously electing President Tubman chairman (a post usually reserved for the host state), the heads of state proceeded to consider and adopt four resolutions. The first and most important resolution (for the complete text, see Appendix 13) concerned "the means of promoting better understanding and cooperation towards achieving unity in Africa and Malagasy."[28] The six principles in this resolution governing relationships between the member states echoed the familiar Tubman philosophy:

(1) Absolute equality of African and Malagasy States, whatever may be the size of their territories, the density of their populations, or the value of their possessions;

(2) Non-interference in the internal affairs of States;

(3) Respect for the sovereignty of each state and its inalienable right to existence and development of its personality;

(4) Unqualified condemnation of outside subversive action by neighbouring states;

(5) Promotion of cooperation throughout Africa, based upon tolerance, solidarity and good-neighbour relations, periodical exchange of views, and non-acceptance of any leadership.

(6) The Unity that is aimed to be achieved at the moment is not the political integration of sovereign African states, but

unity of aspirations and of action considered from the point of view of African social solidarity and political identity.

The heads of state also agreed "that an Inter-African and Malagasy Advisory Organization shall be created, the essential purpose of which shall be to put into effect the above-mentioned principles and to establish this Organization at the next conference" which was scheduled to be held at Lagos, Nigeria. This crucial decision indicated the determination of these states to take immediate and positive steps toward unity. It also placed the Casablanca Powers on the defensive.

Lagos Conference (January, 1962)

The first work session of the Monrovia States was held in Lagos on January 25–30, 1962. As with the Monrovia Conference, invitations were extended to all independent African states (with the exception of South Africa). Again, the Casablanca Powers made a last minute decision not to attend—this time because the provisional Government of Algeria had not been invited. Tunisia, Libya, and Sudan[29] used the same reason for not attending, but the addition of Congo (Léopoldville) and Tanganyika kept the states represented equal in number to the twenty attending the Monrovia Conference.

Besides reiterating their Monrovia positions on colonialism, disarmament, and nuclear testing in the Sahara, the heads of state accepted in principle President Tubman's proposal for the Inter-African and Malagasy Organization. The Liberian draft charter for this organization was subsequently approved at a meeting of foreign ministers.[30] According to the charter, IAMO is "established for the purpose of promoting a better life for the peoples of Africa and Malagasy by enlisting the efforts of member States through cooperative and joint actions." It cites as its goals the following:

(a) accelerate economic and social development and intercourse and to promote the pooling and effective utilisation of their resources;

(b) provide better and broader educational opportunities for its peoples;

(c) raise the level of health and well-being of its peoples; and

(d) concert, as far as possible, political actions and initiate new means of establishing relationships in which the interests of the Continent of Africa and Malagasy will be better defined and served.[31]

Although the Charter marked a high point in Pan-Africanism, it also led to greater inflexibility by the Monrovia and Casablanca groups. During 1962 and the early part of 1963, rapprochement between the two groups was the overriding hope and challenge for Africans. In this respect Secretary of State J. Rudolph Grimes summed up the Liberian viewpoint when he said:

> We regret the groupings which have occurred in Africa, a situation which might not have developed had the advice and warning of President Tubman been given attention in some other capitals. He advised that all African leaders—not a selected few—should be invited to attend any meeting which was to be convened for the purpose of finding solutions to African problems; and he warned that, if this course were not followed, events would be set in motion which would result in divisions in Africa.
>
> Be that as it may, the fact is that the groupings do exist and may be harmful in the long run to the interest of Africa. The task is therefore to eliminate the divisions. I know that President Tubman is resolved to do all that lies within his power to assist in bridging the gap and to work for an intensification of the areas of cooperation in Africa.
>
> He realizes that cooperation among African States can make a change for the better in our general conditions and in our relations with the rest of the world be a positive force for good in shaping these new relations.[32]

The Addis Ababa Conference (May, 1963)

In anticipation of the Addis Ababa Conference, Nkrumah addressed a letter on January 20, 1963, to Tubman, calling for

President Tubman and Emperor Haile Selassie I in front of the Liberian Embassy, Addis Abab, Ethiopia, May, 1963.

a common African foreign policy, joint continental planning for economic and industrial development of Africa, a common currency, a monetary zone and a central bank, a joint defense system, and a central political organization with its own constitution. He added:

> This union of African States should consist of an upper house and a lower house. Each state would have the right to send two representatives to the upper house irrespective of the size and population of the state, while admission to the lower house would be secured on the basis of proportional representation in accordance with the population of each state.

Although this was a new proposal, it still implied surrender of national sovereignty, reflecting Nkrumah's previous pronouncements on unity. It was clearly at odds with the firm Monrovia position that "the Unity that is aimed to be achieved at the moment is not the political integration of sovereign African States, but unity of aspirations and of action considered from the point of view of African social solidarity and political identity."[33] In his reply, President Tubman observed:

> Viewed historically, political concerts and/or world parliaments have offered no permanent solution to international problems of unity. They have never allayed suspicions, fears, subversions and distortions aimed at the destruction of smaller states by more powerful ones. At this stage of our evolution, types of Unity should be carefully thought out in the light of precedents. Unity on a functional basis and geographical approach seems the most realistic and achievable solution if effectively insulated against wanton ambition, centralism and subversion.
>
> Unity, if not integration, becomes more imperative when it is realized that there are twenty-two African Colonies and territories not yet free, some of whom are groaning under the degrading load of oppression and servitude, and are at this time, looking to Addis Ababa for their emancipation. What is taking place in these territories today, the brutal and inhumane treatment meted to black men in those areas because of their color,

is an insult not only to the dignity of humanity but particularly to all African States as well as to the nations of every continent of the earth that regard as inherent in all men, the natural right to freedom.

To promote unity on a cultural, economic and scientific basis, it would appear essential that an accelerated program of cultural, scientific and economic exchange between African States be initiated.

Such a program, if well planned and carefully pursued, would not only cultivate stronger ties of friendship and unity among Africans, but would also lay the foundation for developing closer understanding as the basis for new forms of unity.

As Africans we must realize that we face grim challenges. Africa is not a world unto itself but an integral part of our one world. It is our responsibility to fashion and build a New Africa in which all races of men can live and work together in the great task of reconstruction. The problems are many. The situation is urgent. We cannot but heed the call.

I have no doubt that as we enter upon the business of the conference we shall do so objectively as Africans, and not as members of any particular group—be it Casablanca, Monrovia, French Community or any other. If we do this we shall then raise ourselves above the level of group complex, regional and such other elemental tendencies that might subject us to contracted thinking and selfish actions.

We from Liberia are going to this conference with open minds and hearts permeated and imbued with an impelling urge and a burning anxiety for understanding, friendship and concord on the basis of mutual respect and regard for every State.[34]

When the Addis Ababa Conference convened on May 22, 1963, it was the largest summit conference in African history, with thirty heads of state present.[35] At its closing, it was also the most fruitful, having overcome the two major problems that threatened its success: the aftermath of the assassination of President Sylvanus Olympio of Togo and the delicate problem of drawing up a charter acceptable to all. As it turned out, the first problem helped to solve the second.

The conference began with the troublesome question of whether to seat the Grunitzky government of Togo. The Olympio assassination was widely condemned throughout Africa, and among those who threatened to walk out if Grunitzky was permitted to participate in the conference was Sékou Touré of Guinea. Touré also claimed to have documentary evidence implicating his former ally, Kwame Nkrumah, in the assassination. Besides splitting the Casablanca bloc, the Togo issue pushed Nkrumah's faltering prestige to its lowest point.

At the same time, the question of Togo became a rallying point for the Monrovia Powers, counteracting the separatist tendencies of the U.A.M. and other members of the group. Though there was a risk of a walkout by Guinea, Nigeria, and other African states, Liberia and most of the Monrovia group were ready to admit Grunitzky (with a clear distinction between recognition and approval) in order to have as many African states as possible represented. The Monrovia Powers were also influenced by a persistent rumor that another Togo coup was in the making, led by a group even more favorably disposed to Nkrumah than Grunitzky.

The Togo issue had become so serious as the conference opened that Tubman addressed himself to the threat of walkouts by some of the African heads of state:

> I crave your permission to refer to a practice sometimes indulged in by delegations at conferences such as this, namely, walking out of committee or general assemblies during debates when the trend is contrary to their delegation's views. It appears to me that such actions are harmful to the success of a conference.
>
> If a decision taken is against the view or interest of the delegation, the delegation might ask for its protest to the decision to be noted for the benefit of record and future generations because there may be other matters which may arise when the

interest of the delegation may be affected or when the advice, counsel and assistance of the delegation may be necessary and helpful. We lose the benefit of their advice, counsel and assistance if the delegation has walked out.

We earnestly hope that at such an historic and significant conference, the general and not the personal or purely national interest will influence our thinking and action and thereby enable us to participate dispassionately and selflessly in debates designed to achieve the greatest good for Africa. . . . It is towards this end that we have assembled here; it is for this purpose that we have worked, planned and prepared for the conference. Certainly this is not a conference to end all conferences but it is one to which African leaders imbued with an avid desire for unity have come to find a way.

.   .   .   .

In the great tasks to which we have set ourselves at this crucial moment in our continent's history, let us think like men of action and act like men of thought.[36]

The heads of state, although they did not extend to the Togo regime an invitation to attend the conference, made no formal pronouncements concerning the issue for fear of forcing other delegations to make good their promises of walking out. However, there was a behind-the-scenes agreement that those states wishing to extend diplomatic relations to the Grunitzky government would do so quietly after the conference.

As matters developed, the Togo problem helped to eliminate much of the wrangling anticipated over a conference charter for achieving African unity. At odds with his usual allies, Nkrumah was unwilling to risk further isolation by pushing for the plan he had proposed the previous January. Thus, with Africa's chief proponent of immediate political union quieted, it was a relatively easy task for the Monrovia Powers and the others to agree on the details of a "Charter of the Organisation of African Unity." The Charter clearly echoed Liberia's philosophy of cooperation as a means of achieving eventual union in all spheres, including the political.

The Addis Ababa Charter (see Appendix 15) is almost identical with the proposal for unity first submitted and read to the Lagos Conference in January, 1962, by President Tubman. It is the logical culmination of President Tubman's pronouncements on African unity that date back to the mid-1950's. This is borne out particularly by Article III, the Charter's most critical clause, in which the thirty signatory states affirm and declare their adherence to seven basic principles, namely:

1. the sovereign equality of all African and Malagasy States;
2. non-interference in the internal affairs of States;
3. respect for the sovereignty and territorial integrity of each member and for its inalienable right to independent existence;
4. peaceful settlement of disputes by negotiation, mediation, conciliation or arbitration;
5. unreserved condemnation, in all its forms, of political assassination as well as of subversive activities on the part of neighbouring States or any other States;
6. absolute dedication to the total emancipation of the African territories which are still dependent;
7. affirmation of a policy of non-alignment with regard to all blocs.

This general acceptance of the Tubman approach toward unity underlined the crucial role of Liberia in shaping the New Africa. With its patient, persistent policy, free of flamboyance and extravagant propaganda, Liberia is easily overlooked outside Africa when trends and developments toward unity are weighed. With President Tubman, it is a matter of personal dedication, and he makes a point of stressing commitment to a vision of Africa that surpasses competitive nationalism:

One of the worst alternatives to African Unity is African anarchy. It can be engendered by armed and militant nationalism of "my country right or wrong," by the pride of power, by the penchant for prestige, the lust for conquest, the thirst for glory and the quest for the spotlights. . . .

To say that the salvation of Africa lies in unity is to suggest that divergent interests be reconciled; that common values and African welfare be substituted for exclusive and competitive self-seeking.[37]

Epilogue

President Tubman of Liberia has bridged with his leadership the old and the new Liberia, colonial and independent Africa. He has played a major part in the sudden and dramatic emergence that has placed Liberia and much of Africa at the takeoff point of economic development. He has engineered major social changes in his country and worked to establish stable political patterns throughout the continent. His importance historically is established.

As Tubman entered his fifth term of office in January, 1964, both Africa and Africa's "Lone Star Republic" were at the threshold of further change; both were about to establish patterns of policy that would predominate in the new generation of leadership and would direct the main lines of social and economic development. In only two decades, Liberia, under Tubman, had made revolutionary advances without bloodshed and without sacrificing its democratic heritage. As noted earlier, the national budget soared from less than $1 million to $50 million; health facilities were extended throughout the country; the number of school-age children attending classes regularly rose tenfold to nearly 100,000; political stability was brought about by a campaign for equal opportunity under the Unification Policy; and the Open Door Policy made Liberia a model of rapid African economic development.

But despite these and other advances which have been brought about, some old problems remain almost unchanged. For example, political and economic power is still highly concentrated in the hands of a few. However, it is also true that today's elite differs widely from the Americo-Liberian elite of yesteryear in its open-mindedness and fluidity. Since it is based more on individual friendships than familial ties, even the humblest tribal boy can aspire toward membership. The primary requirements for acceptance into the new elite appear to be either personal wealth, an important job, or a foreign university education, plus membership in one of Liberia's several Masonic lodges. All but a few political appointments and nominations are given to persons inside this elite. Further, it is asserted by some outsiders that True Whig (Liberia's only political party) nominations are more or less agreed to at fraternal lodge meetings long in advance of party conventions. The Moslems and animists, who make up the great majority of the population (there are no statistics available on the exact number), receive relatively little representation. In this way, the minority elite has controlled the government since Liberia's independence in 1847. There is little indication that this situation will change even under the next generation of leaders.

There are also several new problems which have resulted from Liberia's rapid but uneven economic expansion. Easily recognizable signs of new prosperity throughout the country have stirred the material aspirations of the common people far beyond their vocational preparedness. In a qualified sense this is also true with respect to social and political gains. The people hope for greater equality of opportunity but literally lack a sufficient number of qualified persons from among their ranks to take full advantage of that which has already been made available to them over the past two decades. The educational crisis in Liberia is one of the greatest in Africa and no solution in the short run is apparent. The government has already borrowed as much as it can on the strength of future revenues and is presently in debt for over $100 million. The only hope appears to be foreign assistance programs. The United States has already committed itself to financing a large part of the ten-year educational plan, and relative to population there are more Peace Corps personnel in Liberia than in any other African nation.

Regardless of how haphazard progress has been, the sheer fact of change for the better in Liberian society generally has made Tubman a messiah in the eyes of his countrymen. However, it has been his amiability, tolerance, generosity, and sincerity which has kept him in office. There is no question that Tubman can continue as President as long as he wishes. However, when he completes his present term he will be seventy-two years of age and it seems probable that he will retire.

Who will succeed President Tubman?

This represents a major responsibility facing President Tubman, who is required by the nature of the social and political milieu to play the major role in this planning. He must now begin taking the steps necessary to assure that there is a peaceful and orderly transition to effective leadership. Final judgments on his administration will be heavily influenced by the way in which it hands the torch to its successor.

Appendixes

Constitution of the Republic of Liberia
(as amended through May, 1955)

ARTICLE I. DECLARATION OF RIGHTS

The end of the institution, maintenance, and administration of government, is to secure the existence of the body politic, to protect it, and to furnish the individuals who compose it, with the power of enjoying in safety and tranquility, their natural rights, and the blessings of life; and whenever these great objects are not obtained, the people have a right to alter the government, and to take measures necessary for their safety, prosperity and happiness.

Therefore, we the People of the Commonwealth of Liberia, in Africa, acknowledging the devout gratitude, the goodness of God, in granting to us the blessings of the Christian religion, and political, religious, and civil liberty, do, in order to secure these blessings for ourselves and our posterity, and to establish justice, insure domestic peace, and promote the general welfare, hereby solemnly associate and constitute ourselves a Free, Sovereign and Independent State, by the name of the REPUBLIC OF LIBERIA, and do ordain and establish this Constitution for the government of the same.

Section 1. All men are born equally free and independent, and have certain natural, inherent and inalienable rights; among which, are the rights of enjoying and defending life and liberty, of acquiring, possessing and protecting property and of pursuing and obtaining safety and happiness.

146

Section 2. All power is inherent in the people; all free governments are instituted by their authority and for their benefit and they have the right to alter and reform the same when their safety and happiness require it.

Section 3. All men have a natural and inalienable right to worship God according to the dictates of their own consciences, without obstruction or molestation from others: all persons demeaning themselves peaceably, and not obstructing others in their religious worship, are entitled to the protection of law, in the free exercise of their own religion; and no sect of Christians shall have exclusive privileges or preference, over any other sect; but all shall be alike tolerated: and no religious test whatever shall be required as a qualification for civil office, or the exercise of any civil right.

Section 4. There shall be no slavery within this Republic. Nor shall any citizen of this Republic, or any person resident therein, deal in slaves, either within or without this Republic, directly or indirectly.

Section 5. The people have a right at all times, in an orderly and peaceable manner, to assemble and consult upon the common good; to instruct their representatives, and to petition the government, or any public functionaries for the redress of grievances.

Section 6. Every person shall have remedy therefor, by due course of law; justice shall be done without sale, denial or delay; and in all cases, not arising under martial law, or upon impeachment, the parties shall have a right to trial by jury, and to be heard in person or by counsel, or both.

Section 7. No person shall be held to answer for a capital or infamous crime, except in cases of impeachment, cases arising in the army and navy, and petty offences, unless upon presentment by a grand jury; and every person criminally charged, shall have a right to be seasonably furnished with a copy of the charge, to be confronted with witnesses against him—to have compulsory process for obtaining witnesses in his favor; and to have a speedy, public and impartial trial by a jury of the vicinity. He shall not be compelled to furnish or give evidence against himself; and no person shall for the same offence be twice put in jeopardy of life or limb.

Section 8. No person shall be deprived of life, liberty, property or privilege, but by judgment of his peers, or the law of the land.

Section 9. No place shall be searched, nor person seized, on a criminal charge or suspicion, unless upon warrant lawfully issued, upon probable cause supported by oath, or solemn affirmation, specially designating the place or person, and the object of the search.

Section 10. Excessive bail shall not be required, nor excessive fines imposed, nor excessive punishment inflicted. Nor shall the legislature make any law impairing the obligation of contracts; nor any law rendering any act punishable, in any manner in which it was not punishable when it was committed.

Section 11. All elections shall be by ballot, and every citizen (Male and Female) of twenty-one years of age possessing real estate shall have the right of suffrage. When applied to Voters in the Provinces of the hinterland of the Republic, "possessing real estate" shall be construed to include possessing a hut on which he or she pays the hut tax.

Section 12. The People have a right to keep and bear arms for the common defence. And as in time of peace, armies are dangerous to liberty, they ought not to be maintained, without the consent of the legislature; and the military power shall always be held in exact subordination to the civil authority, and be governed by it.

Section 13. Private property shall not be taken for public use without just compensation.

Section 14. The power of this government shall be divided into three distinct departments: Legislative, Executive and Judicial; and no person belonging to one of these departments, shall exercise any of the powers belonging to either of the others. This section is not to be construed to include Justices of the Peace.

Section 15. The liberty of the press is essential to the security of freedom in a state; it ought not, therefore, to be restrained in this Republic.

The printing press shall be free to every person, who undertakes to examine the proceedings of the Legislature or any branch of government; and no law shall ever be made to restrain the rights thereof. The free communication of thoughts and opinions, is one of the invaluable rights of man, and every citizen may freely speak, write and print, on any subject, being responsible for the abuse of that liberty.

In prosecutions for the publication of papers, investigating the official conduct of officers or men in a public capacity, or where the matter published is proper for public information, the truth thereof may be given in evidence. And in all indictments for libels, the jury shall have a right to determine the law and the facts, under the direction of the court, as in other cases.

Section 16. No subsidy, charge, impost, or duties ought to be established, fixed, laid or levied under any pretext whatsoever, without the consent of the people, or their representatives in the legislature.

Section 17. Suits may be brought against the Republic in such manner, and in such cases as the Legislature may, by law, direct.

Section 18. No person can, in any case, be subjected to the law martial, or to any penalties or pains by virtue of that law, (except those employed in the army or navy, and except the militia in actual service) but by the authority of the legislature.

Section 19. In order to prevent those who are vested with authority, from becoming oppressors, the people shall have a right at such periods, and in such manner, as they shall establish by their form of government;—to cause their public officers to return to private life, and to fill up vacant places by certain and regular elections and appointments.

Section 20. That all prisoners shall be bailable by sufficient sureties, unless, for capital offences, when the proof is evident, or presumption great; and the privilege and benefit of the writ of habeas corpus, shall be enjoyed in this Republic, in the most free, easy, cheap, expeditious and ample manner: and shall not be suspended by the legislature, except upon the most pressing and urgent occasions, and for a limited time, not exceeding twelve months.

ARTICLE II. LEGISLATIVE POWERS

Section 1. The Legislative power shall be vested in a Legislature of Liberia, and shall consist of two separate branches—a house of Representatives and a Senate, to be styled the Legislature of Liberia; each of which shall have a negative on the other, and the enacting style of their acts and laws shall be, "It is enacted by the Senate and House of Representatives of the Republic of Liberia, in Legislature Assembled."

Section 2. The representatives shall be elected by, and for the inhabitants of the several counties and provinces of Liberia and shall be apportioned among the several counties and provinces as follows: The County of Montserrado shall have five representatives, the Territory of Marshall shall have one representative, the County of Grand Bassa shall have four representatives, the County of Sinoe shall have four representatives, the County of Maryland shall have four representatives, and three existing

Provinces of the Republic situated in the hinterland thereof shall each have one representative, and all counties which shall hereafter be admitted into the Republic shall have one representative, and for every ten thousand inhabitants one representative shall be added. No person shall be a representative who has not resided in the County or Province two whole years immediately previous to his or her election, and who shall not when elected be an inhabitant of the County or Province, and who does not own unencumbered real estate of not less value than one thousand dollars in the County in which he or she resides, or who in the Provinces shall not own a hut in which he or she resides and for which he or she pays the hut tax, and who shall not have attained the age of twenty-three years. The representatives shall be elected quadrennially and shall serve for four years from time of their election.

Section 3. When a vacancy occurs in the representation of any County or Province by death, resignation, or otherwise, it shall be filled by a new election.

Section 4. The House of Representatives shall elect their own Speaker and other officers; they shall also have the sole power of impeachment.

Section 5. The Senate shall consist of two members from Montserrado County, two from Bassa County, two from Sinoe County, and two from each county which may be hereafter incorporated into this Republic. No person shall be a Senator, who shall not have resided three whole years immediately previous to his or her election in the Republic of Liberia, and who shall not when elected, be an inhabitant of the county which he or she represents, and who does not own unencumbered real estate of not less value than one thousand two hundred dollars in the County, and who shall not have attained the age of twenty-five years. The Senators shall serve for six years and shall be elected quadrennially, and those elected in A.D. 1905 shall retain their seats for six years from the time of their election, and all who are otherwise elected shall serve for six years.

Section 6. The Senate shall try all impeachments; the Senators being first sworn or solemnly affirmed to try the same impartially, and according to law; and no person shall be convicted but by the concurrence of two thirds of the Senators present. Judgments in such cases shall not extend beyond removal from office, and disqualification to hold an office in the Republic: but the party may be tried at law for the same offence.

Section 7. It shall be the duty of the Legislature, as soon as conveniently may be, after the adoption of this constitution, and once at least in every ten years afterwards, to cause a true census to be taken of each town, and county of the Republic of Liberia, and a representative shall be allowed every town, having a population of ten thousand inhabitants, and for every additional ten thousand in the counties after the first census, one representative shall be added to that county until the number of representatives shall amount to thirty: afterwards one representative shall be added for every thirty thousand.

Section 8. Each branch of the Legislature shall be judge of the election returns and qualifications of its own members, a majority of each shall be necessary to transact business, but a less number may adjourn from day to day and compel the attendance of absent members. Each house may adopt its own rules of proceedings, enforce order, and with the concurrence of two thirds, may expel a member.

Section 9. Neither house shall adjourn for more than two days without the consent of the other; and both houses shall always sit in the same town.

Section 10. Every bill or resolution which shall have passed both branches of the Legislature, shall before it becomes a law, be laid before the President for his approval; if he approves, he shall sign it, if not, he shall return it to the Legislature with his objections—if the Legislature shall afterwards pass the bill or resolution by a vote of two thirds in each branch, it shall become a law. If the President shall neglect to return such bill or resolution to the Legislature with his objections for five days after the same shall have been so laid before him—the Legislature remaining in session during that time, such neglect shall be equivalent to his signature.

Section 11. The Senators and Representatives shall receive from the Republic a compensation for their services to be ascertained by law; and shall be privileged from arrest except for treason, felony or breach of the peace while attending at, going to, or returning from the session of the Legislature.

ARTICLE III. EXECUTIVE POWER

Section 1. The Supreme Executive Power shall be vested in a President who shall be elected by the people and shall hold office for a term of eight years. No President may be elected for two consecutive terms of eight years, but should a majority of the ballots cast at a second or any other succeeding election by all of the electors voting thereat elect him, his second or any other succeeding term of office shall be for four years. He shall be Commander-in-Chief of the Army, Navy and Air Forces. He shall in the recess of the Legislature, have power to call out the militia or any portion thereof, into actual service in defence of the Republic. He shall have power to make treaties, provided the Senate concur therein, by a vote of two-thirds of the Senators present. He shall nominate, and with the advice and consent of the Senate appoint and commission, all Ambassadors, and other public Ministers and Consuls, Secretaries of State, of National Defence, of the Treasury, Attorney General, all Judges of Courts, Sheriffs, Coroners, Marshals, Justices of the Peace, Clerks of Courts, Registers, Notaries Public, and all other officers of State civil and military, whose appointment may not be otherwise provided for by the Constitution, or by standing laws. And in the recess of the Senate, he may fill any vacancies in those offices, until the next session of the Senate. He shall receive all ambassadors and other public ministers. He shall take care that the laws be faithfully executed: —he shall inform the Legislature from time to time, of the condition of the Republic, and recommend any public measures for their adoption, which he may think expedient. He may after conviction, remit any public forfeitures and penalties, and grant reprieves and pardons for public offences, except in cases of impeachment. He may require information and advice from any public officer, touching matters pertaining to his office. He may on extraordinary occasions, convene the Legislature, and may adjourn the two houses whenever they cannot agree as to the time of adjournment.

Section 2. There shall be a Vice President who shall be elected in the same manner and for the same term as the President, and whose qualifications shall be the same. He shall be the President of the Senate, and give the casting vote when the house is equally divided on any subject. And in case of the removal of the President from office or his death, resignation, or inability to discharge the powers and duties of said office, the same shall devolve upon the Vice President; and the Legislature may by law provide for the cases of removal, death, resignation or inability, both of the President, and Vice President, declaring what officer shall then act as President, and such officer shall act accordingly, until the disability be removed, or a President shall be elected. When a vacancy occurs in the office of Vice President, by the death, resignation or otherwise, after any regular election of President and Vice President, the President shall immediately call a special election to fill said vacancy.

Section 3. The Secretary of State shall keep the records of the State, and all the records and papers of the Legislative body, and all other public records and documents, not belonging to any other department, and shall lay the same when required, before the President or Legislature. He shall attend upon them when required and perform such other duties as may be enjoined by law.

Section 4. The Secretary of the Treasury or other persons who may by law, be charged with the custody of the public monies, shall before he receive such monies, give bonds to the State with sufficient sureties, to the acceptance of the Legislature, for the faithful discharge of his trust. He shall exhibit a true account of such monies when required by the President or Legislature, and no monies shall be drawn from the Treasury, but by warrant from the President, in consequence of appropriation made by law.

Section 5. All Ambassadors and other public Ministers, and Consuls, the Secretary of State, of National Defence, and of the Treasury, the Attorney General, and Postmaster General shall hold their offices during the pleasure of the President. Justices of the Peace, sheriffs, coroners, marshals, clerks of courts, registers, and notaries public, shall hold their offices for the term of two years from the date of their respective commissions; but may be removed from office within that time by the President, at his pleasure; and all other officers whose terms of office may not be otherwise limited by law, shall hold their offices during the pleasure of the President. The Legislature shall pass a standing law organizing and regulating the Civil Service of the Republic, which law shall declare what offices may be controlled by the provisions of said law. The provisions of this section of the Constitution relating to tenure of office shall not apply to offices falling within the provisions of the Civil Service law.

Section 6. Every civil officer may be removed from office by impeachment, for official misconduct. Every such officer may also be removed by the President, upon the address of both branches of the Legislature, stating their particular reason for his removal.

Section 7. No person shall be eligible to the Office of President who is not a citizen of this Republic by birth or a naturalized citizen of over twenty-five years' residence and who is not possessed of unencumbered real estate of the value of two thousand and five hundred dollars.

Section 8. The President shall at stated times receive for his services, a compensation which shall neither be increased nor diminished during the period for which he shall have been elected: And before he enters on the execution of his office, he shall take the following oath of affirmation.

"I do solemnly swear, (affirm) that I will faithfully execute the office of President of the Republic of Liberia, and will to the best of my ability preserve, protect and defend the constitution, and enforce the laws of the Republic of Liberia."

ARTICLE IV. JUDICIAL DEPARTMENT

Section 1. The Judicial power of this Republic shall be vested in one Supreme Court, and such subordinate courts as the Legislature may from time to time establish. The Judges of the Supreme Court, and all other Judges of Courts, shall hold their office during good behavior; but may be removed by the President on the address of two thirds of both houses for that purpose, or by impeachment and conviction thereon. The Judges shall have salaries established by law, which may be increased, but not diminished during their continuance in office. They shall not receive any other perquisites or emoluments whatever from parties or others, on account of any duty required of them.

Section 2. The Supreme Court shall have original jurisdiction in all cases affecting ambassadors, or other public ministers and consuls, and those to which a County shall be a party. In all other cases the Supreme Court shall have appellate jurisdiction, both as to law and fact, with such exceptions, and under such regulations as the Legislature shall from time to time make.

Section 3. The number of justices of the Supreme Court of the Republic of Liberia shall be limited to One Chief Justice and Four Associated Justices, a majority of whom shall be deemed competent to transact the business of the Supreme Court and from whose Judgment there shall be no appeal.

ARTICLE V. MISCELLANEOUS PROVISIONS

Section 1. All laws now in force in the Commonwealth of Liberia and not repugnant to this Constitution, shall be in force as the laws of the Republic of Liberia, until they shall be repealed by the Legislature.

Section 2. All judges, magistrates, and other officers now concerned in the administration of justice, in the Commonwealth of Liberia, and all other existing civil and military officers therein, shall continue to hold and discharge the duties of their respective offices, in the name and the authority of the Republic, until others shall be appointed and commissioned in their stead, pursuant to this Constitution.

Section 3. All towns and municipal corporations within the Republic, constituted under the laws of the Commonwealth of Liberia, shall retain their existing organizations and privileges, and the respective officers thereof shall remain in office, and act under the authority of this Republic, in the same manner and with like powers as they now possess under the laws of said Commonwealth.

Section 4. The first election of President, Vice President, Senators and Representatives shall be held on the first Tuesday in October in the Year of Our Lord, Eighteen Hundred and Forty Seven, in the same manner as elections of members of the Council are now held in the Commonwealth of Liberia and the votes shall be certified and returned to the Colonial Secretary, and the results of the election shall be ascertained, posted and notified by him, as is now by law provided, in case of such members of Council.

Section 5. All other elections of President, Vice President, Senators and Representatives, shall be held in the respective towns on the first Tuesday in May in every two years, such elections to be held and regulated in such manner as the Legislature may by law prescribe. The returns of votes shall be made to the Secretary of State, who shall open the same, and forthwith issue notices of the election to the persons apparently so elected, Senators and Representatives: and all such returns shall be by him laid before the Legislature at its next ensuing session, together with the list of the names of the persons who appear by such returns, to have been duly elected Senators and Representatives; and the persons appearing by said returns to be duly elected, shall proceed to organize themselves accordingly as the Senate and House of Representatives. The votes for President shall be sorted, counted and declared by the House of Representatives. And if no person shall appear to have a majority of such votes the Senators and Representatives present, shall in Convention by joint ballot, elect from among the persons having the three highest number of votes, a person to act as President for the ensuing term.

Section 6. The Legislature shall assemble once at least in every year, and such meeting shall be on the first Monday in January unless a different day shall be appointed by law.

Section 7. Every Legislator and other officer appointed under this Constitution shall before he enters upon the duties of his office, take and subscribe a solemn oath or affirmation to support the Constitution of this Republic, and faithfully and impartially discharge the duties of such office. The presiding officer of the Senate shall administer such oath or affirmation to the President, in Convention of both houses, and the President shall administer the same to the Vice President, to the Senators, and to the Representatives in like manner. When the President is unable to attend, the Chief Justice of the Supreme Court may administer the oath or affirmation to him at any place, and also to the Vice President, Senators and Representatives in Convention. Other officers may take such oath or affirmation before the President, Chief Justice, or any other person who may be designated by law.

Section 8. All elections of public officers shall be made by a majority of the votes, except in cases otherwise regulated by the Constitution or by law.

Section 9. Offices created by this Constitution which the present circumstances of the Republic do not require to be filled shall not be filled until the Legislature shall deem it necessary.

Section 10. The property of which a woman may be possessed at the time of her marriage, and also that of which she may afterwards become possessed, otherwise than by her husband, shall not be held responsible for his debts, whether contracted before or after marriage.

Nor shall the property thus intended to be secured to the woman be alienated otherwise than by her free and voluntary consent, and such alienation may be made by her either by sale, devise or otherwise.

Section 11. In all cases in which estates are insolvent, the widow shall be entitled to one third of the real estate, during her natural life, and to one third of the personal estate, which she shall hold in her own right subject to alienation by her, by devise or otherwise.

Section 12. No person shall be entitled to hold real estate in this Republic, unless he be a citizen of the same. Nevertheless this article shall not be construed to apply to Colonization, Missionary, Educational, or other benevolent institutions, so long as the property or estate is applied to its legitimate purposes.

Section 13. The great object of forming these Colonies, being to provide a home for the dispersed and oppressed children of

Africa, and to regenerate and enlighten this benighted continent, none but Negroes or persons of Negro descent shall be eligible to citizenship in this Republic.

Section 14. The purchase of any land by any citizen or citizens from the aborigines of this country for his or their own use, or for the benefit of others, or estates or estates in fee simple, shall be considered null and void to all intents and purposes.

Section 15. The improvement of the native tribes and their advancement in the arts of agriculture and husbandry, being a cherished object of this government, it shall be the duty of the President to appoint in each county some discreet person whose duty it shall be to make regular and periodical tours through the country for the purpose of calling the attention of the natives to these wholesome branches of industry, and of instructing them in the same, and the Legislature shall, as soon as it can conveniently be done, make provision for these purposes by the appropriation of money.

Section 16. The existing regulations of the American Colonization Society, in the Commonwealth, relative to immigrants, shall remain the same in the Republic, until regulated by compact between the Society and the Republic; nevertheless, the Legislature shall make no law prohibiting immigration. And it shall be among the first duties of the Legislature to take measures to arrange the future relations between the American Colonization Society and this Republic.

Section 17. This Constitution may be altered whenever two-thirds of both branches of the Legislature shall deem it necessary; in which case the alteration or amendments shall first be considered and approved by the Legislature by the concurrence of two-thirds of the Members of each branch and afterwards by them submitted to the people and adopted by two-thirds of all the electors at a special election called for that purpose.

APPENDIX 2

The National Anthem

All hail Liberia, hail!
All hail Liberia, hail!
This glorious land of liberty
Shall long be ours
Tho' new her name

Green be her fame,
And mighty be her powers.
In joy and gladness
With our hearts united
We'll shout the freedom
Of a race benighted.
Long live Liberia, happy land,
A home of glorious liberty,
By God's command.

All hail Liberia, hail!
All hail Liberia, hail!
In union strong, success is sure
We cannot fail
With God above
Our rights to prove
We will o'er all prevail
With heart and hand
Our country's cause defending
We'll meet the foe
With valor unpretending,
Long live Liberia, happy land,
A home of glorious liberty
By God's command.

The National Anthem was composed by Daniel Bashiel Warner, who later became Liberia's third president. Music for the anthem was subsequently supplied by Olmsted Luca, a Liberian immigrant who came from a family of musicians.

APPENDIX 3

Labour Agreement of 1928

This indenture of agreement made and entered into this 2nd day of April in the year of our Lord nineteen hundred and twenty-eight (A.D. 1928) in the City of Monrovia and the Republic of Liberia by Messrs. Barclay & Barclay, attorneys-at-law under special power of attorney to act for and on behalf of Theodomiro

Avendano, president of the Syndicato Agrícola de los Territorios Españoles del Golfo de Guinea, residing at Santa Isabel, Fernando Poo, hereinafter referred to as the Syndicate, of the first part, and Thomas E. Pelham, Robert W. Draper, E. G. W. King, J. C. Johnson, M. A. Bracewell, and C. Cooper, citizens of the Republic of Liberia, recruiting agents now represented by S. A. Ross, of counsel for the recruiting agents, hereinafter referred to as the Recruiting Agents, party of the second part.

That the party of the first part agrees to pay to the party of the second part nine pounds sterling to cover headmoney, taxes, advances, compensation and food; in other words, including all expenses (except passage to Fernando Poo), which is to be borne by the party of the first part, exclusive of the nine pounds sterling above mentioned. The party of the first part requests the party of the second part to recruit and ship fifteen hundred boys to the Spanish authorities at Fernando Poo in accordance with the laws and regulations of Liberia government shipment labourers.

On arrival of these boys at Fernando Poo to the Curadoo, the Curadoo and the Liberian Consul shall engage these boys to the Syndicate, which the Syndicate undertakes to see done according to Spanish law, the Liberian Consul being present and superintending the engagement of said boys as per laws of the colony.

The fifteen hundred boys above mentioned should be shipped within one calendar year from the date of the signing of this agreement, and the party of the second part should do their level best to have these boys shipped.

The boys shipped by the Recruiting Agents are contracted for the period of two years, one year's salary to be paid each boy in cash at Fernando and the remaining salary to be paid each boy when returning to Liberia, cheque on the Bank of British West Africa, Ltd., in Monrovia, or the agency in Sinoe or Cape Palmas.

The party of the first part agrees and faithfully promises not to inflict any inhumane punishment upon these boys but to treat them kindly and feed them properly, furnishing quarters for said boys, and in case of sickness to give said boys proper medical treatment.

The party of the first part empowers the party of the second part to make advances to each boy in the sum not exceeding three pounds sterling, which is allocated within the nine pounds sterling above mentioned, and will be the only sum chargeable to the boy. All other sums within the nine pounds sterling is free to the boy and paid by the party of the first part.

The party of the first part further agrees to pay to the head man of each gang of 25 boys the sum of $10.00 money of the colony in cash per month; and to each common labourer the sum of $6.00 money of the colony in cash per month; and, at the expiration of the period contracted for, the boys are to be returned to the place from whence they were shipped in Liberia.

Should any of the boys die, whatever amount may be due said boy at the time of his death will be paid over to the Liberian Consul. The party of the first part and their assignee further agree that at any time that the Liberian Consul desires to visit any of the farms where these boys are engaged for the purpose of inspecting and looking after the welfare as well as the interests of said boys he shall be permitted to do so without any objection on the part of the party of the first part, or their assignee.

The party of the first part further agrees to remit the sum of nine pounds sterling through the Bank of British West Africa, Ltd., as agreed upon to the party of the second part on each boy on return of the steamer conveying these boys to Fernando Poo without failure, said cheque to be drawn in the name of S. A. Ross, counsel for the party of the second part.

The party of the first part agrees and will pay to the counsel of the party of the second part the sum of one thousand pounds sterling as a bonus at the signing of this agreement; and further agrees to pay another sum of a thousand pounds sterling in British coin, to the party of the second part for every additional fifteen hundred boys shipped to the party of the first part.

In consideration of the above stipulations above mentioned the party of the second part promises and agrees to recruit and ship to the Curadoo at Fernando Poo, fifteen hundred labourers and more if possible, under the laws of Liberia made and provided for, as long as there be no intervention on part of the government to prohibit the recruiting of boys to Fernando Poo said boys should be shipped within one calendar year from date.

The party of the second part further agrees and accepts from the party of the first part the sum of nine pounds sterling to be sent through the Bank of British West Africa, Ltd., to the party of the second part as full expenses on each boy so recruited and shipped to Fernando Poo.

The party of the second part further agrees and accepts from the party of the first part the sum of one thousand pounds sterling as a bonus on the fifteen hundred boys to be shipped, on the signing of this agreement; and also further agrees to accept from the party of the first part another sum of a thousand pounds sterling on a further additional shipment of fifteen hundred whenever shipped as stipulated on the above agreement.

The party of the second part further agrees to recruit boys and ship same to the Curadoo at Fernando Poo within the space of two calendar years, providing there be no objection on the part of the government of Liberia.

After two years, either party being dissatisfied, may serve notice on the other party as to their intention of serving this agreement, said notice to be in writing.

And should there be any indebtedness to the party of the second part by the party of the first part at the terminus of this agreement same shall be paid, and all indebtedness on part of the parties of the second part to the party of the first part shall also be refunded.

It is further agreed, and the party of the second part so requires, that the party of the first part not presenting any authorization showing their status, before signing this agreement, shall be guaranteed by the Spanish Consul duly accredited to the Liberian government at Monrovia.

It is duly agreed that the party of the first part shall cause the Spanish steamer to call at the Ports of Greenville and Harper or any other port within Sinoe and Maryland Counties, the party of the second part furnishing port charts, where these boys may be recruited according to the laws of Liberia, monthly, and that no delay should be occasioned on the part of the party of the first part by said Spanish steamers not calling.

All inconveniences and expenses which the party of the second part may be exposed by such steamer not calling shall be chargeable to the party of the first part, and the party of the first part, hereby agrees to pay all damages incurred on account of delay of steamer, such damages and delays to be settled by arbitrations. (Arbitrators to be appointed in the usual legal way.)

It is mutually agreed between the parties that the party of the second part shall also operate within the County of Maryland, either in person or by appointment of subsidiary agencies in Maryland County, to carry out the intention of this agreement, and will do all in their power to recruit and ship to Fernando Poo, fifteen hundred boys or more, making a grand total of three thousand boys, under the laws of Liberia made and provided so long as the government of Liberia places no obstruction in the way.

The party of the first part further agrees to pay to the party of the second part the sum of nine pounds sterling per boy for all expenses incurred on laborers from Maryland County as above stated and further to pay the sum of one thousand pounds sterling, gold or silver coin, as a bonus for this privilege, making a total of two thousand pounds sterling to be paid at the signing of this agreement.

In witness whereof the parties hereto and hereunto have set their hands and seals this 2nd Day of April, A.D. 1928.

For the Syndicato Agrícola of Fernando Poo:

(Sgd) Barclay and Barclay,
Party of the first part.

For the Recruiting Agents:

(Sgd) S. A. Ross,
Party of the second part.

Witnesses: J. A. Dougan
J. W. Howard
E. A. Monger.

APPENDIX 4

*A Joint Resolution Authorizing the President
of Liberia To Complete Negotiations in Connection with
the League's Plan of Assistance to Liberia*

WHEREAS the Government of Liberia did appeal to the League of Nations to render assistance to Liberia on the lines of education, finance, economics and native administration; and

WHEREAS the League of Nations in a form of protocol adopted by the majority on October 13th, 1933, has submitted a Plan of Assistance for the consideration of the Liberian Government in compliance with her request for assistance; Therefore

It is resolved by the Senate and House of Representatives of the Republic of Liberia in Legislature assembled;

Section 1. That the President of Liberia be hereby authorized to accept on behalf of the Government of the Republic of Liberia in principle the basis outlined in the said proposed Plan of Assistance laid down in the protocol with the following reservations:

1. The bases of the scheme shall, by the League of Nations, be

declared to be the political integrity and economic independence, of the Republic of Liberia.

2. That the Chief Advisor shall not be appointed from any State to whose Nations the Liberian Government has financial obligations, or is under economic commitments, nor from any State having territory contiguous to Liberia.

3. That to avoid any infringement of the sovereignty of Liberia, and the full responsibility of its Government, the power and rights of the Chief Advisor shall be carefully defined so as to restrict him to the precise objects to which they apply—namely: To give the Central Government the benefit of his advice and to supervise the execution of the Plan of Assistance.

4. That the Deputy Provincial Commissioners shall be Liberians.

5. That no power be granted to any advisor appointed under the Plan which will be in derogation of the powers and authority of the President, Legislature, or courts constitutionally established.

6. That no question affecting the interest of the State shall be subject to the decision of any outside or alien authority unless the Liberian Government freely decides same.

7. That no body of troops or gendarmerie shall be placed under the command of foreigners; nor shall any force of police or messengers be armed for any purpose except upon the authority of the President of Liberia.

8. That no official shall be engaged in the service of Liberia even if supervised or administered by the Foreign Experts except upon the prior approval or, and appointed by, the President of Liberia, and, where required by the Constitution, confirmation by the Senate of Liberia.

9. That the foreign experts shall be attached to the Departments; and work in association with the Head of said Department who shall follow the advice of said experts under such sanctions as the Legislature may approve.

10. The cost of the execution of said Plan shall involve neither temporary nor permanent increase in the capital indebtedness of the Republic either to the Finance Corporation of America or otherwise, and the cost of said Plan shall be within the actual financial capacity of the Government of Liberia.

11. That a moratorium on interest and sinking fund on the 1926 7 per cent Gold Loan shall be maintained until such period when, in the opinion of the Chief Advisor in collaboration with the Government of Liberia, the interest, sinking fund, or both, may be met out of current revenues without increasing the capital

indebtedness of Liberia and without recourse to the issuance of bonds.

12. The Government will not concede any limitations upon its power to grant concessions to foreigners; although the Government will undertake to submit to the Chief Advisor and Financial Advisor any proposals for concessions that may be made and give due consideration to any advice they may offer thereon.

Section 2. The Legislature of Liberia does not approve of the provisions of the proposed supplementary agreement between the Government of the Republic of Liberia and the Finance Corporation of America as attached to the League of Nations protocol as an annex thereto; but inasmuch as Section 2 of Article 24, page 11, of the said protocol makes the operation of the Plan of Assistance contingent upon a conclusion between the Government of Liberia and the Finance Corporation of America of adequate arrangements for financing said Plan of Assistance, the President of Liberia is hereby authorized and directed to send a mission of two competent Liberian citizens to America with the least possible delay to treat with the Finance Corporation of America on the spot with a view to adjusting the differences existing between the Government of Liberia and said Corporation and arriving at an arrangement by which the Plan of Assistance might become operative.

Section 3. That the Secretary of the Treasury, R.L., be and he is hereby authorized to expend out of the public revenues a sum not exceeding $8,000.00 for the purpose of defraying the expenses (travelling) of said special mission to America, upon warrant of the President of Liberia from any funds of the Government not otherwise appropriated or assigned.

This Joint Resolution shall be published in handbills and take effect immediately.

Any law to the contrary notwithstanding.

Approved January 12, 1934.

APPENDIX 5

Toward Better Standards in Liberian Education
(Text of a speech broadcast on Flag Day, August 24, 1962,
by Dr. William V. S. Tubman, President of Liberia)

Fellow Citizens:

On the one hundred and fifteenth anniversary of the raising and unfurling of the nation's flag, I consider it an appropriate time to address you and in particular the parents and guardians, and the professors, teachers and students of the institute of learning of the nation on the subject of EDUCATION IN LIBERIA.

Education is an essential and indispensable element in the life and progress of a nation. It is one of the safeguards of the liberties of a people and the index finger pointing to the future prospect of the continued survival, progress and life of any nation. Within this context, I feel very strongly that an assessment of the educational system of the country is highly desirable and essential as it will determine the basis of our national outlook, efficiency and preparedness, constitute our underlying philosophy and give a clearer revelation of the relative importance which we place upon education in the valued hierarchy of our society.

My confidence in education and a well organized school system as the basis and sheet-anchor of our democracy is derived from my awareness of the extraordinary need for its present and future service to the nation and its growth out of a comprehensive vision, a willing spirit and an intelligent cooperation by all concerned in its (socially desired) end-results.

The story of our educational advancement is one of sublime faith and daring perseverance in the face of imponderable odds. On the long road to nationhood and the resultant social progress and economic advance, both Government and foreign philanthropy and benevolent agencies as well as foreign and local enterprises have played important roles in shaping the educational standards which today guide the nation. Born of an ardent passion and a rugged determination to establish schools for the training and education of their children, our Pioneer Fathers laid the foundation which was to popularize education as the priceless possession of a free people. For even with the meagre financial resources available at that time, they never ceased their constant concern for, nor did they ever relinquish, the hope that education would always be the bulwark of their political freedom.

More than this, they entertained the reassuring conviction that religious education would enable them to create a new society in an atmosphere different from the one in which their bodies had been incarcerated but one in which their soul and minds had been sustained amidst the trials and tribulations through which they had passed and were able to endure. For in the religious songs which have become the great heritage of the Negro, the spirituals brought them hope, consolation, courage and patience. They dreamed. They laboured. They waited. They confided in themselves and looked to God and friendly peoples to help them find solutions for their problems. They profited from their experiences. They kept faith with those who had led the way to a fuller life through a better educational process.

It is a tribute to our past leaders and people, their vision, their unselfishness, their sacrifices, that they struggled to give their children better educational opportunities which had been denied themselves, for despite the fact that their schools were scanty, equipment almost non-existent, standards shockingly low, teachers few, inadequately prepared and poorly paid, the light of learning was kept burning in the schools of this nation even though many times with an uncertain and flickering glow.

Throughout the years there has been a continuing and consistent interest shown in, and more support given to, education, even when the finances of the nation were inadequate and salaries and allowances of officials and employees of Government were unpaid for as much as five and six months successively, but as conditions progressively changed and resources and revenues increased, greater appropriations have been provided. Foreign contributions and support for the extension of education have increased with the result that there are now more improved and better facilities as well as a higher standard of teachers and administrative personnel in our schools. There is a more favorable atmosphere for learning and what is most gratifying, men and women, boys and girls everywhere in the nation are responding enthusiastically to, and clamoring for, the improved educational opportunities and taking advantage of the facilities at hand. We are happy for this, and proud of the awakening interest in, and support given to, education.

But this imposes an even greater challenge to Government, to professors, teachers and educational institutions of every kind to cope with this nation-wide urge and demand of the young people for better facilities, greater opportunities and better standards of education.

Despite all this, there are, it seems to me, some vital missing links in our educational system. In the first place, I have a feeling that emphasis is being placed only on the mere academic type of education while a great amount of indifference is shown to the cultivation of the finer and more lasting disciplines of life—the moral, spiritual, and aesthetic values.

I note with growing concern the lack of emphasis on the teaching of classics, poetry, music, drawing, painting and other works of art which nourish the mind, broaden the understanding, deepen the intellect and awaken appreciation for love and beauty from which the possessor finds joy and significance in human existence and achievement. While it may be that not all of these areas are being neglected *per se,* their visible results in the lives of the young people of our nation are not eloquent enough to be functional and vitalizing forces. The challenge to achieve, the joy in creativity, the love of scholarship, the genuine pursuit of truth and the discovery of knowledge have become almost lost in the superficialities of the age, often under the misconstrued semantics of progressive education.

Consequently, education has become, in the view of many, so sugar-coated that it has been bereft of its challenge, mysterious enchantment and wonder of discovery.

Secondly, religious education as literature has been entirely eliminated from our schools.

Under the declaration of the religious rights of the citizen, the Constitution of Liberia provides that no sect of Christians shall claim exclusive privileges or preference over any other sect. If we construe this to mean that in a community which is predominantly Christian, the Bible, which is the sacred book of that sect, should not be permitted to be taught in the public schools, then it would be a deprivation of the constitutional rights of those Christians living in that community. Similarly, in a community where the population is for the most part Moslem, it could be a violation of religious freedom to prevent the Koran, which is the sacred book of that sect, from being taught.

I agree that in the public schools no religious dogmas, canons or rubrics of any particular denomination may be expounded, but I contend that the teaching of the Bible, the reading of the Koran or of any other sacred writing in our schools, colleges and universities is no violation of the provisions of the Constitution in respect of religious freedom.

Furthermore, it seems to me that objections to conducting devotional exercises and reading the Bible, the Koran or any other religious literature in schools, colleges and universities involve a question which is individual in character and could be raised only by the individual who conscientiously objects because of his disbelief in, or objections to the Bible or any other religious literature. But a whole community of students who profess any religious belief should not be deprived of the right and privilege of their religious worship in our institutions of learning because of the objections of one or two persons with atheistic or agnostic attitudes.

The next question on which I desire to speak is corporal punishment in the elementary schools. This we consider to be also important, but there are those who are inclined to talk a lot about child psychology. To know the psychology of a child is a hyperbole similar to the utterance of the apostle Paul, "O to know the love of God that passeth knowledge." To know the psychology of a child passeth all knowledge; for it is my opinion that a child actually has no psychology. Psychology must be stimulated or instilled in the child by its parents, its teachers and those who are charged with the responsibility of nurturing the child in its immediate environment, in the home, and in its contacts with neighbours and friends. All of these influences tend to create and develop its outlook, its psychology, its character and its attitude.

In any case, I must admit that this is a specialized subject and may better be left with the experts; but from a layman's point of view, I do know that in the days when children were not left to be governed, trained and controlled by the psychologists but by the use of what Solomon, the wise man, calls in his proverbs "the rod" and we in Liberia call the switch or whip, there were fewer juvenile delinquents, fewer wayward children and fewer truants in our land and in the world generally than we have today when so much emphasis is placed on child psychology.

The wise man in his proverbs has declared: "Spare the rod and spoil the child." He said further: "The rod is made for the back of the fool," and in Proverbs, Chapter 19, verse 18, he declared: "Chasten thy son while there is hope and let not thy soul spare him for his crying."

These are the admonitions of wisdom, handed down by that wise man, which were followed and practised since the incipience of our nation until in recent years, when, having an apparent desire to imitate or emulate what is known as the modern educational practices of other countries, we abandoned this tried, tested and proven educational system with the result that we are beginning to have on our hands unruly, criminally-minded and delinquent young people. The responsibility attaches to us who are responsible for elimination of the rod or switch from the elementary schools; to us parents who fail to cooperate with teachers in disciplining our children; to us who threaten physical combat with teachers who attempt, in the interest of the correct upbringing of the children, to admonish them rightly; to us parents who threaten legal action against teachers and professors who rebuke and chastise our children.

In consequence and in recognition of our responsibility in this respect, I appeal to all leaders of state, parents, guardians, prelates, clerics, professors, teachers, wards and the students themselves to cooperate with us in our efforts to stamp out rudeness, criminal tendencies and delinquency by supporting teachers and all those having to do with the training, up-bringing and nurturing of children and youth of the nation in administering corporal punishment in the elementary schools, when necessary, and in rebuking and punishing students in the high schools when expedient as well as in imposing disciplines by suspension or even expulsion when needed in colleges and universities in the interest of the maintenance of a higher standard of discipline and a moral course of conduct.

Let us support them in the way that my father did in a particular case of mine when I was coming up, if I may be permitted to narrate it here. It is an incident in my school life when my professor in music was teaching tonic solfa on the blackboard: I mischievously gave falsettoes and although he called my attention to this immediately, I repeated the falsettoes and on me he jumped with a switch and whaled me properly, inflicting one lash on my head which brought the blood streaming down. I rushed out of school to my parents, as mad as I could be, and reported this incident, crying. My mother became annoyed, as is more characteristic of mothers than of fathers, but my father said, "You must have done something that caused the teacher to do this to you." I said, "I did nothing." He said, "Come let us go up to the school." We went and when we arrived there my father inquired of the teacher, "You whipped this boy and cut his head; why did you do it?" The professor replied, "I was teaching tonic solfa on the blackboard and Shad gave falsettoes. When I called his attention to it he persisted and so I whipped him and mistakenly cut his head which I did not intend to do. I meant to whip him severely for his misconduct but I didn't mean to wound him." My father turned to me and said, "Boy, I knew that you had done something wrong." Turning to the professor, he said, "Beat him again in my presence." The professor ordered some of the strong boys in the school to take hold of me, put me on the back of one of them; whereupon he gave me another severe whipping in the presence of my father. Thereafter, my father took me home, cut the hair from around the wound and applied alcohol and plaster.

This was the kind of training and up-bringing we of our generation and those before and after us had until recently when corporal punishment was outlawed and the knowledge of the psychology of children as a means of training and up-bringing took its place.

The Government, parents, teachers and professors of educational institutions and all those who have to do with the training and nurturing of the young people of this country, have created and offered virtually nothing to occupy their minds outside of the classrooms; and even when they are in the classrooms, there is hardly anything to keep them occupied except their academic subjects.

In the days past, there were rhetorical exercises and social programs in all of the schools. There were exercises when the students had the opportunity to appear on the stage and debate some topic of current interest. There were spelling matches which were commonly called "spelling bees." There were mental arithmetic drills and both vocal and instrumental music classes. There were spelling definers when the student spelt the word and gave its definition. There was competition in the correct pronunciation of words. Then there was a practice that after school hours when work was done, the older folks in the communities saw to it that from four to six o'clock in the afternoon the young people engaged in such games as leap-frog, baseball, quoit-pitching, wrestling, "chordor," "bleh," and tug-of-war.

The children were so well disciplined that regularly in the evenings at different seasons of the year, all of the school bells rang at seven o'clock for those students not in boarding schools to assemble in their homes for study and parents were responsible, and did see that this was done. Thereafter, another bell rang at nine o'clock for the children to cease study and retire to bed. Thus there was not much time left for the children to engage in degrading and demoralizing practices during their tender years.

It is therefore a sad commentary on the age that today lads and lasses [teenagers] are permitted to wander about at night, attend parties, bars and cafes and remain out of the home until one and two o'clock in the morning without any restraint, restriction or scoldings. It seems that we are afraid of our own children.

I appeal to all of us to cooperate in the interest of the church, of society, of our children and of the future of the nation, to advocate and resuscitate reforms not only along the lines mentioned herein but such other means and methods that any of us, each of us or all of us may envisage or perceive as salutary to the benefit of reforms.

The Government, on its part, has given serious attention to, and taken positive action in, trying to retrieve its negligence toward the youth of the nation and is therefore inaugurating special schemes for the young people under special arrangements and provisions with the Israeli Government. Already a number of Liberians over the past three or four years have been sent to Israel for specialized training and are now back in the country with Israeli experts who have come to assist us in inaugurating and executing this program.

Here is a brief outline of what the program envisions:

1. That the Liberian National Youth Organization be a part of the national educational framework. It will function in close coordination with the Department of Public Instruction and the Department of National Defense.

2. The Organization will educate the young people of Liberia to be ready, both morally, and physically, to answer the call of their country for its present and future needs.

3. The Organization will deal with youth—male and female—between the ages of fourteen and twenty, in two age groups: fourteen to sixteen and seventeen to twenty.

4. Pre-military subjects will be introduced for the seventeen to twenty age group in addition to the normal subjects for young people with which the Organization will deal.

Organizational Structure:

The structure of the Liberian National Youth Organization shall answer in a practical way the needs of the above-mentioned aims. There shall be an Executive Office consisting of the following functionaries: Leader of the Organization, Deputy Leader, Education and Youth Activities Officer, Organization and Administrative Officer.

The Organization shall have a National Training Center for courses and youth training and sectional units shall be established in the various areas (schools, clubs, etc.).

Proposed Framework of Activities:

Activities in the organization will be carried out on a voluntary basis, boys and girls together (except for special activities) according to age groups, as follows:

a. In the framework of existing youth organizations (sports

clubs, community centers, youth clubs, boy scouts, girl guides, etc.) with whom there shall be close coordination and cooperation.

b. In the framework of formal educational institutions (secondary schools, vocational and agricultural schools, evening classes, etc.).

c. In the framework of proposed activities for as yet unorganized youth (youth centers, youth clubs, etc.) which are to be established.

d. Two senior youth instructors' courses annually.

e. Junior youth instructors' course during school vacation.

f. Special group courses for specific needs (sea and air).

Subjects for Youth Activities:

a. Camping
b. Foot Drill
c. First Aid
d. Outdoor Games
e. Recreational Subjects (folklore, singing, dancing, etc.)
f. Handicrafts
g. Physical activities
h. "Know Your Country and Your People"

The additional pre-military subjects for the seventeen to twenty age group will be as follows:

a. Foot and Rifle Drill
b. Use of weapons, stressing rifle and sports, marksmanship with small bore rifles
c. Topography
d. Fieldcraft and outdoor field life
e. Physical fitness—obstacle course

Ways of Working:

a. Regular local activities once or twice a week (1-2 hours)
b. One full day's activities once a month (Saturdays or Holidays)
c. Intensive training in a national youth center, 1-2 weeks a year during school vacation, for the fourteen to sixteen age group
d. Two weeks to one month of annual national service in development areas for the seventeen to twenty age group. This will be for the reclamation of the land, for road building, cultivation and other manual work of national importance.

All of the above proposed ways of working will stress the bringing together of youth in Liberia from the various counties and provinces, for the strengthening of national unity.

It is expected and requested that all educational institutions and other organizations concerned with the nurturing and training of the young people of the country, as well as all parents and guardians, will cooperate to the fullest extent in making this program a success.

I must emphasize what I consider to be some of the vital needs of our society and some of the things that our educational institutions can do in this advancing age of science and technology to achieve comparable results in a highly complex and competitive society. I believe that education should:

1. make of educatees changed agents who are serviceable not only as great scholars but as outstanding citizens;

2. extend the horizons of the possessors, quicken their understanding and deepen their appreciation for the past and present history of our race and country and make them visualize more realistically their individual contribution and contemplate the role which the nation can and must play in contemporary civilization;

3. renew the will and steel the determination to make society better than what it was yesterday so that the noble ends of democracy may be furthered more assuredly.

It is toward the achievement of such objectives that we can look with optimism and determination that our institutions of learning will steer the way clearly in the critical days that are upon us and ahead of us and of all mankind.

Such, in brief, is the story of our educational progress over the years. Our program is still expanding, being strengthened and improved from within and without and enriched in proportion as the resources of the country permit. Consequently, the educational budget has continued to climb steadily but even now the resources available are negligible. We need more and more funds so as to enable more and more up-to-date schools to be opened and staffed by competent and qualified teachers; trained personnel to be employed; educational experts and foreign agencies to share their knowledge in the service of our nation; more school equipment to be bought; foreign and local scholarships to be given additional boosts, and a better learning climate to be created.

To top all this, the State University must enlarge its program which may well evolutionize education in Liberia and give it new dimensions.

All in all, the fruits of one hundred and thirty-nine years of educational endeavours have been encouraging, if not satisfactory.

It appears to me to be a coincidence that just at this time, on the anniversary of our National Flag Day, the members of the Peace Corps from the United States are arriving in the country under the United States' program of assistance to developing countries, to assist us in this all-important national program for education.

We express our gratitude to that Government, private corporations, concessionaries, business enterprises, foreign missions and foundations as well as individual foreign citizens for their contributions toward our struggle for the education of the people of this nation.

The Department of Public Instruction is optimistic that in less than ten years roughly all children of school age in Liberia will be in organized schools, with a modern elementary school in every town and a high school in every district. This is indeed an ambitious program but the pace has been set and must be pursued with bold imagination and dedicated service.

Summing up, then, I have reviewed the story of our educational struggle and the importance which our forefathers attached to education; abridged the story of our progress and portrayed the opportunites and achievements of the present. I have spoken of the lack of emphasis on the moral, spiritual and aesthetic values in our schools, the absence of religious training, and the constitutional safeguards. I have stressed the need for corporal punishment in our elementary schools, and finally, I have called the attention of old and young, boys and girls, to the enriched opportunities of the present. I urge you in the saying of the old Latin Master, *Carpe diem*—seize the day.

Today, our budding university, our improved colleges, our enriched curricula offerings in the high and elementary schools and other educational adjuncts stand as a testimony to the reinforcement of the ideas of our fathers in education and our own determination that it will continue to be the bulwark of our society— now and forever. The challenge is great. We cannot renege, nor must we compromise it in a single detail.

The Executive Mansion
Monrovia, Liberia.

APPENDIX 6

Speech Delivered by President William V. S. Tubman to the
National Unification Council Held at Kolahun, Liberia,
February 14, 1963

Nine years ago we embarked with faith and determination upon a program of unifying and integrating the people of the country into a united whole. The policy that led to this program is referred to as the Unification Policy.

Twelve years earlier we repudiated publicly any idea that any section or segment of the nation was entitled to political and social preference or right over any other, and we declared that it was impossible to build a powerful and progressive nation with divided loyalties, suspicion and fear. This was in our statement of policy when we first stood for election to the office of President in 1943.

In our first Inaugural we outlined our social philosophy, declaring that we would take little or no pleasure in being called President of a nation of vassals and sycophants and calling for an educational program for all the people of the nation in order that they may be better prepared for the responsibility of intelligent government. We then avowed that all Liberians are entitled to the same rights and privileges.

Immediately we embarked upon a program which brought universal suffrage to the people of Liberia and nine years ago the first unification council was convoked in Maryland County and we challenged those who had constantly believed or entertained the idea that one segment of the population should live apart from, rather than as a part of, the whole people of the nation. In thus establishing this policy we threw out a challenge also to all sections and elements of the nation to unite and contribute to building a strong and progressive nation.

That the people have picked up the gauntlet and accepted that challenge is indicated by the progress that has been made.

Two years ago, a monument was erected here commemorating the national endorsement of the Unification Program. You may recall that the resolutions presented to the Legislature by you advocated the erection of a monument in each of the provinces as a mark of the concurrence in the unification policy and program by all the people, but the Legislature decided to erect only one monument in the Western Province, it being the first to petition it with the request.

It is our hope that the idea for which the Unification Monument stands will perpetually endure and that the monument so long as the elements hold it together will be a constant reminder and a covenant symbolizing the concurrence of all the elements and sections of the population, that through the unification of the nation we stand in strength and justice.

Today the Unification Program is near the end of one era and the beginning of another era that we hope will be greater and nobler. It is our hope that this present Council will be the final one held whilst the nation is divided into counties, provinces and territories. At our next convocation the nation should be divided principally into counties, with all the rights and privileges which go with county administration under our system of government. This is the new era to which we look hopefully forward in the immediate future, an era which will call upon all of us to share an even greater responsibility in the day-to-day life of the country. Whatever the task therefore we are to perform for the national progress, we should happily give our best.

We feel gratified that all sections of the country, and the people have cooperated in making the Unification Policy a success. During the last twenty years there have been no inter-tribal wars. All tribes, segments and elements of the country have stood together in support of the nation and the Unification Policy. No better, greater or more eloquent testimonial to the support of this policy could be demonstrated than that the people have given their approval to the policies of the administration and their constant demand that we remain their National Leader, often over and above our objections, re-inforced by their unanimous nomination of us a week ago today.

There is no question that the Unification Policy has been successful and that it has brought manifold benefits to the nation. This gives much satisfaction to all those who had anything to do with the inauguration, the shaping and execution of the policy as well as to every citizen who has cooperated in making the practical application of the policy a reality.

This policy could not have been successful without the Open Door Policy and vice versa the Open Door Policy could not have succeeded without the Unification Policy. The Open Door Policy brought about better and numerous roads to almost every part of the country, airfields and other means of communication and transportation which made the remotest parts of the country accessible to traders and businessmen and thereby activated development in these areas, as well as affording to the people in different sections of the country the means whereby they could communicate with, visit and get to know more about each other. The Open Door Policy also brought greater advantages in education, health, social and other benefits to the citizens of the country. It made possible the coming of various concessions such as the mining and agricultural concessions which enable more of our people to be gainfully employed and to receive practical on-the-job training, higher wages and other benefits.

Moreover, we felt that not only should the Government and the concessionaires share in the profits of these concessions but that the people themselves should also obtain direct benefits therefrom. In this connection we enunciated the policy that wherever possible Liberian citizens, without regard to station, tribe or clan inhabiting the littoral or the hinterland, be offered the privilege to purchase stocks in these concessions. Many of the chiefs and the citizens living in their chiefdoms are holders of share certificates in one or more concessions.

In the case of the LAMCO stock when the people of the hinterland and remote parts of the littoral failed to purchase shares on time because of the distances to be traversed the Government concerned itself to have the time extended so that all may benefit by participating in the wealth of their nation. I personally, as President, made a broadcast to the people throughout the country trying to persuade them to invest in this enterprise.

The purpose for all of these has been our wish to raise the standard of living of the people of the nation and to develop a middle class which is so necessary in a democracy and free enterprise system of government.

However, there is no doubt or question that human nature in its various aspects and propensities manifests itself in different ways under almost any circumstance. Indeed sometimes these human frailties even invade the realm of the deities. The story is told of Lucifer, the angel of light in heaven, who not satisfied with this high station became a traitor, causing confusion and war in heaven itself and had to be hurled into the bottomless pit of hell.

Traitors have arisen ever and anon in society, the church, in nations and in the family which is the smallest unit of the state. However the man, however the institution, however the people may decide, treachery at some time will show its monstrous head.

And so just at the time when the nation and people are seeking to conclude arrangements for the review of the territorial subdivisions of the nation, as when the sons of God appeared before the throne Satan also appeared in their midst and attempted to challenge God, so also at this time He appeared in our midst and attempted to challenge the Unification Policy, all that it stands for and has accomplished and to disrupt the peace, unity and stability with which this Government has been credited through the Unification Program.

It is perhaps interesting and even necessary to mention that even when there were internecine wars, uprisings and rebellions within the country they were not aimed at the assassination or murder of the Chief of State and the change of the frame and system of government but were waged in opposition to some wrong which the belligerents believed to have been committed against them, whether right or wrong. What is generally known is that most of these wars and uprisings that occurred in the early history of the country did not have their origins in disputes and disagreements between the Government and the tribes but between the tribes themselves and one or both of them then brought their complaints to Government for investigation and decision. Generally these complaints were mostly over boundary disputes and the tribe against whom Government decided to be in error objected and refused to submit to the decision of Government, which being the Supreme authority of the nation, was compelled to enforce its decisions and in such cases the tribe in whose favour the decision was rendered generally became an ally of Government in executing the decisions.

Now, a new, strange and traducing concept seems to be attracting some of our people, particularly some of the young, impressionable and irresponsible ones who seem still to be obsessed with the idea of tribalism and fall easy prey to the propaganda and indoctrination that is secretly and stealthily being disseminated amongst them that the land and territory of Liberia belong to them and that they have been deprived of their heritage; that the only way to retrieve the situation is to engage in subversive activities, treason and sedition and overthrow the Government, by force and murder, establish a socialist system of government, expropriate the properties of those who by their many years of labour, sacrifices, toil and sweat acquired their possessions and then distribute these properties among themselves.

We have no quarrel; we wage no war against socialism if it is kept within the territories and among the people that are socialistically inclined and who desire it. Each nation has the right to pursue the way of life it prefers and we will never attempt to impose our way of life on any other nation or people. But we shall fight to the death any attempts to impose and force upon us what we consider a mystical illusion. Our democracy has stood the test for almost a century and a quarter. Let us wait and see what reward socialism will bring to socialist countries within a century or a half century and then strike the balance sheet; perhaps at that time what now seems attractive to some of the young in this new, splashy ideology may prove itself.

This doctrine is being disseminated by certan foreign agencies and it is finding its way into some of the schools of the country, particularly Cuttington College, the College of West Africa, the University of Liberia and other schools. The authorities of these institutions are, or should be in knowledge of the infiltration and unless they take appropriate action, Government will be constrained to do so. I must in fairness, however, state that Bishop Harris of the Protestant Episcopal Church has sensed this situation and has been very active in trying to trace and stamp it out; but even that is not enough, it must be completely exterminated. But from the University of Liberia and the College of West Africa no official intimation or action has been forthcoming. To the contrary, we get the impression that the Nelson's Eye seems to be placed on these activities in the University of Liberia and the College of West Africa and unless it is stamped out completely the managements of these two institutions will be changed; if that is not enough, then they will be closed down at any cost.

That some of the youths of our nation seem to be attracted by these traducing ideologies is somewhat astounding for never before in the history of the country have the young people of Liberia had such splendid opportunities for education in many and various specialized fields without regard to tribe or origin as at this time, including scholarships, both foreign and local, medical facilities and other necessities of life.

But to be more specific, less than two weeks before the convocation of this Unification Council, the hydra-headed plot to assassinate the President and other officials of Government and thereby overthrow the Government by force was unearthed, the designated executor of the plot being the Acting Commander of the National Guard, Colonel D. Y. Thompson. This officer not being able to induce a sufficient number of officers and men of the Army to join in the conspiracy, moved arms and ammunition from the arsenal kept by Lieutenant Jenkins, organized a civilian group called "the club," composed principally of Klemoweh Greboes, some Vais, Krus and a few citizens of Arthington whose brother, Booker T. Bracewell, was convicted of treason but pardoned but who immediately thereafter committed the identical crime for the second time, whereupon he was again arrested, imprisoned and now awaits trial.

The present plot is a survival and revival of the one discovered about eighteen months ago by a number of young men, principally students, such as Appleton, Thompson, Sherman, etc., who were arrested, indicted and imprisoned and now await trial for treason.

The fact remains, nevertheless, that with the trial of that case not yet consummated the same sources from which that movement started found fertile soil in Colonel D. Y. Thompson whose brother is involved, has been indicted and imprisoned for trial. Colonel Thompson himself, an old criminal suspect in the 1955 assassination attempt, an adversary of democracy and orderly government and a natural miscreant, unable to move the army or even the unit that he commanded, resorted to the organization of a civilian movement to activate his designs. He and Lieutenant Jenkins, also a suspect of the 1955 conspiracy, together with Lieutenant Joseph T. Gibson who was charged with and convicted of larceny but were permitted to find their way back into the Army, all officers of the Liberian National Guard having access to government's arsenal, undertook to arm these men with arms and destructive weapons to execute their despicable plan.

When intimation of the organization of the plot was received, action was at once taken to penetrate it and sufficient evidence being accumulated, arrests were made. The inquiry and penetration continue and if convicted, everyone involved in the plot, whether as principal, accessory before or after the fact, shall receive the full penalties of the law because from little acorns great oaks grow.

Notwithstanding all this, the Unification Policy will go on and the development of the nation will move forward in ever increasing momentum, and nothing can or must stop or retard it because it has the support of you, the people of the nation.

We are determined to continue the various programs of social, economic, cultural and political reforms and progress which we enunciated and began implementing upon our induction into office. And why have we pursued these programs? To see them dissipated through the efforts of a few irresponsible and treasonable persons, and a few vain and ambitious men? Have we invited foreign capital into the nation to have the sacredness of contracts and our obligations violated and abused and make the nation the object of ridicule and scorn of the civilized world? Shall our promises be words of expedience with no more value than the paper on which they are written? This cannot be! It shall never come to pass!

The Government, I and others owe a special debt of gratitude and tribute to the Chiefs and people of the interior and hinterland, some of whom having heard of this plot almost at the same time as I, came down to the Capital, assured me of their support and of their condemnation of this subversive movement and took certain actions on their own to ensure the safety of the State as well as my personal security.

The Unification Policy is founded on our sincere belief that all citizens are entitled to the basic guarantees of the Constitution. It is our opinion that an axiom should be that if I demand respect from every man I should respect myself; but I cannot respect myself if I do not respect my fellow man since to demand respect from someone I do not respect is meaningless and does nothing for me as it is no honour to be thus respected; however, to be respected by someone for whom I have respect is to be honoured. Thus I honour myself when I respect my fellow man and am in return respected by him. It follows that the nation must be composed of men who are equal under the law and have the same rights and privileges. This is fundamental to the Unification Policy.

And so as we are about to embark upon a new era in the political life of the nation, when counties will comprise the basic sub-divisions of the nation, this step will demand that an even greater sacrifice be made by the citizens in order that our nation may continue her forward march. We must be vigilant and ever watchful that we do not fruitlessly chase mirages and utopias. We should remember that there is much to be done if our country is to grow, prosper and retain the fundamental principles of the love of liberty and respect of the individual.

Clearly, this is a time for firmness in resolution, a time for the enlargement and deepening of our national vision and dedication to the things which we cherish most. For a nation which has always believed in and subscribed to equality and justice, freedom and independence must always be our priceless heritage. This will require every man and every woman, every chief and official, every boy and every girl to be eternally vigilant and an individual watchdog against subversion and traducing ideologies and intrigues, make immediate reports and trace down any who may be engaged therein.

Within the past few years, very significant changes have taken place on the continent of Africa. The new nationalism which sparked the emergence of many nations, the phenomenal developmental strides now taking place, the comprehensive programs for economic expansion and greater educational opportunities and the insistent talk of African Unity and Solidarity are issues upon which the fate of two hundred and fifty million African peoples may well depend. Everywhere I travelled in and outside the continent, in discussions with African and world leaders and peoples my conviction has been strengthened that in unity of purpose and action lies our greatest hope. The greatest challenge, therefore, which confronts us in this country and in other African nations is our ability to comprehend the nature of our responsibilities and our willingness and readiness to shoulder the tasks which will lead to the solution of these problems.

The experiences through which our nation has gone, the lessons of history we are eager for this generation to learn, and the indivisibility of a unified Liberia which we have tried to convey to the people of the nation express more than anything else our determination that we will stand ready to fight for and die for these cherished goals of liberty and freedom which have always been encouraged and taught in our social and political institutions. To these ends my faith in you, the people of the country, has always been unshakable and unshaken, and in spite of actions which have recently brought shame and infamy to the history of our nation, I urge you to set high the ideals of Liberia, the realization of which will bring us more happiness, greater prosperity and peace within our borders and with all mankind.

I offered my life upon the altar of my country in three or four battles and therefore, being used to alarm, I declare that "none of these things move me, neither count I my life dear unto myself if it is necessary that my life be offered up again in the interest of the principles and ideas for which our nation was founded and for which it stands."

When the new arrangement for the territorial sub-division of the nation that we envisage materializes and additional counties are established and if this new arrangement inures to the best interest of the nation, the possibility exists for still another step to be taken for the benefit of greater and more effective integration and as a measure of decentralization of Government. There could be established states within the Republic with a certain amount of sovereignty in each. As a tentative or arbitrary suggestion, for instance, Montserrado County, Grand Cape Mount County and the New Lofa County could comprise one state; [Grand Bassa County and the new Bong County, another state]; Sinoe County and the new Nimba County, still another and Maryland County and the new Jede County, a fourth state. This arrangement is only hypothetical and may not comprise the actual combination of counties to form states in the order that I have suggested, should it become desirable to do so. This, however, I expect to be after my day and generation.

Fellow citizens of the Western Province, what great transformation has come to your Province because of your foresight, your hard labour, your loyalty and devotion to the ideals of yourselves and your fellowmen! For you, your children, your wives and those surrounding you, life can never return to what it was heretofore. The new day of prosperity and progress of which you dreamed, worked and fought for has begun coming to you. By your splendid cooperation and constant loyalty, you have blazed the trail to national unity and progress. The congratulations of the Government and people of Liberia go to you today and always for this great pace which has been set in the history of your Province and in the annals of our nation.

In the light of these accomplishments, one might be tempted to suggest that the objectives of the Unification Program have been achieved and therefore that other national goals need to be set and pursued. But the end is not yet; we are just beginning to begin. For while appreciable gains have been made, there are psychological barriers which must be overcome, for Unification is a thought process as much as it is a coming together of peoples of different elements, sections and tribes as part of the constitutional requirements of the nation. More than this, it must become a thought pattern, since it is in the hearts of men that ideas originate, and be constantly nourished so that it will spread to all areas of our national undertakings. This policy must continue until even our critical foreign critics can no longer discern the difference among the peoples of this nation.

Unification must become a way of life deriving its greatest support from the innermost conviction that the strength of all societies is resident in the contributions which are culled from all classes and levels of the society. It is with this thought and this conviction that we continue to work toward a more prosperous nation and a happy and enlightened citizenry.

Fellow citizens, after everything we will say and do at this Council is forgotten, the ideal and idea of unification must become a part of us and remind us continually of our united will and determination to become one people—Liberians.

Remember that a stronger and greater Liberia of tomorrow will depend upon your share and my share now and in the future in the great political program which has served the nation so well and which has greater possibilities for the future of the country.

We have all been tremendously thrilled by the wonderful reception and demonstrations accorded us since our arrival here. Thank you for your continued interest and unflinching loyalty to our administration and the State, and we hope that the same spirit which marked our joint efforts and which has borne abundant fruits will continue in the future for the benefits of our common country, Africa and the world, even when we have passed away.

May we from this meeting and from this day adopt a new frame of mind towards our country's future, its progress and development and thereby take greater courage for its continued welfare, safety and perpetuity in the community of nations and may the vision of a united Liberia be perpetually before us so that we may all work constantly and conscientiously toward the fulfillment of our true destiny as a nation and people.

APPENDIX 7

Liberia Official Gazette, XLVI, No. 2x (Extraordinary)
(January 26, 1959)
(Liberia's Proposal for the Associated States of Africa)

With the emergence of newly independent states in Africa, Liberia is happy that she no longer stands alone as she did in the age of colonial expansion and exploitation. In that age she lost over half of her territory and suffered unspeakable indignities, discrimination and perils. But never for once have the Liberian people lost sight of the fact that they are inseparably engaged in the great total human struggle for freedom and independence taking place everywhere and more particularly in Africa.

Liberia has consistently maintained that every people have an inherent right to be free to decide upon the type or form of Government they desire as well as the political machinery they wish to employ in the solution of their problems in their own way without interference.

However, when the Liberian Government speaks of non-interference in the affairs of member-countries, this cannot be construed to mean that it advocates the principle that any Government can violate Fundamental Human Rights of its citizens without such violation being the common concern of the entire world community. Neither can it be interpreted to refer to Governments which have not been voluntarily created by the people of their own free will and accord.

Therefore in the United Nations and elsewhere Liberia has sought every opportunity in a constructive manner to advocate the cause of African freedom and independence. She has always maintained that Africa should not be half-slave and half-free. She has felt that Africa must be totally free so that her peoples might become masters of their own destinies. Thus, even at great risks to her own safety, Liberia has remained an asylum for the oppressed peoples of Africa. But the Liberian people are convinced that only friendly cooperation among all nations and races will ensure that degree of peace and prosperity necessary for universal progress.

The Liberian Government and people believe that there is no substitute for freedom except it be greater freedom through equal participation and unlimited fulfillment of the whole purpose of a people. They also believe that any hasty or superficial semblance of unity in areas where conflicting issues are not carefully resolved may undermine the entire structure of any permanent political unity and retard real cooperative effort.

Hence, taking into consideration differing economic systems, differing political allegiances and preferences, differing cultural backgrounds and differing social customs; and not wishing to superimpose any artificial unity upon these differences, it is the opinion of the Liberian Government that the peoples of Africa should resolve to achieve close association and cooperation, without prejudice to their national or international identities, in the following or some similar manner:

1. That a single Convention which would provide for a permanent organization to be known as The Associated States of Africa, be concluded among the independent African nations and those which have fixed dates upon which they shall achieve independence, with the understanding that other non-independent countries of Africa shall have the right to join the organization upon attaining independence.

2. That The Associated States of Africa provide for continuing consultation on problems of common interest and for the peaceful solution of all disputes which may arise among its members.

3. That, within said organization, Regional Associations be recognized where they already exist or be organized to develop closer unity and provide uniform and common solution to specific problems in certain areas. For instance, it is suggested that in West Africa:

(a) A regional health authority should be created which would concentrate on the eradication of diseases common to the area.

(b) An agency should be developed to direct regional scientific research and training projects.

(c) A common cultural institute for the region should be developed.

(d) A uniform reduction of tariffs and a Customs Convention should be undertaken.

The Liberian Government feels that these political, social, cultural and economic actions should be achieved in consonance with the aims of the United Nations and in support of its endeavours to achieve peace and raise the level of living of the inhabitants of the earth.

BY ORDER OF THE PRESIDENT

(Sgd) J. RUDOLPH GRIMES
Acting Secretary of State

APPENDIX 8

*Correspondence Between President Kwame Nkrumah and
President Tubman in May, 1959, Concerning the
Sanniquellie Conference*

Dr. William V. S. Tubman
President of the Republic of Liberia
The Executive Mansion
Monrovia, Liberia

15th May, 1959

My dear and esteemed friend,

In your letter of the 7th April, 1959, you proposed that a conference be held between President Sékou Touré, you and me to discuss matters of interest to our respective countries and the unity of the continent of Africa. In my interim reply of the 20th April, I stated that I would discuss the matter with President Touré. I am happy to be able to say that President Touré agrees with me that a meeting between the three of us will be most useful.

I have now reviewed my programme for the next few weeks and any time in June that fits in with your own arrangements will be convenient for such a meeting. It is my view also that the meeting should be held in Liberia, provided that you are willing to act as host. Further, I consider that we should, if possible, keep private those meetings at which serious discussions will take place. The great importance of our deliberations to our respective countries and to Africa will require that our discussions are held in an atmosphere of complete frankness and calm. For that reason, if you agree, it may be convenient for the serious discussions to take place outside Monrovia City itself. A statement can be issued to the public at the conclusion of our discussions.

I trust that you will find my proposal regarding this conference acceptable and that you will let me know as early as possible what your final proposals are as regards the time and place.

I am sending a letter in similar terms to His Excellency President Sékou Touré.

With assurances of my highest esteem,

Yours sincerely,
(Sgd) KWAME NKRUMAH

His Excellency
Dr. Kwame Nkrumah
Prime Minister of Ghana
Accra, Ghana

May 27, 1959

My dear and esteemed friend:

It is with pleasure that I acknowledge the receipt of your letter of May 15, in which you refer to my letter of April 7, regarding my proposal for a conference to be held between President Sékou Touré, you and me to discuss matters of interest to our respective countries and the unity of the Continent of Africa.

I note with satisfaction that you agree that the meeting between the three of us will be most useful. I also note that after reviewing your program for the next few weeks, any time in June will be convenient for you for the meeting. However, after I had suggested June, and not hearing from you until I received your letter now under reply, I accepted an invitation to visit Sierra Leone in June.

Having just come through with the General Elections which were held throughout the country and having to visit Sierra Leone in June, I would be glad if you found it convenient for the meeting to be postponed until the 15th of July or, if that date will still not suit your convenience, I shall be willing to adjust my engagement schedule to suit whatever date which might be convenient for you on or about July 15th. You may inform me if this is acceptable to you by radiogram either through the Liberian Embassy in Accra or through your Embassy here.

You suggest that the meeting be held in Liberia, provided I am willing to act as host. Since you recommend the meeting to take place in Liberia, it follows as a normal sequence that I will in that case become host.

I am in agreement that some of the discussions which we expect to have should be kept private and also welcome your suggestion that these discussions should be held in an atmosphere of complete frankness and calm. I have always advocated and practiced frankness, calm and poise in all deliberations; hence I heartily concur with your suggestion.

Since it is felt that the conference should be held outside of Monrovia, I go along with you in this respect and will arrange a place outside of Monrovia for that purpose.

I shall be glad to know, as soon as possible, the names and official status of those who will be accompanying you to the conference.

Looking forward to seeing you in July and with assurances of my highest esteem, I remain,

Sincerely yours,

(Sgd) WILLIAM V. S. TUBMAN

APPENDIX 9

Correspondence Between President Sékou Touré and President Tubman in May, 1959, Concerning the Sanniquellie Conference

His Excellency, President Tubman
President of the Republic of Liberia
Monrovia

May 4, 1959

Excellency:

1: The Ambassador of the Republic of Guinea accredited to your Government will comment on this correspondence, so as to keep you informed about certain details of the situation in your Country.

After my return from the agreeable and important mission which I had the honour to accomplish near you in the name of the people of Guinea, the National Assembly of Guinea has ratified unanimously the understanding signed by both of us. By so doing, they have affirmed our common decision of cooperation and assistance between our two Republics.

2: In order to enhance the spirit of this agreement, and taking this into consideration in all my activities inside and outside of our Young Republic, the Declaration made on May 1, by Dr. Nkrumah, Prime Minister of Ghana, and myself, relative to the constitution of the Union of Independent African States, indicates the provisional character of this action which will ultimately regulate the relations between Members States of this Union and could function until such time when this instrument is ratified by our Parliament.

3: As your vast experience permits you to know, this Union, which you also have been advocating on several occasions, is destined to play an important role in the life of our Continent. The Declaration mentions also the agreement concluded between our two Republics on November 20 last, and also at the same time the conference of African States which was organised last year in Accra.

4:     I am personally convinced that you would be willing to accept the Role of "Dean" of the Independent African States, so that rapidly the hopes which have come into existence in the various African Territories by the birth of this Union should be fulfilled and thus we engage ourselves resolutely on the basis of achievements thus far realized in an Inter-African cooperative movement on the one hand and between Africa and the world on the other hand.

5:     I would like to emphasize the peculiar position of the Republic of Guinea, which cannot submit to any Colonial Power, and by this fact our Union would have as its first duty to assist the movement of emancipation of all African peoples against illegitimate privileges of the Colonial Powers.

6:     A certain press organized in France has started a campaign of diversion and untruths indicating that our Country is subject to orders from the Communist Bloc. This is wholly untrue, because our Government could not accept such a position as this would be neither in the interest of Guinea nor in the interest of the entire African Continent. As you know this campaign to discredit our Government is caused by a gift of arms, which has been made gratuitously by Czechoslovakia. While we have also received gifts from the U.S.A., and the Federal German Republic, of which the French Press has not made any mention, yet the 3,000 rifles which were offered us by this Country of the East, with whom we have established a trade for the sale of our bananas has given rise to all sorts of malicious and untrue commentaries.

7:     I beg to recall that during my visit I have requested you personally to be kind enough to intervene to the U.S.A. in order to obtain equipment for our young army which was demobilized by France, and placed in complete lack of weapons which I have not failed to explain to you. I regret that your intervention to the U.S.A. in our behalf has not been followed with such speed as the situation required. I therefore, and in order to save the honour of our Army, could not refuse such assistance which was offered and this, more so, as the Country which made the gift has not been asked by us to do so, and as there have been no political or Diplomatic conditions attached to this gift.

Your Representative accredited to us has been kept informed in all details of the situation prevailing inside Guinea, as he was kind enough to accompany me during eleven days which permitted him to make contact with the populations of the various regions.

8:      Finally, I wish to confirm the talks which we had in November and to assure you that the Republic of Guinea is far from any thought that its personal experience alone could be adequate and is convinced of the idea that only together our States can accomplish the historic mission to enhance the happiness of the Peoples of all Africa.

9:      Your correspondence re: Conference in Monrovia in the near future, was received and I expressed agreement with the suggestions therein.

10:      In the hope that nothing could affect adversely our fraternal and trusted relations, and expressing the conviction that you will use all your African and International Authority and Weight to support the early creation of the Union of Independent African States on the basis of respect for the personality and the institutions of each Member State, I beg you to accept for yourselves, Madame Tubman, the Members of your Government and your Peoples the expression of the confidence of the Government, National Assembly and the Peoples of Guinea.

Fraternally,
(Sgd) Sékou Touré

His Excellency Sékou Touré
President of the Republic of Guinea
Conakry, Guinea

May 27, 1959

Your Excellency:

I am the happy recipient of your letter of May 4, 1959, in which you inform me that the National Assembly of the Republic of Guinea has unanimously ratified the understanding signed by both of us, and has thereby affirmed our joint will and decision of cooperation and assistance between our two republics. That's grand!

It seems to me that the next step should be for both governments to appoint plenipotentiaries to sign, on their respective behalf, the treaty and protocol be signed in Conakry, Guinea, since the negotiations took place in Monrovia, Liberia. If you are in agreement, let me know your reaction so that I may designate the plenipotentiary on behalf of Liberia to conclude and sign the treaty in Conakry.

Referring to your observations on the declaration made on May 1, 1959, by Dr. Nkrumah, Prime Minister of Ghana, and yourself relative to the Constitution of the Union of Independent African States and the indication of the provisional character of this action which you suggest will ultimately regulate the relations between member states of this Union until such time when this instrument is ratified by their respective Parliaments; it is my feeling that that question requires serious discussions which could take place between us at the proposed conference.

Your advocacy of the President of Liberia as the Dean of the Independent African States seems plausible; but how can that be considered practicable when Guinea and Ghana have already for themselves developed a Constitution and a Flag for the African Independent States without reference to or consultation with the Government of Liberia? This is a question that could also be discussed at our prospective meeting.

Commenting on the emphasis which you place on the peculiar position of the Republic of Guinea submitting to any colonial power, I am in full agreement with you. Liberia has always stood against the repressive methods of colonialism and has been compelled to fight against the colonial powers throughout the last century to be able to survive. She is therefore committed to the task of supporting and advancing the crusade for emancipation of all peoples of Africa against not only the illegitimate powers of colonialism, but the exercise of undue authority over them by any foreign power.

The tirades of the foreign press against Guinea in which it is suggested, as you have mentioned in your letter, that your country is a satellite of the communist bloc, is not surprising to me. My own experience has taught me that that is the course of conduct some foreign powers take when they desire to malign and misrepresent other nations and peoples less fortunate or less powerful than themselves. Consequently, if I were you, I would completely disregard these vile and false allegations, but would boldly pursue my course in the interest of my country, its people, the peoples of Africa and democracy, thereby proving to the world the fallacy of the accusations.

In your letter you state that these allegations that your country is a satellite of the communist bloc are wholly untrue. This is ac-

cepted by me as being an honourable and forthright rebuttal to
the false accusations attempted to be levelled against the good
name of Guinea by some of the colonial powers because I have
vivid recollections that when I had the pleasure of your visit last
November, we discussed this identical question and you convinced me at the time that this was not so. I still remain firmly
convinced that charges of communism have been contrived simply
to place you and your country in an unfavorable light.

When it comes to the gift of arms made to you gratuitously by
Czechoslovakia, you had no alternative but to accept the offer because you did all you could, with the Liberian Government's assistance, to have the United States assist you with arms, but they
delayed action and failed to give favorable consideration to your
request. I can understand their reticence at the time which was, I
am sure, due to their tedious negotiations with France to have
them recognize your government.

I am in complete agreement with you that the gift of arms from
Czechoslovakia to you at a time when you were in direct need of
them could not justify any allegations or suspicions that you are
communist inclined. You can be well assured that I will, to the
limits of my ability, stand by and support you against any such
attempts to malign you and your government, because I am fully
conversant with the facts.

My representative, Ambassador Edward Peal, has, as you mention in your letter, been kept *au courant* with the situation and
has reported to me on the whole affair. I appreciate the confidence which you repose in me and assure you that that confidence will never be violated.

I am pleased that you agree to a conference between the three
of us. Prime Minister Nkrumah has also indicated his agreement
and has suggested June for the conference; but because I did not
receive a reply from either of you as to your acceptance of my
suggestions for this conference before now, I accepted an invitation to visit Sierra Leone in June. I have therefore written to the
Prime Minister suggesting that the conference be held in July beginning on the 15th or any time within that octave. I shall be
pleased to have your suggestion for a date in July or any time
other than June for the meeting and I will adjust my schedule so
as to harmonize with your wishes.

Prime Minister Nkrumah has also suggested that the conference
be held in Liberia. I have replied to him accepting his suggestion,
and arrangements are being made therefor.

I would be glad to know, as soon as possible, the names and official status of those who will be accompanying you to the conference so that arrangements may be made for their reception and entertainment.

You may be reassured that nothing can adversely affect our mutually fraternal and trusted relations as expressed by you in your letter to me.

Thank you very much for your kind expressions of solicitude for Mrs. Tubman, the members of my government and myself on behalf of the Government and peoples of Guinea; and I extend to you, Mrs. Touré, the Government and people of Guinea, on behalf of my Government, people of Liberia, Mrs. Tubman and myself, our abiding faith, confidence and steadfast feelings of fraternity and oneness for the Government and people of Guinea.

With assurances of my highest esteem and fraternal greetings, I remain,

Faithfully,

(Sgd) WILLIAM V. S. TUBMAN

APPENDIX 10

Joint Declaration by the Governments of Liberia, Ghana and Guinea Issued at Sanniquellie, Liberia, July 19, 1959

Resolved to assist, foster and speed up the total liberation of African non-independent territories whose peoples are struggling for national independence and self-determination, racial equality and human dignity:

CONSCIOUS of the fact that freedom, equality, justice and dignity are noble objectives of all peoples and are essential to the achievement of the legitimate aims and aspirations of the African peoples;

DETERMINED to bring about unity, co-operation, harmony, coherence and mutual understanding among ourselves;

BEARING in mind the historical differences among the peoples of Africa in various fields, but convinced that joint action is necessary to attain our common purpose;

THE PRESIDENT OF THE REPUBLIC OF LIBERIA, THE PRESIDENT OF THE REPUBLIC OF GUINEA AND THE PRIME MINISTER OF GHANA, after a frank change of views, have agreed on the necessity for immediate action and, in the light of this, they have reviewed the two communiques issued by Ghana and Guinea, on the one hand, and the Official Gazette Extraordinary issued by Liberia, on the other hand, and have proposed the holding of a Special Conference in 1960 of all independent States of Africa as well as non-independent States which have fixed dates on which they will achieve independence to discuss and work out a Charter between independent African States.

These Principles are:

1.   The name of the organisation shall be THE COMMUNITY OF INDEPENDENT AFRICAN STATES.

2.   Africans, like all other peoples, have the inherent right to independence and self-determination and to decide the form of Government under which they wish to live.

3.   Each State or Federation, which is a member of the Community, shall maintain its own national identity and constitutional structure. The Community is being formed with a view to achieving unity among independent African States. It is not designed to prejudice the present or future international policies, relations and obligations of the States involved.

4.   Each member of the Community accepts the principle that it shall not interfere in the internal affairs of any other member.

5. (a) The acts of States or Federations, which are members of the Community, shall be determined in relation to the essential objectives which are Freedom, Independence, Unity, the African Personality, as well as the interest of the African Peoples.

   (b) Each member State or Federation shall, in its acts or policies, do nothing contrary to the spirit and objectives of the Community.

6. (a) The general policy of the Community shall be to build up a free and prosperous African Community for the benefit of its peoples and the peoples of the world and in the interest of international peace and security.

   (b) This policy shall be based essentially on the maintenance of diplomatic, economic and cultural relations, on the basis of equality and reciprocity with all the States of the World which adopt a position compatible with African interest and African independence.

   (c) Its main objective will be to help other African territories subjected to domination, with a view to accelerating the end of their non-independent status.

7. The Community shall set up an Economic Council, a Cultural Council and a Scientific and Research Council.

8. Membership in the Community shall be open to all independent African States and Federations, and any non-independent Country of Africa shall have the right to join the Community upon its attainment of independence.

9. The Community shall have a flag and an Anthem to be agreed upon at a later date.

10. The motto of the Community shall be "INDEPENDENCE AND UNITY."

(Sgd) WILLIAM V. S. TUBMAN
President of the Republic of Liberia
SÉKOU TOURÉ
President of the Republic of Guinea
KWAME NKRUMAH
Prime Minister of Ghana

APPENDIX 11

Joint Communiqué of the Sanniquellie Conference, July 19, 1959

Issued by the President of the Republic of Liberia, the President of the Republic of Guinea, and the Prime Minister of Ghana, at Sanniquellie, Liberia, July 19, 1959.

We, the President of the Republic of Liberia, the President of the Republic of Guinea and the Prime Minister of Ghana, meeting at Sanniquellie, Republic of Liberia, from 15th to 18th July, 1959.

Having reviewed matters of common concern to our respective States and Africa in General,

HAVE DECIDED THAT:

1. *Cameroons*

We deplore the present situation in that Territory and we consider that free elections under United Nations supervision before independence is the most effective and democratic means of solving the present crisis. We appeal to the conscience of the world and the members of the United Nations to support our efforts to bring the matter before the next session of the General Assembly of the United Nations.

2. *Algeria*

We reaffirm the terms of the resolution adopted at the Conference of Independent African States held in Accra in April, 1958, and support the inscription of the Algerian Question on the Agenda of the next session of the General Assembly of the United Nations. We will consider the recognition of the Provisional Government of Algeria at the forthcoming Conference of the Foreign Ministers of the Independent African States to be held in Liberia in August, 1959.

3. *Racial Discrimination*

We condemn racial discrimination in any form wherever it exists and in particular the policy of apartheid practised in South Africa and will do all in our power to implement the provisions of the Universal Declaration of Human Rights.

4. *South West Africa*

We maintain that this Territory is in fact a Trust Territory of the United Nations, and as such the United Nations cannot relinquish its legal and moral responsibilities to the indigenous inhabitants who are entitled to the same treatment given to other Trust Territories. Consequently, we will request the United Nations to give further consideration to this question, declare the Territory not a part of South Africa and fix a date for the independence of the Trust Territory of South Africa.

5. *Nuclear Tests in the Sahara*

We deprecate France's insistence on carrying out these tests in Africa, and appeal to all African peoples including those in the French Community, and to all members of the United Nations to realize the destructive effects of such tests and associate themselves with us in our endeavor to dissuade France from embarking upon such a devastating course. We express our strong disapproval of all nuclear tests and appeal to the conscience of all peoples to condemn the production and use of nuclear weapons. We specifically appeal to these nations which produce such weapons to put an end to such tests.

6. *Cooperation and Unity of Action*

Touching our mutual relationships, we agree to consult together on all international questions, and to ensure unity of action at the United Nations.

7. *African Culture*

Considering African Culture as one of the essential elements in the struggle against colonialism and the assertion of African dignity and personality, we have decided to make the rehabilitation and diffusion of African culture an imperative national duty.

APPENDIX 12

Opening Speech of President Tubman to the Monrovia Conference, May 8, 1961

My Fellow Colleagues and Brothers, Excellencies, Ladies and Gentlemen:

It is with a sense of deep humility and profound personal and public pleasure that I welcome, on behalf of the Government and people of Liberia, our brothers and friends from the other sections of Mother Africa. I welcome you with the sincerity and warmth of a brother and member of the African family.

Although faced with varying political vicissitudes, the sponsors of this Conference have not been unmindful of their responsibilities as individuals and as a group for the total liberation of their Continent from the debasing state of national dependence and serfdom to the exhilarating status of political independence and equality. In an earnest endeavour, therefore, to resolve some of the disturbing issues of our times, we thought it expedient to request a congress of this kind to which all heads of African States were invited. Your presence here today is indicative of the common interest we hold in the purpose of our gathering and how generously and enthusiastically you responded to this invitation.

We live in a period of Conferences. But this Conference, we hope, will be labelled the STOCKTAKING CONFERENCE of 1961. We do not want our endeavours to be construed in the light of personal rivalries or ambition for recognition or leadership. We have no desire to seek fame for ourselves, nor is this conference intended to undermine the conclusions of previous conferences; nor will we fail to endorse and support such decisions of other conferences which we know to be in the best interest of Africa and the World. Rather, all that we seek to achieve is to bring all African leaders to reason together towards determining a consensus in the interest of peace and better understanding and to endeavour to provide a climate in which large as well as small states will participate as equal partners in building a New Africa and a new world order.

In our long struggle for respect for the sovereignty and independence of all states, and for the total liberation of the peoples of the Continent, we have come to believe that unity, understanding and tolerance are the principal means of achieving and perpetuating our objectives. Unity, therefore, should be the watch-word of this conference.

With this frame of reference, we can seek to utilize our potentialities, our combined forces, our best talents and our opportunities to more useful and practical advantages; we can employ the knowledge of our common racial background, the history of our common struggles and the fact of the identity of our aspirations and struggles to work towards a better and securer future for the present and future generations; we can stand on the ideals and ideas which now find unanimity among us as a prelude to seeking possible solutions to those in which we differ and also resolving those problems which plague us and mankind; we can come together, we can deliberate, we can reason together, we can plan and work together and thus engender mutual understandings and establish lasting friendships. In all these endeavours, nothing must be permitted to stand in the way of our attaining these objectives.

For these and other reasons, the sponsors of this conference realize that as in military operations, after a major success in battle is achieved, good strategy dictates the necessity for the coming together of the generals and other arms of the various services for conferences and discussions on the causes of the success, to consider the mistakes that were made, to find solutions to the problems involved and to lay the foundation and plans from which to proceed and to follow, to consolidate their position so as to enable them to continue their struggles with confidence and certainty for complete victory. This also obtains in all well organized businesses.

We have assembled here today, as representatives of African States to consider the successes that have been ours over the last five years, to discuss some of the pressing problems that confront us, to seek solutions to these problems and to prepare for pushing forward toward the cause we represent, the cause of African Freedom, to the goal of engendering a better understanding among ourselves and the nations of the earth, to pose suggestions for easing world tension and to formulate plans aimed at reconciling and bridging as fast as possible the gap between conflicting international ideologies which have created tensions and persist in dividing the world into opposing and apparently irreconcilable political blocs.

Just as the interdependence of nations has never been more apparent than at present, so too the fear of annihilation has never been more ominous than today. We sincerely believe that African States should have a mission of new dimensions to the old world otherwise our struggle for liberation in an atomic age will be the more difficult. We should be the harbingers and proponents of a changed world order. And to do this effectively we need to shoulder our task without personal ambition but only in the interest of the greatest good to the greatest number. It is in this light that we have grave concerns that should a nuclear war occur it would virtually destroy mankind, and those nations which recently won their freedom and independence would be affected beyond measure, for their independence would have been ephemeral.

It should be crystal clear to every leader that Africans cannot live in isolation if they expect to allay suspicion, fear and tension. The idea of *primus inter pares*, first among equals, is destructive to African Unity and Peace. Tolerance, good faith, honour, good neighbourliness, justice, equality and mutual respect are the most vital constituents of Unity and Solidarity.

The sense of oneness should be deeply rooted in the breast of every African. But the whirls of circumstances and ambition can make it difficult for us to fit ourselves into the picture of a unified Africa, the foundation for which we hope will be laid before this conference closes.

Recent trends in human affairs reveal an insatiable tendency to short cuts in the achievement of social progress. In the process men lose their poise and self-control and become enmeshed in enmity, rancor, and revenge, the conflict and confusion from which have marked the state of human affairs in the world.

It is our heart's most fervent wish that the State of Africa, individually and collectively, will set a new pattern of social and political behaviour and thus work out a changed social reconstruction. Whether this pattern takes the form of democracy, socialism, communism or African nationalism should be determined by the voluntary choice of the people affected. Whatever may be its form, it should ever be dedicated to the peace and prosperity of all peoples in all lands.

Africa, once considered the cradle of world civilization, can by our combined efforts again become the pivot of a changed social-political order directed to world peace, in which faith in moral and spiritual forces would supersede the fear of even atom bombs.

The greatness of states up to the present has been predicated on military power and possessions rather than on justice and morality, hence their conceptions of right and wrong have been governed generally by expediency. The world has, as a consequence, been in perpetual turmoil of wars and rumors of wars. If this mistaken conception is adopted by African States as a policy it is bound to rupture good relationships and the mutual cooperation we so ardently seek.

According to some recent writers who have given much thought to world politics, we learn that a nation's greatness lies neither in the abundance of its possessions nor in the strength of its arms. In this connection, Straus Houpe writes: "A people finds greatness in its response to the historical challenge—by how it manages to harness its strivings to the aspirations of the age. Thus to be great is to fulfill a promise that surpasses the national interest." The greatness of the new Africa should be demonstrated in the creative use of the forces at our disposal in solving the great problems of our time and of ensuring a new order out of the present disorder.

We have met as representatives of free, sovereign and independent States to design policies to secure the perpetuity of our national existence, friendship and amity among ourselves and all peoples. May our deliberations be richly blessed and so yield abundant harvests in the years ahead.

It is unfortunate that while we are enjoying the benefits of freedom our brothers in Angola, Mozambique, Algeria, South Africa and other parts of this great continent are still smarting under the heel of oppression and tyranny; their fight for freedom is our fight. They must know in unmistakable terms that we stand with and behind them and will not desert them by the plans we evolve for their assistance.

Our deliberations at this conference will be a mere rhetorical exercise if we do not seek to formulate principles of conduct which will be realistic, rational and an effective contribution to the eradication of the last vestige of domination, discrimination and social inequality in Africa and the world.

There is not a man present who is undisturbed by recent events in the Congo and Angola and the dread and despair those events arouse in all men of good-will. After mature reflection upon the gravity of those events and their consequences, and convinced that their possible solution is not within the competence of any one nation, or even a few of the heads of State or Government, a conference of all heads of state was considered the most competent authority in the present circumstances.

I come now to the question of leadership of Africa. On this issue I repeat what I said in an Independence Day Message delivered on July 26, 1957, when there were fewer independent African States. "In this connection I have observed that there seem to be three schools of thought on this subject. There are those who feel that Liberia should assume leadership based on the fact that she is the oldest African Republic and is riper in political experience; but it will require more than age and political experience to assume leadership of Africa. There are others who hold that Ghana should assume that role because she is physically more developed and embraces larger territories. It will require more than development and larger territory to assume leadership of Africa. And there are yet those who opine that Egypt with its rich traditions dating back to the remotest antiquity, should do so. It will require more than rich traditions of antiquity. It will require, in my opinion, the aggregate of all three of these and more besides. It will require the aggregate of the best that is in all compounded in such a manner as to represent the divisibility of Africa indivisible."

Excellencies, on the long road of human evolution from international disorder and confusion to systems of global international cooperation, the United Nations, we believe, offers the best hope and the means whereby we can strengthen the ties that bind nations and preserve those things which are necessary for peaceful progress among mankind.

The turbulent speed of events which have transformed the political status of our Continent imposes upon us the responsibility of setting up a new guide-post toward an international society, buttressed by wisdom and knowledge adequate to overcome the failures, pitfalls and fumblings that brought the world to the rim of the abyss.

In the fifteen years of its existence, which is indeed a relatively short period in the life of a nation, the United Nations has brought together ninety-nine independent States to deliberate as equals in a meaningful partnership to implement and enforce decisions where necessary, and by so doing has averted wars.

By the adherence to the principle of self-determination and the fundamental principle of human rights it has accelerated the liberation of many countries in Asia, Africa and Europe from colonial status. While we do not underwrite every item of its activities in the fifteen years of its existence we feel that it is entitled to our support and the affirmation of its fundamental tenets and everything must be done to ensure its continuity, and nothing must be done by any State or group of States to undermine its great objectives.

Some of the leading considerations this Conference should discuss revolve around such issues as:

1. Contributions of the African States to World Peace.
2. Threats to Peace and Stability in Africa.
3. Promotion of Better Understanding, Unity and Cooperation among African States.
4. Development of a Permanent Machinery to Provide Consultation Among the African States.
5. Formulation of a General Policy Attitude toward Peoples Striving for Independence.
6. The Situation in the Congo.
7. Working out General Principles for the Settlement of Frontier and Border Disputes which may arise from the Emergence of Independent States.

Let me conclude by reiterating that while the idea of a universal political order is debatable at this stage of our political experience, the necessity for better cooperation among us is obvious. But any form of unity must be a voluntary process. Political Union is attained by virtue of agreement. In the absence of a free agreement, any form of political union is but imperial domination.

The unsettled state of affairs in the Republic of the Congo matter of grave concern to all African nationalists. The presence of the soldiers of many of the African States as well as other nations in that country in an endeavour to assist in preserving peace and keeping the country from being torn by civil war is an eloquent testimony that we cherish freedom and independence and are determined to fight for it if needs be. And so we hope that eventually conditions in the Congo will return to normal so that its peoples may enjoy the blessings of liberty and freedom in common with the rest of mankind. This situation should be one of the items for our deliberation.

We are striving for cohesion, for a changed social-political order, for individual states retaining their own way of life, united by mutual exchange of peoples, goods and ideas in the common defense of our heritage, and a just and lasting peace.

Excellencies, this Conference will, I doubt not, concern itself with all Declarations and Resolutions of previous Conferences relating to this Continent. The Decisions of previous Conferences of African States, including the Casablanca Conference, should be studied and such aspects which require more time and perhaps conscientious study referred to a subsequent Conference.

This suggestion reminds me of an incident recorded in the sacred history of the Christians where it is reported that on one occasion the disciples of Christ reported to Him that they saw one casting out devils in His name and yet he did not follow them. Christ replied, "Forbid him not; for there is no man which shall do a miracle in my name, that can lightly speak evil of me. For he that is not against us is our partner." Thus although previous conferences have convened at different times, the general aims have not been entirely contradictory nor are they completely inimical to the basic objectives we are now trying to pursue.

Excellencies, we should be guided by history and manifest justice so that we do not repeat the mistakes that laid the foundation for the intervention of great European States in the affairs of other states. What we should do is to strive to strengthen the independence of all States regardless of their alignments into Communities or Commonwealths, for no one can say with any degree of truth—*I am holier than thou.* We must remember that nations grow from lower to higher forms of association.

History has clearly demonstrated that political Union as opposed to Political Domination can be more rapidly achieved where there is a community of economic interest, cultural cross-fertilization as well as free social intercourse and association.

It would probably be unreasonable to expect that we can at this Conference work out a complete pattern of mutual action in this respect. However, we trust that agreement can be reached on the guiding principles which would enable technical experts representing us to concretize proposals for economic cooperation and collaboration as well as the establishment of common identities toward which we may strive in the immediate future. In this way we believe steps can be taken now to reach goals which will enable each member country to make a distinctive contribution to lasting, natural unity in Africa.

Again, Excellencies, I welcome you and may our deliberations lead to a consensus of values and methods that will constitute the social, economic, cultural, political and moral foundation of a changed world.

APPENDIX 13

Resolutions Adopted at the Monrovia Conference,
May 8–12, 1961

I. Resolution on the Means of Promoting Better Understanding and Cooperation Towards Achieving Unity in Africa and Malagasy.

The Conference of Heads of States and Government of Africa and Malagasy meeting at Monrovia on 8th to 12th May, 1961.

RECOGNIZING the historic importance of the Conference at Monrovia, because of the number of participating States;

NOTING with deep regret the absence of some of our sister states;

CONFIDENT in their intense desire for African solidarity and expressing the hope that they may find it convenient to attend subsequent meetings;

ANXIOUS to promote henceforth a full and brotherly cooperation between Independent African and Malagasy States;

CONSIDERING the need for pooling resources and coordinating efforts in order to overcome the barriers of growth which confront all African and Malagasy countries on their way to development;

A. SOLEMNLY AFFIRMS AND ADOPTS the following principles, which shall govern the relationship between the African and Malagasy States:

(1) Absolute equality of African and Malagasy States, whatever may be the size of their territories, the density of their populations, or the value of their possessions;

(2) Non-interference in the internal affairs of States;

(3) Respect for the sovereignty of each state and its inalienable right to existence and development of its personality;

(4) Unqualified condemnation of outside subversive action by neighbouring states;

(5) Promotion of cooperation throughout Africa, based upon tolerance, solidarity and good-neighbour relations, periodical exchange of views, and non-acceptance of any leadership;

(6) The Unity that is aimed to be achieved at the moment is not the political integration of sovereign African States, but

unity of aspirations and of action considered from the point of view of African social solidarity and political identity;

B. URGES that all African and Malagasy States shall refrain from encouraging, directly or indirectly, dissident groups or individual of other states in subversive activities by permitting their own states to be used as bases from which such dissidents may operate, or by financing dissidents in other countries or otherwise;

C. ACCEPTS, in principle, that an inter-African and Malagasy Advisory Organization shall be created, the essential purpose of which shall be to put into effect the above-mentioned principles and to establish this Organization at the next conference;

D. DECIDES,

(1) That a technical commission of experts designated by the respective States shall be created and that these experts shall meet in Dakar, Senegal, within three months after the close of this Conference for the purpose of working out detailed plans for economic, educational, cultural, scientific and technical co-operation, as well as for communications and transportation among African and Malagasy States;

(2) That the existing research and technical institutions shall constitute effective machinery for the collection of data and the dissemination of the results of research among African and Malagasy States, and that all States shall so direct;

(3) That all African and Malagasy States shall recognize the desire to promote the revival of African culture and traditions in the interest of preserving the real African heritage;

(4) That all African and Malagasy States shall make a special effort to include in addition to their respective national and official languages the teaching of the French and English languages;

E. DECIDES, finally, that the next Conference of Heads of African and Malagasy States shall be held in Lagos, Nigeria.

II. THREATS TO PEACE AND STABILITY IN AFRICA AND THE WORLD

The Conference profoundly disturbed by the serious threats which hang over peace and stability in Africa and the world,

CONSIDERING that the principle of non-interference in the domestic affairs of African States applies only to States already independent and sovereign;

AFFIRMS its unanimous determination to give material and moral assistance to all dependent territories of colonial powers with a view to accelerating their accession to independence.

The Conference, as concerns the Algerian question, welcomes the improvement of the situation in Algeria and the decision of the two parties to open negotiations on 20th May, 1961; and

APPEALS to the Government of France and the Provisional Government of the Algerian Republic to conclude at the earliest moment an agreement putting an end to the war and accord to Algeria its independence and territorial integrity.

The Conference, as concerns the CONGO,

RE-AFFIRMS its faith in the United Nations as the only organization which, in spite of past weakness and mistakes in its work, is best adopted to achieve a real solution of the Congo problem;

CALLS ON all African States to desist from such activity as the hasty recognition of break-away regimes in the Republic of the Congo, and generally from taking sides with rival groups in any form or manner;

CONDEMNS assassinations as a means to attain political power.

CONDEMNS the action of certain non-African states which encourage subversion in other African States.

The Conference, as concerns ANGOLA,

CALLS ON all African and Malagasy States to pledge their whole-hearted material and moral support to the Africans in Angola in their struggle for autonomy;

APPEALS to the universal conscience against the atrocities and the bloody repression of the Angolan population.

The Conference, as regards to UNION OF SOUTH AFRICA,

CONDEMNS unreservedly the theory and practice of *Apartheid* by the Government of the Union of South Africa;

CALLS ON all African and Malagasy States to apply immediately political and economic sanctions, collectively and individually, against the Government of the Union of South Africa, not only to demonstrate our resentment of the ruthless degradation of the non-whites there, but also ultimately to compel the Government of the Union of South Africa to abandon the iniquitous practice of *Apartheid;*

CALLS ON all African and Malagasy States to take all necessary steps to give all material and moral support to the Africans and Asians of South Africa in their struggle to regain the stature of man;

AFFIRMS that all the participating African States strongly support the reiterated decision of the Trusteeship Council of the United Nations that the Government of the Union of South Africa must acknowledge the authority of the Council as guardian of the mandate over the Territory of South West Africa.

The Conference, as concerns DISARMAMENT,

APPEALS to all the nuclear powers to stop the manufacture and stockpiling of nuclear weapons and all further nuclear explosions anywhere in the world;

DECIDES that the Chairman should make a written appeal in the name of the Conference to the Commission on Nuclear Disarmament, now in session in Geneva, to use their best endeavours to secure the objective stated in the preceding paragraph;

NOTES the assurances given by the French Government that they will cease all further nuclear explosions in Africa.

The Conference, as concerns the UNITED NATIONS,

URGES to send a cablegram to members of the Security Council asking them to take a decision in favour of the admission of Mauritania in the United Nations Organization in conformity with the last Resolution of the General Assembly;

CONDEMNS all attempts to weaken or undermine the authority of the United Nations;

RECORDS the intention of all African and Malagasy States to present a united front in the future, to all world problems with which Africa might be faced at the United Nations.

III. SETTLEMENT OF CONFLICTS WHICH MAY ARISE BETWEEN AFRICAN STATES

This Conference of Chiefs of African and Malagasy States and Governments, meeting at Monrovia from 8th to 12th May, 1961,

RECOMMENDS:

(1) That the settlement of dispute shall be by peaceful means;
(2) That a commission shall be created which shall be attached to the Organization of Cooperation of the African and Malagasy States.
(3) RECOMMENDS that this Conference unanimously resolves that a written appeal be made through the executive authority of the present Conference to their Excellencies The Emperor of Ethiopia and the President of Somalia to make renewed efforts toward a sincere and early solution of all their existing frontier and any other disputes.

IV. An Expression of Gratitude to the President, Government and People of Liberia.

The Conference of Heads of African and Malagasy States, Meeting in Monrovia from 8th to 12th May, 1961:

Having accepted the gracious invitation of the five sponsoring countries to convene a conference of heads of African and Malagasy States;

1. Expresses its gratitude and sincere thanks to the President, Government and People of Liberia for the hospitality extended the Delegations during its historic and fruitful Meeting in Monrovia;

2. Expresses its profound admiration for President William V. S. Tubman, who has persistently worked for African solidarity, brotherhood and unity.

APPENDIX 14

Charter of the Inter-African and Malagasy Organisation

PREAMBLE

We, the African and Malagasy Heads of States and Governments assembled in Lagos, Nigeria;

INSPIRED by the aim of our peoples for brotherhood, solidarity and unity, as evidenced by the previous historic conferences held in furtherance of this aim;

ANXIOUS to reaffirm the faith of our people in the principles of the Charter of the United Nations and the Universal Declaration of Human Rights;

DEDICATED to the progress of a renascent Africa forever freed from colonialism;

DESIROUS that all Africa and Madagascar should henceforth unite for the preservation and consolidation of independence and freedom without which the welfare and well-being of its people cannot be assured;

CONSCIOUS of the responsibility of our governments and peoples to demonstrate the capacity of the human race to overcome ethnic and national differences in the interest of peace and to direct all knowledge towards the promotion of human progress;

CONVINCED that all the independent African and Malagasy States are desirous of creating an African solidarity to which each State can contribute its experience and achievements;

WILLING to welcome in a spirit of fraternity any concrete proposal intended to promote effective participation of all independent African and Malagasy States in a common organization;

RESOLVED to avoid rivalry or conflict among all independent African and Malagasy States by consciously creating and maintaining institutions capable of furthering a common destiny;

HAVE AGREED to the present Charter and by these presents establish an organisation of African and Malagasy States.

CHAPTER I

PURPOSES AND PRINCIPLES

Article 1

1. The High Contracting Parties of African and Malagasy States do by the present Charter establish the organisation to be known as the Inter-African and Malagasy ORGANISATION.
2. This Organisation is established for the purpose of promoting a better life for the peoples of Africa and Malagasy by enlisting the efforts of member States through co-operative and joint actions, in order to:

   (a) accelerate economic and social development and intercourse and to promote the pooling and effective utilisation of their resources;

   (b) provide better and broader educational opportunities for its peoples;

   (c) raise the level of health and well-being of its peoples; and

   (d) concert, as far as possible, political actions and initiate new means for establishing relationships in which the interests of the Continent of Africa and Malagasy will be better defined and served.

Article 2

The High Contracting Parties, in pursuit of these and similar purposes, agree to attain these essential objectives:
   (a) Economic Co-operation
   (b) Educational and Cultural Co-operation
   (c) Health and Nutritional Co-operation

(d) Scientific and Technical Co-operation
(e) Co-operation for Defence

Article 3

For the realisation of the objectives stated in Articles 1 and 2, the High Contracting Parties adopt and affirm these principles:

(a) sovereign equality of African and Malagasy States, whatever may be the size of their territories, the density of their populations, or the value of their possessions;

(b) non-interference in the internal affairs of Member States;

(c) respect for the sovereignty and territorial integrity of each State and for its inalienable right to independent existence;

(d) peaceful and harmonious settlement of all disputes arising among the African and Malagasy States;

(e) unqualified condemnation of any subversive activity on the part of neighbouring or other States;

(f) the constant promotion and fostering of all available means of co-operation in the fields of economics, health, nutrition, education and culture; and

(g) dedication to the total emancipation of the remaining dependent territories of Africa.

CHAPTER II

MEMBERSHIP: ITS RIGHTS AND DUTIES

Article 4

The High Contracting Parties are independent, sovereign States in Africa and Malagasy under indigenous African rule.

Article 5

The High Contracting Parties have solemn and Sacred duty and responsibility to respect the rights enjoyed by other States under international law. Each State has the right of defence of its territorial integrity.

CHAPTER III

INSTITUTIONS

Article 6

The High Contracting Parties agree to establish the following institutions:

(a) an Assembly of Heads of States and Governments;

(b) A Council of Ministers; and
(c) A General Secretariat.

CHAPTER IV

ASSEMBLY OF HEADS OF STATE AND GOVERNMENT

Article 7

The Assembly shall be the supreme organ of the Organisation. It shall meet at least once a year to consider and decide upon general policies and actions of the Organisation and, if necessary, to review the structure, functions and acts of all the Organs and the Specialised Agencies. It may consider all matters affecting the relations between African and Malagasy States.

Article 8

1. The High Contracting Parties agree that each Member State shall have the right to propose items for the agenda of session of the Assembly.

2. The General Secretariat shall circulate to all Member States of the Organisation at least two months in advance of each meeting, except in case of an extraordinary session, a complete list of all suggestions which are intended as items of the agenda.

Article 9

1. The High Contracting Parties agree that each Member State of the Assembly shall have one vote.

2. The High Contracting Parties further agree that all resolutions, including resolutions to hold extraordinary sessions of the Assembly, shall be determined by a four-fifths majority vote of those present and voting. Questions of procedure shall require a simple majority of all Members present and voting.

3. Three-fifths of the total membership of the Organisation shall form a quorum at any meeting of the Assembly.

4. The Assembly shall have the power to determine its own rules of procedure, including the election of a Chairman for each session.

CHAPTER V

THE COUNCIL OF MINISTERS

Article 10

1. The High Contracting Parties agree that the council of Ministers shall consist of such Ministers as are designated in that behalf by the Governments of Member States.

2. The Council of Ministers shall meet at least twice a year to consider, review, and determine matters concerning the areas of co-operation referred to in Article 2 of the present Charter.

3. The Council shall be generally responsible to the Assembly.

4. The Council shall have power to determine its own rules of procedure, including the election of a Chairman for each session.

Article 11

1. The High Contracting Parties agree that any member State of the Organisation may, at any time, request an extraordinary session of the Council on giving not less than two weeks notice before the date of the proposed meeting.

2. Such a request shall be submitted to the Secretary-General for circulation to all member States, and shall be accompanied by a provisional agenda of the proposed session.

3. The approval of not less than four-fifths of all the member States is required for the holding of such a session.

Article 12

1. In the event of a threat to peace and security in any part of Africa and Malagasy, the Chairman of the Council of the immediately preceding session shall have power to convene an extraordinary session of the Council.

2. The Secretary-General may invite the attention of the Chairman of the Council to any situation which, in the opinion of the Secretary-General, constitutes a threat to the peace and security of the continent of Africa and Malagasy.

Article 13

1. The High Contracting Parties agree that each member State of the Council of Ministers shall have one vote.

2. The High Contracting Parties further agree that all resolutions to hold an extraordinary session of the Council of Ministers, shall require a two-thirds majority vote. Questions of procedure shall be determined by the simple majority of the member states.

3. Two-thirds of the total membership of the Council shall form a quorum at any of its meetings.

Article 14

The Council of Ministers shall have power to set up such special commissions and committees as it shall consider necessary from time to time.

CHAPTER VI

GENERAL SECRETARIAT

Article 15

The High Contracting Parties agree that the Assembly shall determine the headquarters of the Secretariat and such administrative branches of it as the Assembly may from time to time deem desirable.

Article 16

The High Contracting Parties agree that the General Secretariat shall be the central administrative organ of the Organisation. It shall be headed by a Secretary-General and shall contain the technical and other departments of the Organisation.

Article 17

The Secretary-General shall be elected by the Assembly. His term of office shall be for a period of three consecutive years, provided that the outgoing Secretary-General shall be eligible for re-election.

Article 18

The Secretary-General shall have no vote, but may participate in all the deliberations of the organs of the Organisation.

Article 19

The High Contracting Parties agree that there shall be an Assistant Secretary-General of the Organisation. He shall be elected by the Assembly and shall be the chief assistant to the Secretary-General. His term of office shall be for a period of two consecutive years. The outgoing Assistant Secretary-General shall be eligible for re-election. Whenever the Secretary-General is English-speaking, the Assistant Secretary-General shall be French-speaking, and vice versa.

Article 20

In case of death of the Secretary-General or of a vacancy in that office for any other reason, or because of any incapacity of the Secretary-General to perform the functions of his office, the Assistant Secretary-General shall assume the office for the unexpired term.

Article 21

Subject to the provisions of this Charter, the Secretary-General shall perform the following functions:

(a) submit to the Assembly an annual report on the activities of the Organisation and the work accomplished by the various organs during the year;

(b) establish with the approval of the Assembly such branches and administrative and technical offices as may be necessary to achieve the objectives and purposes of the Organisation;

(c) prepare the budget of the Organisation;

(d) determine in consultation with the Council of Ministers the number of officials and employees of the Secretariat, regulate their functions, and fix their remuneration in accordance with internationally accepted standards;

(e) submit proposals to the Council with a view to furthering co-ordination between and among the organs and specialised agencies and the programme of the Organisation;

(f) implement such resolutions of the Organisation as are entrusted to him;

(g) make available technical and other information and forward it to Member Governments;

(h) transmit to each member State all documents and other materials on the results, decisions and recommendations reached at all meetings;

(i) serve as registry for copies of agreements entered into between member States of the Organisation;

(j) perform all such other functions as properly pertain to the office of the Secretary-General or such as may be imposed by the Organisation on the Secretariat from time to time.

CHAPTER VII

ORGANISATION OF CO-OPERATION AND SPECIALISED AGENCIES

Article 22

In order to establish conditions favourable to economic co-operation and joint economic endeavours, the High Contracting Parties hereby establish The Association of AFRICAN AND MALAGASY ECONOMIC CO-OPERATION AND DEVELOPMENT, which shall function in accordance with a treaty which shall be regarded as an integral part of the present Charter.

Article 23

The High Contracting Parties agree to promote and accelerate the consolidation of our African and Malagasy cultures and traditions in the interest of preserving our heritage, and shall use their efforts in creating the machinery for their fulfilment.

Article 24

The High Contracting Parties agree to engage in programmes through joint actions to eradicate disease; to co-ordinate their respective health, medical and nutritional policies; and to provide appropriate services and training for these purposes. The High Contracting Parties agree to conclude a separate treaty for co-operation in the fields of health and nutrition.

Article 25

1. The High Contracting Parties agree that those member States which have medical institutions shall serve the Organisation in training medical and paramedical personnel and shall also undertake research, the nature and scope of which shall include continuous inquiry into and study of problems of health and nutrition.
2. Information derived from these inquiries shall be made available to all.

Article 26

The High Contracting Parties further agree that a scientific research organisation shall be co-operatively established, developed and supported. Towards this end, they agree to conclude a separate treaty establishing a SCIENTIFIC TRAINING AND RESEARCH INSTITUTION, which shall seek further co-operation among the member States in the various fields of scientific research as a means of promoting their scientific and industrial growth.

Article 27

The Assembly shall have the power to establish such Specialised Agencies as it may deem necessary from time to time, and the officials of such Agencies shall be appointed by the Council of Ministers acting in consultation with the Secretary-General.

CHAPTER VIII

PACIFIC SETTLEMENT OF DISPUTES

Article 28

The High Contracting Parties pledge themselves to settle all disputes among themselves by peaceful means and, to this end, agree to conclude a separate treaty establishing a PERMANENT CONCILIATION COMMISSION, which shall function in accordance with the said treaty and which shall be regarded as forming an integral part of the present Charter.

CHAPTER IX

RELATIONSHIP TO THE UNITED NATIONS

Article 29

The High Contracting Parties agree that nothing herein shall be understood or interpreted as impairing the commitments or other rights and obligations of the member States of the Inter-African Malagasy Organisation under the Charter of the United Nations Organisation.

CHAPTER X

RATIFICATION OF THE CHARTER

Article 30

1. The present Charter shall be subject to ratification by member States in accordance with their respective constitutional processes and procedures.
2. The original instruments, done in English and French—both texts being equally authentic—shall be deposited with the [not selected] Government.
3. The [not selected] Government shall transmit certified copies of the original instruments to all member governments for ratification and to the Secretariat.

Article 31

The present Charter shall have provisional application when signed by the High Contracting Parties. It shall come into force and effect thirty days after three-fifths of the signatory States have deposited their instruments of ratification with the [not selected] Government, which shall notify all member States which have ratified the Charter.

CHAPTER XI

THE BUDGET

Article 32

The Budget of the Organisation established by the General Secretariat shall be approved by the Council of Ministers at its first sitting after ratification by at least four-fifths of its signatories. This Budget shall be provided by contributions from the member States on a pro rata basis of fractions of their National Budgets. The High Contracting Parties agree to pay their respective contributions regularly and shall deposit at the instrument of ratification the rate of contribution fixed by the Secretariat.

CHAPTER XII

REGISTRATION OF THE CHARTER

Article 33

The High Contracting Parties agree that the present Charter shall after due ratification be registered with the Secretariat of the United Nations through the Government of [not selected] in conformity with Article 102 of the Charter of the United Nations.

CHAPTER XIII

INTERPRETATION OF THE CHARTER

Article 34

The High Contracting Parties agree that any question which may arise concerning the interpretation of this Charter shall be submitted for adjudication of the International Court of Justice at the Hague.

CHAPTER XIV

ADHESION OF NEW STATES

Article 35

1. Any independent sovereign State in Africa under indigenous African rule may at any time notify the Secretary-General of its intention to adhere or accede to the present Charter.
2. The Secretary-General shall, on receipt of such notification communicate a copy of it to all member States. Admission shall be determined by a four-fifths majority of all member States by

the Council of Ministers within a period of six months. The decision of the Council shall be transmitted by the Secretary-General to the State concerned.

CHAPTER XV

MISCELLANEOUS

Article 36

The Official languages of the Organisation and all its organs shall be English and French.

Article 37

The High Contracting Parties agree to undertake to negotiate agreements to provide for privileges and immunities of the personnel of the Organisation in their respective territories.

Article 38

1. All Heads of Departments of the Secretariat shall be appointed by the Council of Ministers on the recommendation of the Secretary-General.
2. The other categories of personnel shall be appointed by the Secretary-General in accordance with Rules to be framed by the Council of Ministers.

Article 39

The Secretary-General and his staff are responsible to the Council of Ministers.

Article 40

The Secretary-General may accept on behalf of the Organisation gifts, bequests and other donations made to the Organisation, provided that the conditions attached to such gifts or bequests are consistent with the objectives and purposes of the Organisation.

CHAPTER XVI

CESSATION OF MEMBERSHIP

Article 41

The High Contracting Parties agree that the present Charter shall remain in force indefinitely. Any member State which desires to renounce its membership shall forward a written notification to the Secretary-General. At the end of one year from the date of such notification the Charter shall cease to apply with respect to the renouncing State, which shall thereby cease to belong to the Organisation.

CHAPTER XVII

AMENDMENT TO THE CHARTER

Article 42

The High Contracting Parties agree that this Charter may be amended or revised if any member State of the Organisation makes a written request to the Secretary-General to that effect, but so that the proposed amendment is not submitted to the Assembly for consideration until all the member States have been duly notified of it and a period of one year has elapsed. Such an amendment shall not be effective unless approved by at least four-fifths of all the Member States.

In faith whereof the High Contracting Parties have signed the Present Charter.

Done in the City of Lagos, Nigeria
this December 21, 1962

APPENDIX 15

Charter of the Organisation of African Unity

We, the Heads of African and Malagasy States and Governments assembled in the City of Addis Ababa, Ethiopia;

CONVINCED that it is the inalienable right of all people to control their own destiny;

CONSCIOUS of the fact that freedom, equality, justice and dignity are essential objectives for the achievement of the legitimate aspirations of the African peoples;

CONSCIOUS of our responsibility to harness the natural and human resources of our continent for the total advancement of our peoples in spheres of human endeavour;

INSPIRED by a common determination to strengthen understanding and cooperation among our States in response to the aspirations of our peoples for brotherhood and solidarity, in a larger unity transcending ethnic and national differences;

CONVINCED that, in order to translate this determination into a dynamic force in the cause of human progress, conditions for peace and security must be established and maintained;

DETERMINED to safeguard and consolidate the hard-won independence as well as the sovereignty and territorial integrity of our States, and to fight against neo-colonialism in all its forms;

DEDICATED to the general progress of Africa;

PERSUADED that the Charter of the United Nations and the Universal Declaration of Human Rights, to the principles of which we reaffirm our adherence, provide a solid foundation for peaceful and positive co-operation among states;

DESIROUS that all African and Malagasy States should henceforth unite so that the welfare and well-being of their peoples can be assured;

RESOLVED to reinforce the links between our states by establishing and strengthening common institutions;

HAVE AGREED TO THE PRESENT CHARTER.

ESTABLISHMENT

Article I

The High Contracting Parties do by the present Charter establish an Organisation to be known as the "Organisation of African Unity." The Organisation shall include the Continental African States, Madagascar and all the islands surrounding Africa.

PURPOSES

Article II

1. The Organisation shall have the following purposes:
   a. to promote the unity and solidarity of the African and Malagasy States;
   b. to coordinate and intensify their co-operation and efforts to achieve a better life for the peoples of Africa;
   c. to defend their sovereignty, their territorial integrity and independence;
   d. to eradicate all forms of colonialism from Africa; and
   e. to promote international co-operation, having due regard to the Charter of the United Nations and the Universal Declaration of Human Rights.

2. To these ends, the Member States shall coordinate and harmonise their general policies, especially in the following fields:
   a. political and diplomatic co-operation;

b. economic co-operation, including transport and communications;
c. educational and cultural co-operation;
d. health, sanitation, and nutritional co-operation;
e. scientific and technical co-operation; and
f. co-operation for defence and security.

PRINCIPLES

Article III

The Member States, in pursuit of the purposes stated in Article II, solemnly affirm and declare their adherence to the following principles:

1. the sovereign equality of all African and Malagasy States;
2. non-interference in the internal affairs of States;
3. respect for the sovereignty and territorial integrity of each member and for its inalienable right to independent existence;
4. peaceful settlement of disputes by negotiation, mediation, conciliation or arbitration;
5. unreserved condemnation, in all its forms, of political assassination as well as of the subversive activities on the part of neighbouring States or any other States;
6. absolute dedication to the total emancipation of the African territories which are still dependent;
7. affirmation of a policy of non-alignment with regard to all blocs.

MEMBERSHIP

Article IV

Each independent sovereign African State shall be entitled to become a Member of the Organisation.

RIGHTS AND DUTIES OF MEMBER STATES

Article V

All Member States shall enjoy equal rights and have equal duties.

Article VI

The Member States pledge themselves to observe scrupulously the principles enumerated in Article III of the present Charter.

INSTITUTIONS

Article VII

The Organisation shall accomplish its purposes through the following principal institutions:

1. The Assembly of Heads of State and Government;
2. the Council of Ministers;
3. the General Secretariat;
4. the Commission of Mediation, Conciliation and Arbitration.

THE ASSEMBLY OF HEADS OF STATE AND GOVERNMENT

Article VIII

The Assembly of Heads of State and Government shall be the supreme organ of the Organisation. It shall, subject to the provisions of this Charter, discuss matters of common concern to Africa with a view to co-ordinating and harmonising the general policy of the Organisation. It may in addition review the structure, functions and acts of all the organs and any specialised agencies which may be created in accordance with the present Charter.

Article IX

The Assembly shall be composed of the Heads of State, Government or their duly accredited representatives and it shall meet at least *once a year*. At the request of any Member State, and approval by the majority of the Member States, the Assembly shall meet in extraordinary Session.

Article X

1. Each Member State shall have one vote.
2. All resolutions shall be determined by a two-thirds majority of the members of the organisation.
3. Questions of procedure shall require a simple majority. Whether or not a question is one of procedure shall be determined by a simple majority of all Member States of the Organisation.
4. Two-thirds of the total membership of the Organisation shall form a quorum at any meeting of the Assembly.

Article XI

The Assembly shall have the power to determine its own rules of procedure.

THE COUNCIL OF MINISTERS

Article XII

The Council of Ministers shall consist of Foreign Ministers or such other Ministers as are designated by the Governments of Member States.

The Council of Ministers shall meet at least twice a year. When requested by any Member State and approved by two-thirds of all Member States, it shall meet in extraordinary session.

Article XIII

The Council of Ministers shall be responsible to the Assembly of Heads of State and Government. It shall be entrusted with the responsibility of preparing conferences of the Assembly.

It shall take cognisance of any matter referred to it by the Assembly. It shall be entrusted with the implementation of the decision of the Assembly of Heads of State and Government. It shall co-ordinate inter-African co-operation in accordance with the instructions of the Assembly and in conformity with Article II (2) of the present Charter.

Article XIV

1. Each Member State shall have one vote.
2. All resolutions shall be determined by a simple majority of the Council of Ministers.
3. Two-thirds of the total membership of the Council shall form a quorum for any meeting of the Council.

Article XV

The Council shall have the power to determine its own rules of procedure.

GENERAL SECRETARIAT

Article XVI

There shall be an Administrative Secretary-General of the Organisation, who shall be appointed by the Assembly of Heads of State and Government, on the recommendation of the Council of Ministers. The Administrative Secretary-General shall direct the affairs of the Secretariat.

Article XVII

There shall be one or more Assistant Secretaries-General of the Organisation, who shall be appointed by the Assembly of Heads of State and Government.

Article XVIII

The functions and conditions of services of the Secretary-General, of the Assistant Secretaries-General and other employees of the Secretariat shall be governed by the provisions of this Charter and the regulations approved by the Assembly of Heads of State and Government.

1. In the performance of their duties the Administrative Secretary-General and the staff shall not seek or receive instructions from any government or from any other authority external to the organisation. They shall refrain from any action which might reflect on their position as international officials responsible only to the organisation.

2. Each member of the organisation undertakes to respect the exclusive character of the responsibilities of the Administrative Secretary-General and the Staff and not to seek to influence them in the discharge of their responsibilities.

COMMISSION OF MEDIATION, CONCILIATION AND ARBITRATION

Article XIX

Member States pledge to settle all disputes among themselves by peaceful means and, to this end, decide to establish a Commission of Mediation, Conciliation and Arbitration, the composition of which and the condition of service shall be defined by a separate protocol to be approved by the Assembly of Heads of State and Government.

SPECIALISED COMMISSIONS

Article XX

The Assembly shall establish such Specialised Commissions as it may deem necessary, including the following:
1. Economic and Social Commission;
2. Educational and Cultural Commission;
3. Health, Sanitation and Nutrition Commission;
4. Defence Commission;
5. Scientific, Technical and Research Commission.

Article XXI

Each Specialised Commission referred to in Article XX shall be composed of the Ministers Concerned or other Ministers or Plenipotentiaries designated by the Governments of the Member States.

Article XXII

The functions of the Specialised Commissions shall be carried out in accordance with the provisions of the present Charter and of the regulations approved by the Council of Ministers.

THE BUDGET

Article XXIII

The budget of the Organisation prepared by the Administrative Secretary-General shall be approved by the Council of Ministers. The budget shall be provided by contributions from Member States in accordance with the scale of assessment of the United Nations; provided, however, that no Member State shall be assessed an amount exceeding twenty percent of the yearly regular budget of the Organisation. The Member States agree to pay their respective contributions regularly.

SIGNATURE AND RATIFICATION OF CHARTER

Article XXIV

This Charter shall be open for signature to all independent sovereign African and Malagasy States and shall be ratified by the signatory States in accordance with their respective constitutional processes.

The original instrument, done in African languages, in English and French, all texts being equally authentic, shall be deposited with the Government of Ethiopia which shall transmit certified copies thereof to all independent sovereign African and Malagasy States.

Instruments of ratification shall be deposited with the Government of Ethiopia, which shall notify all signatories of each such deposit.

ENTRY INTO FORCE

Article XXV

This Charter shall enter into force immediately upon receipt by the Government of Ethiopia of the instruments of ratification from two-thirds of the signatory States.

REGISTRATION OF THE CHARTER

Article XXVI

This Charter shall, after due ratification, be registered with the Secretariat of the United Nations through the Government of Ethiopia in conformity with Article 102 of the Charter of the United Nations.

INTERPRETATION OF THE CHARTER

Article XXVII

Any question which may arise concerning the interpretation of this Charter shall be decided by a vote of two-thirds of the Assembly of Heads of State and Government of the Organization.

ADHESION AND ACCESSION

Article XXVIII

1. Any independent sovereign African State may at any time notify the Administrative Secretary-General of its intention to adhere or accede to this Charter.

2. The Administrative Secretary-General shall, on receipt of such notification, communicate a copy of it to all the Member States. Admission shall be decided by a simple majority of the Member States. The decision of each Member State shall be transmitted to the Administrative Secretary-General, who shall, upon receipt of the required number of votes, communicate the decision to the State concerned.

MISCELLANEOUS

Article XXIX

The working languages of the Organisation and all its institutions shall be, if possible, African languages, English and French.

Article XXX

The Administrative Secretary-General may accept on behalf of the Organisation gifts, bequests and other donations made to the Organisation, provided that this is approved by the Council of Ministers.

Article XXXI

The Council of Ministers shall decide on the privileges and immunities to be accorded to the personnel of the Secretariat in the respective territories of the Member States.

CESSATION OF MEMBERSHIP

Article XXXII

Any State which desires to renounce its membership shall forward a written notification to the Administrative Secretary-General. At the end of one year from the date of such notification, if not withdrawn, the Charter shall cease to apply with respect to the renouncing State, which shall thereby cease to belong to the Organisation.

AMENDMENT TO THE CHARTER

Article XXXIII

This Charter may be amended or revised if any Member State makes a written request to the Administrative Secretary-General to that effect; provided, however, that the proposed amendment is not submitted to the Assembly for consideration until all the Member States have been duly notified of it and a period of one year has elapsed. Such an amendment shall not be effective unless approved by at least two-thirds of all the Member States.

In faith whereof, We, the Heads of African and Malagasy State and Government, have signed this Charter.

Done in the City of Addis Ababa, Ethiopia, this 25th date of May, 1963.

Notes

CHAPTER 1

1.

Province	Districts
Western	Bopolu, Kolahun, Voinjama, Zorzor
Central	Gbarnga, Sanniquellie, Tappita, Salala
Eastern	Nyaake, Zwedru

In 1964 these provinces and districts will be eliminated in favor of the county system. In keeping with an Act of the Legislature passed on February 25, 1961, the President appointed a commission to study and make recommendations on the change. In mid-1963 it was announced that four counties would be created out of the three provinces.

2. Scientists differ on the number, the classification, and even the names of Liberian tribes. The four divisions used in this chapter are ones more or less generally accepted. For a fuller appreciation of the problems involved here, the reader should consult the following:

Charles Schwab and George Harley, *Tribes of the Liberian Hinterland* (Cambridge, Mass.: Harvard University Press, 1947).

Abayomi Karnga, *History of Liberia* (Liverpool: D. H. Tyte and Co., 1926). One other point: the Mandingo and Fanti tribes, while not from Liberia, do have a large number living in the country on a semipermanent basis. The Moslem Mandingoes come in from Guinea on the north and live in Liberia for several years as traders. Their hard-working and frugal manner is famous in West Africa. The other tribe, the Fanti, are fishermen from Ghana who live along the Liberian coast for periods of perhaps five years and then return home with their savings.

3. The Bureau has been under the newly created Office of National Planning since May 28, 1962. The Office is headed by Director-General J. Milton Weeks, who is a close adviser of President Tubman.

4. His assistants were Wologbe, Duala, Tamia, Jalla, Jaarve, Zolu, Tabaku, and Jalla Belekole.

5. Today the script contains 7 vowels and 198 consonants, or a total of 205 characters. A more reasonable explanation of its development is that the characters represent an abbreviated form of the picture-like signs often carved by the Vais on trees in the interior to inform future adventurers of what to expect ahead. The characters produced by Bukele would appear to have been

merely a systemization and slight improvement of what already existed.

6. Actually the Bandi have two small enclaves in Gola country. One is located in the heart of the Gola and the other on the Sierra Leone border just south of the Kissi tribe. The Deys, who are sometimes placed in the Kru group, are located on a coastal strip of land 20 miles wide between the Lofa and St. Paul rivers.

7. Robert Earle Anderson, *Liberia: America's African Friend* (Chapel Hill: University of North Carolina Press, 1952) p. 10.

8. The Bureau of Folkways of the Department of the Interior recently compiled a study entitled *The History and Folklore of the Glebo Tribe* (Monrovia, 1957), an excellent research document which is part of an expanding series on all of Liberia's hinterland tribes. The Bureau has since been transferred to the Liberian Information Service, Cultural Division.

9. Names given to the Poro differ according to dialect; for example,

Dialect	Name
Belle	Finyer
Bandi	Polongi
Gola	Bohn
Dey	Bohn
Kissi	Toma-Polondo
Vai	Belli (alternate, Poro)
Kpelle	Poron

10. The instruments used in these ceremonies are usually old razor blades and a hooked knife. Cicatrization is generally done in several parallel rows down the spine and around the sides just below the ribs. Some tribes (e.g., the Kpelle) scarify both the back and the chest.

11. The precise date is uncertain, since it is not known whether the Hanno in question was the father or son of General Hamilcar. A fuller explanation can be found in Sir Harry Johnston, *Liberia* (London: Hutchinson and Co., 1906), Vol. I, pp. 18 ff. This work is the most comprehensive study of pre-colonial Liberian history and the author acknowledges his indebtedness to it as a major source of data for this section.

12. Johnston, *op. cit.*, p. 42.

13. Nathaniel R. Richardson, *Liberia's Past and Present* (London: Diplomatic Press and Publishing Co., 1959), p. 14.

14. Johnston, *op. cit.*, p. 63.

15. Quoted in Johnston, *op. cit.*, pp. 98–101.

16. George Washington's nephew. Bushrod Island, near Monrovia, is named in his honor.

17. Statement by a group of free Negroes in Philadelphia to their representative in Congress, Joseph Hopkinson.

18. See the interesting account of this point in Charles Henry Huberich, *The Political and Legislative History of Liberia* (New York: Central Book Co., 1947), Vol. I, pp. 77 ff. For a thorough explanation of the constitutional problems posed by the quasilegal nature of the Society, see pp. 23–26.

19. Ashmun was born on April 21, 1794, to a white Methodist family. He studied for the ministry but later turned to teaching. According to Ralph R. Gurley in his *Life of Ashmun*, written in 1835, he took up missionary work as a means of escaping domestic difficulties (he had an affair with another woman and his wife found out about it). At the time, the Society was in

desperate need for someone to handle the fumbling colony, and Ashmun volunteered.

20. Ernest Jerome Yancy, *Historical Lights of Liberia's Yesterday and Today* (New York: Herman Jaffe, 1954), p. 22.

21. Ernest Eastman, *A History of the State of Maryland in Liberia* (Monrovia, 1956). This is a comprehensive and scholarly account of the founding and growth of the Maryland Colony.

22. A. Doris Banks Henries, *Father of the Republic: Joseph Jenkins Roberts* (Monrovia, 1962), 13 pp.

23. Johnston, *op. cit.,* p. 258.

24. President Roye's family subsequently moved to Australia, where Roye had extensive business interests. Roye himself was a millionaire before his inauguration, and it seems unlikely that he would have risked his life for such a small sum of money. It is possible that the loan debacle was used as an excuse to remove Roye. His family later claimed that he did not drown but was dragged through the streets in the most brutal fashion and left to die on the beach. His widow was even denied a plea that she be allowed to cover his naked body. A similar account of Roye's death is rumored to be found in a *Life of E. J. Roye* written by ex-President Edwin Barclay, which remains unpublished in deference to the author's wish. President Tubman, in an interview with this writer, pointed out that Roye was the first black (as opposed to brown or mulatto) Negro to be elected President. He interpreted Roye's death as an attempt by the non-black Negro minority to regain control of the government.

25. Anderson, *op. cit.,* p. 85. See the interesting account of boundary encroachments in Chapter 6, pp. 83–96.

26. The text of this address may be found in Richardson, *op. cit.,* p. 122.

27. Author of the two-volume study cited earlier. Johnston was critical of the way in which the London brokers took unfair advantage of Liberia in the Roye Loan of 1871. He was in large part responsible for the 1906 loan debacle and, it has been asserted, he personally amassed a small fortune from the deal.

28. Raymond Leslie Buell, *The Native Problem in Africa* (New York, 1928), Vol. 2, p. 779. For more information on Liberia's loan difficulties, see George W. Brown, *The Economic History of Liberia* (Washington, D.C.: Associated Publishers, Inc., 1941), Section E; Frederick Starr, *Liberia: Description, History and Problems* (Chicago: Chicago Book Co., 1913), pp. 200 ff.; Yancy, *op. cit.,* Chapter 8; Richardson, *op. cit.,* pp. 117–27.

29. Yancy, *op. cit.,* p. 110.

30. A. Doris Banks Henries, *The Liberian Nation: A Short History* (New York: Herman Jaffe, 1954), p. 112.

31. The name has been changed to the Liberian National Guard. Today it is about 5,000 strong and used primarily in maintaining internal security.

32. Anderson, *op. cit.,* p. 92.

33. *Ibid.,* p. 127.

34. As was noted above, according to the Liberian Constitution only citizens can own property. The concession has been criticized on the grounds that a ninety-nine-year lease is contrary to the spirit of Article V, Section 12.

35. The 1926 concession agreement contained a provision that "the leasee shall use its best efforts to secure either from the government of the United States or, with the approval of the Secretary of State of the United States, from some other person or persons a loan of not less than five million dollars

to establish a credit for public developments. Such loan shall be upon terms and conditions negotiated by a commission appointed by the President of Liberia who shall proceed promptly to the United States for this purpose. It is understood that such terms and conditions as may be agreed upon shall be subject to the approval of the Legislature." Harvey Firestone, in keeping with this agreement, personally interceded with the U.S. Secretary of State and the Congress. He was unable to convince either party of the urgency of the loan. He subsequently suggested that his company make the loan directly. The Liberian Government took exception to the idea of being indebted to a company which was itself liable to taxation (i.e., export duties). Thus, the Finance Corporation of America came into existence, though the distinction was of little practical significance.

36. Yancy, *op. cit.*, pp. 111–12.

37. Article III, Section 2 of the Constitution (see Appendix 1 for complete text) reads in part: "the Legislature may by law provide for the cases of removal, death, resignation or inability, both of the President and Vice President, declaring what officer shall act accordingly, until the disability be removed, or a President shall be elected." President Edwin Barclay assumed power on the strength of a 1901 act that empowers the Secretary of State to take control in such circumstances. However, during the course of the following two years, several foreign governments, including the United States and Britain, dealt with the Barclay administration as the *de facto* government only and diplomatic representations were made on the charge d'affaires, instead of the ministerial, level.

38. Anderson, *op. cit.*, p. 111.

39. Yancy, *op. cit.*, p. 221.

40. *Ibid.*

41. The Moratorium Act—*A Joint Resolution to a Joint Resolution Authorizing the President of Liberia to Suspend Payment of Interest and Amortization of the 7 Percent Gold Loan of 1926 and for Other Purposes, Being Chapter 2 of the Acts of the Legislature of Liberia Approved January 12, 1934.* The quotation is taken from Section 1 of this Act.

42. Louis Arthur Grimes served as Secretary of State from 1931 till 1933, after which he was appointed Chief Justice of the Supreme Court. The Louis Arthur Grimes School of Law at the University of Liberia is named in his honor. His son, J. Rudolph Grimes, is the present Secretary of State.

43. The quotations are taken from *A Joint Resolution Authorizing the President of Liberia to Complete Negotiations in Connection with the League's Plan of Assistance to Liberia,* Sections 5 and 6. See Appendix 4 for full text.

44. The actual number of years from Liberia's independence to the end of President Edwin Barclay's term was ninety-six.

45. The text of the address may be found in Richardson, *op. cit.*, p. 180. Also refer to Richardson's work for more detail on the Barclay administration.

CHAPTER 2

1. Charles Henry Huberich, *The Political and Legislative History of Liberia* (New York: Central Book Co., Inc., 1947), Vol. II, pp. 1230–31.

2. *Ibid.*, pp. 1232–33.

3. *Outline of Policies* (ms. submitted to the True Whig Party), 1943, Section 3.

4. *Ibid.*, Section 4.

5. *President Tubman of Liberia Speaks,* ed. E. Reginald Townsend (London: Consolidated Publications, 1959), p. 16.

6. *Ibid.*, p. 20.

7. *Ibid.*, p. 108.

8. *The National Unification Program* (Monrovia: Bureau of Information, Department of State, 1954), pp. 9–10.

9. *Ibid.*, p. 10.

10. The quotation is from the President's opening speech before the National Unification Council at Kolahun, February 14, 1963. The full text of the speech is included in Appendix 6.

11. *Ibid.*

12. From a speech made by President Tubman in 1955 entitled "The Open Door vs. the Closed Door."

13. The Free Port of Monrovia is one of the better ports on the West African Coast. In 1962, it handled nearly 2,000 vessels with a combined cargo of about 4 million tons. Liberia's flag vessels number 886 with a total displacement of 6.5 million tons. The registry is one of the largest in the world: in 1960, ships under the Liberian flag carried more cargo in the foreign trade of the U.S. than those under the U.S. flag. This is due chiefly to Liberia's liberal regulations and lower fees.

14. 1954 Independence Day Message, quoted in *President Tubman Speaks.*

15. J. Milton Weeks, *1962 Annual Report* (Monrovia: Office of National Planning, October 30, 1962), p. 14.

16. The budget bill, however, contains a provision under which the President has authority to cut where necessary in order to meet foreign debt commitments. The total national debt is presently $112 million in short-term loans. Nearly half of this amount matures prior to 1966, in inverse proportion to projected national income increases. The result may be an austerity budget during the 1963–65 fiscal years. The remainder of the debt matures prior to 1973.

17. Fourth Inaugural Address, January 2, 1960.

18. As recorded by Arnold Beichman in an article entitled "Free Enterprise in Liberia," *Christian Science Monitor* (Boston), June 14, 1962.

CHAPTER 3

1. *President Tubman of Liberia Speaks,* ed. E. Reginald Townsend (London: Consolidated Publications, 1959), pp. 86–87.

2. Cousin of the late President Edwin J. Barclay. He is the second Liberian doctor to head the Department. The first, Dr. J. N. Togba, was appointed in 1947.

3. The Department is currently considering requests made by several of its doctors that they be allowed to carry on part-time private practices. Director-General Edwin M. Barclay has suggested that, if their requests are approved, they will suffer a 25 per cent reduction in pay.

4.

Firm	*Hospital Location*
Liberian Mining Co.	Bomi Hills
B. F. Goodrich	Klay District
Firestone Plantations	Cavalla and Harbel
LAMCO	Buchanan

The Bong Mining Company, with headquarters at Bong, will have its hospital in operation in 1964.

5. Protestant missionaries operate the Phoebe Curren Hospital at Zorzor; the Methodist Hospital and Leper Colony at Ganta; and the Hope Leper Settlement at Barrobo.

6. The Research Institute was set up in 1952 with a $250,000 gift made by Harvey Firestone, Jr., in memory of his father. Subsequent contributions have come from the Republic of Liberia, the United States Government, and many firms connected in some way with the tropics.

7. *1962 Annual Report* (Monrovia: National Public Health Service, 1962), p. 17.

8. *Ibid.*

9. Congotown is a suburb of Monrovia.

10. It must be noted that, even if Liberia were to undertake the DDT program immediately, it would not be completely effective because the neighboring countries would not be matching the effort. Until such time as regional spraying can be arranged, total eradication is an impossibility.

11. Vaccinations are also made free of charge to the general population. However, in the case of medical treatment, financial need must be established.

12. *Towards Better Standards in Liberian Education,* speech made by President W. V. S. Tubman on August 24, 1962. See Appendix 5 for the full text. Other addresses made by the President on education in Liberia may be found in *President Tubman Speaks,* pp. 33–72.

13. Figures computed from sundry statistics found in the annual reports of the Department of Public Instruction.

14. There is a growing consensus that the money spent sending students abroad would in most cases be better used in the long-term development of more adequate educational facilities at home. Many private scholarships offered to Liberian students have gone unfilled year after year because government grants are so numerous and usually better paying. On page 4 of his *1962 Annual Report,* Secretary Mitchell pointed out: "If we are to make the best use of government funds this program must be continually reviewed and brought into line with national demands. Because internal conditions have been improved it is possible to do many things at home which formerly could be achieved only by sending persons abroad. It seems advisable to carefully select candidates for foreign study in terms of national needs and the capacity of the individuals to be prepared to meet these needs. Furthermore, when students complete the required work they should return home promptly. Those who fail to measure up to their obligations in institutions abroad should also be brought home. Too many students remain away for indefinite periods of time at government expense." In September, 1962, the Secretary recalled thirty-seven students who, in his estimation, were abusing the program.

15. Speech made to the graduating class of Booker Washington Institute, November 21, 1957. *President Tubman Speaks,* p. 68.

16. According to law, a company cannot hire foreign labor unless it is demonstrated that there are no qualified Liberians to fill the job.

17. His predecessor, the late Nathaniel V. Massaquoi, had been in poor health for several months. Mitchell previously held the post of Under-Secretary of Education.

18. *1962 Annual Report* (Monrovia: Department of Education, 1962), p. 2.

19. In addition to the School of Liberal and Fine Arts, the colleges and schools are as follows:
Louis Arthur Grimes College of Law and Government
W. V. S. Tubman College of Teacher Training
College of Forestry
College of Agriculture
The Laboratory High School
The People's College
The Benjamin J. K. Anderson School of Commerce and Business Administration

20. At the time of this writing the plans are not yet complete. A United States architectural firm has been employed to draw up the plans. Preliminary estimates on the total cost go as high as $40 million. The student body will be about 2,500 in 1970.

21. In that year 129,275,000 pounds (dry rubber content) were exported and the value was $36.2 million. The latter figure represents a 20 per cent drop from the previous year, due to a decline of prices in the world market. Palm kernels were the second largest export, with a quantity of 28.5 million pounds and a dollar value of almost $1.2 million.

22. The following is a brief report on Liberia's six foreign rubber concessionaires:

FIRESTONE PLANTATIONS CO.
Location: Harbel and Cavalla
Agreement Date: 1925
Duration: 99 years
Reserve: 1,000,000 acres
Source of Capital and Management: U.S.A.
Employment: 21,000 Liberians and 200 foreign
Operation: 102,000 acres planted; 100 million trees, a quarter of which are
           not yet producing; buys privately produced latex at lower than
           world prices; has processing plant.
Other Activities: soap factory; foreign and American Ford distributors
           through wholly-owned subsidiary, United States Trading
           Co. (which also bottles and distributes Coca-Cola and
           Fanta soft drinks)

B. F. GOODRICH CORP.
Location: Klay and Gbarnga
Agreement Date: 1954
Duration: 80 years
Reserve: 600,000 acres
Source of Capital and Management: U.S.A.
Employment: 980 Liberians and 24 foreign
Operation: 60,000 acres being developed, a sixth of which will begin pro-
           ducing in 1967; building a rubber-processing plant.

LIBERIAN AGRICULTURAL CO.
Location: Grand Bassa and Tappita
Agreement Date: 1959
Duration: 70 years
Reserve: 600,000 acres
Source of Capital and Management: Italy and Netherlands, respectively

Employment: 800 Liberians and 19 foreign
Operation: Plan to have 100,000 acres planted by 1976; production will not
        be significant before 1970.
LIBERIA COMPANY
Location: Cocopa
Agreement Date: 1949
Duration: 40 years
Reserve: 150,000 acres
Source of Capital and Management: U.S.A. and Germany
Employment: 1,200 Liberians and 16 foreign
Operations: developing 25,000 acres, 3,000 of which will start producing in
        1967; plant being constructed
Other Activities: Has 14,000 acres of coffee (robusta) and 600 acres of cacao
        now producting; sells lumber, some 170,000 board feet in
        1961.

AFRICAN FRUIT CO.
Location: Greenville
Agreement Date: 1952
Duration: 80 years
Reserve: 600,000 acres
Source of Capital and Management: Germany
Employment: 750 Liberians and 21 foreign
Operation: currently developing only 5,000 acres
Other Activity: Banana growing was original aim but crop failed.

SALALA RUBBER CO.
Location: Salala
Agreement Date: 1959
Duration: 70 years
Reserve: 100,000 acres
Source of Capital and Management: Netherlands and Germany
Employment: 800 Liberians and 12 foreign
Operation: 14,000 acres being developed; production will begin in 1968;
        rubber-processing plant being constructed.

23. The difference is attributed to processing and transport costs. A few of
the larger independent growers have begun shipping their raw latex to
various countries (including the Eastern bloc) to take advantage of the
higher prices. But this requires a substantial investment in specially equipped
ocean freighters, and not many can afford this outlay.

24. Based on map published in 1957 by the Joint Liberian–United States
Commission for Economic Development.

25. A survey made by a group of specialists from the United States in 1944
placed the figure at 235. Since then several others, some previously unknown,
have been identified. For example, the *Tetraberlinia Tubmania,* named after
the President, is a wood similar to mahogany which was discovered in the late
1940's. Among the types of wood now being used for large-scale commercial
purposes in the world, Liberia has the following: mahogany, cherry, white oak,
walnut, corkwood, red and white cedar, black gum, and camwood.

26. One possible exception to this statement is the Mim Timber Company,
which may be able to use the Buchanan-Nimba railroad. The six major timber
concessions operating in Liberia are:

SIGA LUMBER CO.
Location: Tappita and Grand Bassa
Agreement Date: 1959
Duration: 60 years
Reserve: 40,000 acres
Source of Capital and Management: Switzerland and England
Operation: Developing 20,000 acres in Grand Bassa; 1963 estimated production 1.5 million board feet.

LIBERIAN TIMBER INDUSTRIES CORP.
Location: Central and Eastern Provinces
Agreement Date: 1959
Duration: 60 years
Reserve: 350,000 acres
Source of Capital and Management: U.S.A.
Operation: not yet producing

MARYLAND LOGGING COMPANY
Location: Maryland County
Agreement Date: 1960
Duration: 60 years
Reserve: 500,000 acres
Source of Capital and Management: Germany and Spain
Operation: 3,000,000 board feet in 1961 exports; ceased operation due to change in ownership.

LIBERIAN INDUSTRIAL FORESTRY CORP.
Location: Western Province
Agreement Date: 1957
Duration: 20 years
Reserve: 40,000 acres
Source of Capital and Management: Spain
Operation: annual production of 3,000,000 board feet.

MIM TIMBER CO.
Location: Central Province
Agreement Date: 1961
Duration: 60 years
Reserve: 325,000 acres
Source of Capital and Management: England
Operation: company previously operated in Ghana but is now putting investments into Liberia.

MORRO RIVER LUMBER CO.
Location: Tappita and Grand Bassa
Agreement Date: 1957
Duration: 60 years
Reserve: 100,000 acres
Source of Capital and Management: not disclosed
Operation: development has not yet begun.

27. There are eight national forests, the Gbi, Gio, Gola, Gola Maher, Grebo, Kpelle, Krahn-Bassa, and Lorma.

28. The value of iron exports in that year was $29.4 million; nearly $4 million more than that of rubber.

29. This range extends into the Republic of Guinea. It is significant that Sékou Touré has followed the Tubman formula (i.e., 50 per cent) and has granted the concession to a West European banking consortium called Consafrique. The ore will be shipped via Liberian ports and a railroad will probably be built to connect with the Buchanan-Nimba line owned by the LAMCO Joint Venture.

30. The only projects exceeding the scale of the LAMCO Joint Venture is the Volta River Project, which is owned by the Ghanaian Government, and the Aswan Dam project, which is owned by the United Arab Republic.

31. Officers of the LAMCO Joint Venture Enterprise are:

President, Johnston Avery, New York
Executive Vice President, Erik Lionhead, Stockholm
Secretary-Treasurer, Jan Ekmann, Stockholm
Chairman of the Board, Marc Wallenberg, Stockholm

The Venture awarded its management contract to the Grangesberg Co., a member of the Swedish Syndicate and the largest ore-exporting organization in the world.

32. Bethlehem and LIO are each putting up $60 million; $50 million is derived from a pre-financed contract from Erzkontor (Ruhr Steel Mills); $30 million from the Export-Import Bank, and $5.7 million from the First National City Bank of New York.

33. Liberia Mining Company was incorporated in Liberia. Ownership is divided as follows: Republic Steel Corp., 60 per cent; Lansdell Christie, 25 per cent; remainder undisclosed. The officers are:

President, Lansdell Christie
Vice President and General Manager, Walter K. Scheibe
Vice Presidents, R. A. Eldridge, E. R. Johnson, C. H. Dewey
Treasurer, W. W. Hancock
Secretary, Vernon R. Y. Lynn
Chairman of the Board, Thomas F. Patton, President, Republic Steel

34. Ownership is evenly split between the government and a consortium made up of five German steel interests. Officers are:

Board Chairman, Dr. Friedrich Elshoff
President, Dr. Eugen Plotzki, Duesseldorf
Director, Dr. Hans Guenther Sohl (also Chairman of the German Iron
        and Steel Association)

35. It is owned by Consortium Liberia (75 per cent) and Societa Finanzi-aria Liderurgica (25 per cent) (Finsider, Rome). The chief officers are:

Chairman of the Board, Dr. Karl Kaup
President, Dr. Eugen Plotzki

36. Government owns 50 per cent; Liberian Enterprises, Ltd., 35 per cent; and Liberia Mining Company, 15 per cent. Liberian Enterprises is owned by some 1,700 Liberian stockholders. Officers of NIOC are:

President, Charles D. Sherman, Secretary of the Treasury, R.L.
Vice President, Lansdell Christie, President, LMC
Secretary, Richard A. Henries, Speaker of the House of Representatives, R.L.
Treasurer, William R. Tolbert, Jr., Vice President of the Republic of
   Liberia.

Financing is as follows: Liberia Mining Company, $1.5 million; Government
of Liberia, $5 million; Liberian Enterprises, $3.5 million. There are also two
loans of $7 million each; one from the Export-Import Bank and the other
from Dutch brokers.

37. Officers of Mine Management Associates are:

President, Floyd W. Erickson
Vice President and General Manager, S. A. Hanson
Vice President and Secretary, Garland R. Farmer
Treasurer, George Wizer

CHAPTER 4

1. President Sékou Touré, speech on the occasion of the Liberian Independence Day Celebration, July 26, 1959, in Conakry.

2. Quoted by Secretary of State J. Rudolph Grimes in a statement to the
Fifteenth Session of the U.N. General Assembly, September 29, 1960.

3. For more detail on the proceedings and decisions concerning the Angola
question, refer to the *Report of the Sub-Committee on the Situation in Angola*
(A/4978), Agenda Item 27, Sixteenth Session, U.N. General Assembly, November 22, 1961, Part I.

4. Quoted in Thomas P. Melady, *The White Man's Future in Black Africa*
(New York: Macfadden Bartell Corp., 1962), p. 115. Chapter Seven of this
work gives the historical developments, background, and racial implications of
the Angola situation.

5. *Report of the Sub-Committee on the Situation in Angola*, p. 10.

6. *Verbatim Record of the Nine Hundred and Fifteenth Meeting, United
Nations Security Council* (S/PV. 950), June 6, 1961, p. 16.

7. United Nations General Assembly (A/PV. 033), October 11, 1961, p. 62.

8. This choice was made because of the geographical closeness of the Union
to South West Africa, because South African troops under General Botha had
seized the territory from the Germans on behalf of the Allies in 1916, and because the union had close ties with Britain traditionally and economically.

9. *Mandate for German South West Africa* (Document) December 17, 1920,
Article 2.

10. There was a move by South Africa in 1934 to incorporate the territory
as a fifth province of the Union, but the Mandates Commission ruled
against it.

11. There were two other advisory opinions:

(1) On June 7, 1955 the Court ruled that the General Assembly could use
its normal voting procedures (as set forth in the Charter) in deciding questions relating to South West Africa.

(2) On June 1, 1956, the Court upheld the General Assembly's authorization of
the Committee on South West Africa to hear petitioners.

12. Statement before the General Assembly on September 26, 1962.

13. Statement before the seventeenth Session of the General Assembly,
September 29th, 1962.

14. *Loc. cit.*

15. *Loc. cit.*

16. *President Tubman Speaks,* pp. 185–86. The quotation is from the President's July 26, 1957 Independence Day Address to the nation.

17. *Liberia Official Gazette,* XLVI, No. 2X (Extraordinary), (January 26, 1959). See Appendix 7 for text.

18. See the full text of the letters in Appendixes 8 and 9.

19. President Tubman's opening speech at the Sanniquellie Conference, July 15, 1959.

20. See Appendix 10 for text.

21. Represented at this conference were: Liberia, Ghana, Libya, Ethiopia, Morocco, Tunisia, United Arab Republic, Sudan, and the Provisional Government of Algeria.

22. Attending were: Cameroon, Ethiopia, Ghana, Guinea, the Provisional Government of Algeria, Libya, Liberia, Morocco, Nigeria, Somalia, Sudan, Tunisia, and the United Arab Republic.

23. Quoted from *Second Conference of Independent African States* (Addis Ababa: Ministry of Information of the Imperial Ethiopian Government, 1960), p. 42.

24. Members are: Cameroon, Central African Republic, Congo (Brazzaville), Ivory Coast, Dahomey, Gabon, Upper Volta, Madagascar, Mauritania, Niger, Senegal, and Chad.

25. Members are the United Arab Republic, Morocco, Algeria, Ghana, Guinea, and Mali.

26. The idea for the conference emerged from a meeting between Sékou Touré, Modibo Keita, and President Tubman in January, 1961. The latter two had traveled to Conakry in honor of Sékou Touré's first inauguration as President. The three agreed that all of Africa should meet around the same conference table and Tubman was asked to call the conference. The President agreed on the condition that Touré and Keita agree to act as co-sponsors.

27. Tunisia attended as an observer because Algeria had not been invited.

28. The island state of Madagascar (Malagasy Republic) insisted, as she had at Brazzaville, on being acknowledged as a distinct entity which was voluntarily cooperating with the African nations.

29. Sudan attended no conferences and joined no African grouping until 1963, when it joined the Organisation of African Unity at Addis Ababa.

30. See final draft of the Charter of the Inter-African and Malagasy Organisation (IAMO) in Appendix 14.

31. Charter of IAMO, Chapter I, Article 1, Section 2.

32. In his Independence Day Address, July 26, 1962.

33. Resolution 1, part A, section 6, adopted by the Monrovia Conference. (See Appendix 13 for text.)

34. President Tubman's broadcast to the Liberian nation on the eve of his departure for the Addis Ababa Conference of Heads of African States (May 13, 1963).

35. Hassan II, of Morocco objecting to Mauritania's presence, did not attend; the Grunitzky government of Togo was not invited; and South Africa, which is not considered to be independent, was not invited. Those attending were: Algeria, Burundi, Cameroon, Central African Republic, Chad, Congo (Brazzaville), Congo (Leopoldville), Dahomey, Ethiopia, Gabon, Ghana, Guinea, Ivory Coast, Liberia, Libya, Madagascar, Mali, Mauritania, Niger, Nigeria,

Rwanda, Senegal, Sierra Leone, Somalia, Sudan, Tanganyika, Tunisia, Uganda, United Arab Republic, and Upper Volta.

36. Address by President Tubman to the Addis Ababa Summit Conference, May 22, 1963.

37. President Tubman's broadcast to the Liberian Nation (see note 34).

Bibliography

ANDERSON, ROBERT EARLE, *Liberia, America's African Friend* (Chapel Hill: University of North Carolina Press, 1952).

AZIKIWE, BENJAMIN NNAMDI, *Liberia in World Politics* (London: A. H. Stockwell, Ltd., 1934).

BANE, MARTIN J., *The Catholic Story of Liberia* (New York: D. X. McMullen Company, 1950).

BROWN, GEORGE WILLIAM, *The Economic History of Liberia* (Washington: Associated Publishers, Inc., 1941).

BUELL, RAYMOND LESLIE, *Liberia: A Century of Survival* (Philadelphia: University of Pennsylvania Press, 1947).

COLE, HENRY B. (ed.), *The Liberian Yearbook for 1962* (Monrovia: A Liberian Review Publication, 1962).

DAVIS, STANLEY A., *This is Liberia* (New York: William Frederick Press, 1953).

DE LA RUE, SIDNEY, *The Land of the Pepper Bird* (New York: Putnam, 1930).

DONNER, ETTA, *Hinterland Liberia* (London: Blackie and Son, 1939).

FIRESTONE, HARVEY S., *Views in Liberia* (Chicago: R. R. Donnelley and Sons Co., 1937).

GREENE, BARBARA, *Land Benighted* (London: Saunders Co., 1938).

GREENE, GRAHAM, *Journey Without Maps* (Toronto: W. Heinemann and Co., 1950).

GREENWALL, HARRY JAMES, and WILD, ROLAND, *Unknown Liberia* (London: Hutchinson and Co., 1936).

HARLEY, GEORGE W., *Native African Medicine* (Cambridge, Mass.: Harvard University Press, 1941).

————, *Notes on the Poro in Liberia* (Cambridge, Mass.: Harvard University Press, 1941).

HAYMAN, ARTHUR, and PREECE, HAROLD, *Lighting Up Liberia* (New York: Creative Age Press, 1943).

HENRIES, A. DORIS BANKS, *The Liberian Nation: A Short History* (New York: Herman Jaffe, 1954).

HENRIES, RICHARD and DORIS, *Liberia, the West African Republic* (New York: Herman Jaffe, 1958).

HUBERICH, CHARLES HENRY, *The Political and Legislative History of Liberia* (New York: Central Book Co., 1947).

JOHNSON, S. J., *The Traditional History and Folklore of the Vai Tribe* (Monrovia: Bureau of Folkways, Department of the Interior, 1954).

JOHNSTON, HARRY H., *Liberia* (London: Hutchinson and Co., 1906).

JUNGE, WERNER, *African Jungle Doctor* (London: George C. Harrap and Co., Ltd., 1952).

KARNGA, ABAYOMI, *Liberia Before the New World* (Liverpool: D. H. Tyte and Co., 1923).

————, *History of Liberia* (Liverpool: D. H. Tyte and Co., 1926).

LAWRENCE, JAMES COOPER, *The World's Struggle with Rubber* (New York: Harper, 1931).

LIEF, ALFRED, *The Firestone Story* (New York: Whittlesey House, 1951).

MAUGHAM, REGINALD CHARLES F., *Republic of Liberia* (New York: Scribner, 1920).

MAYER, KARL RODNEY, *Forest Resources of Liberia,* Bulletin 67 (Washington: U.S. Government Printing Office, 1951).

MCCAUGHREY, LAWRENCE, *Liberian Interlude* (New York: Pageant Press, 1954).

MOORE, BAI T., *The Tribes of the Western Province and the Denwoin People* (Monrovia: Bureau of Folkways, Department of the Interior, 1955).

PHILLIPS, HILTON A., *Liberia's Place in Africa's Sun* (New York: Hobson Book Press, 1946).

RICHARDSON, NATHANIEL R., *Liberia's Past and Present* (London: Diplomatic Press and Publishing Co., 1959).

SADLER, WESLEY, *Untangled Loma: A Course of Study of the Loma Language of the Western Province of Liberia* (Baltimore: Board of Foreign Missions of the United Lutheran Church of America for the Evangelical Lutheran Church of Liberia, 1951)

SCHWAB, GEORGE, and HARLEY, GEORGE W., *Tribes of the Liberian*

244   BIBLIOGRAPHY

Hinterland (Cambridge, Mass.: Harvard University Press, 1947).

SEEBACK, MARGARET R., *Man in the Bush* (Philadelphia: Board of Foreign Missions, 1945).

SIMPSON, CLARENCE L., *Symbol of Liberia: Memoirs of C. L. Simpson* (London: Diplomatic Press and Publishing Co., 1961).

STARR, FREDERICK, *Liberia: Description, History, Problems* (Chicago: Chicago Book Co., 1913).

TAYLOR, WAYNE C., *The Firestone Operations in Liberia* (Washington: National Planning Association, 1956).

TOLSON, MELVIN B., *Libretto for the Republic of Liberia* (New York: Twayne Publishers, 1953).

TOWNSEND, E. REGINALD (ed.), *President Tubman of Liberia Speaks* (London: Consolidated Publications, 1959).

WALKER, THOMAS HAMILTON, *History of Liberia* (Boston: Cornhill Publishing Co., 1921).

WARNER, ESTHER S., *The Silk-Cotton Tree* (New York: Doubleday, 1958).

WOODSON, CARTER G., *African Heroes and Heroines* (Washington: Associated Publishers, Inc., 1939).

YANCY, ERNEST JEROME, *Historical Lights of Liberia's Yesterday and Today* (New York, Herman Jaffe, 1954).

———, *The Republic of Liberia* (London: George Allen & Unwin, Ltd., 1959).

YOUNG, JAMES CAPERS, *Liberia Rediscovered* (New York: Doubleday, Doran, 1934).